THE 4 YEAR OLYMPIAN

JEREMIAH BROWN

THE 4 YEAR OLYMPIAN

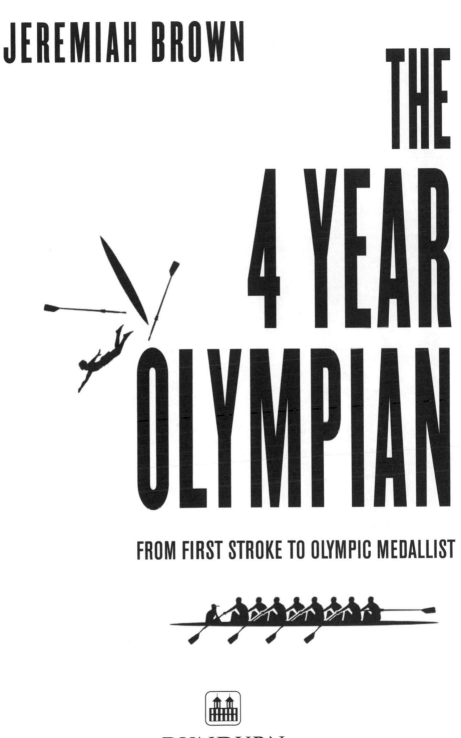

FROM FIRST STROKE TO OLYMPIC MEDALLIST

DUNDURN
TORONTO

Cover image: Kostis Pavlou
Printer: Webcom

Library and Archives Canada Cataloguing in Publication

Brown, Jeremiah, 1985-, author
The 4 year Olympian : from first stroke to Olympic medallist / Jeremiah Brown.

Issued in print and electronic formats.
ISBN 978-1-4597-4131-7 (softcover).--ISBN 978-1-4597-4132-4 (PDF).--
ISBN 978-1-4597-4133-1 (EPUB)

1. Brown, Jeremiah, 1985-. 2. Rowers--Canada--Biography. 3. Olympic Games (30th : 2012 : London, England). I. Title. II. Title: Four year Olympian.

GV790.92.B76A3 2018 797.12'3092 C2017-907134-3
C2017-907135-1

1 2 3 4 5 22 21 20 19 18

Conseil des Arts du Canada Canada Council for the Arts Canada ONTARIO ARTS COUNCIL CONSEIL DES ARTS DE L'ONTARIO an Ontario government agency un organisme du gouvernement de l'Ontario

We acknowledge the support of the **Canada Council for the Arts**, which last year invested $153 million to bring the arts to Canadians throughout the country, and the **Ontario Arts Council** for our publishing program. We also acknowledge the financial support of the **Government of Ontario**, through the **Ontario Book Publishing Tax Credit** and the **Ontario Media Development Corporation**, and the **Government of Canada**.

Nous remercions le **Conseil des arts du Canada** de son soutien. L'an dernier, le Conseil a investi 153 millions de dollars pour mettre de l'art dans la vie des Canadiennes et des Canadiens de tout le pays.

Care has been taken to trace the ownership of copyright material used in this book. The author and the publisher welcome any information enabling them to rectify any references or credits in subsequent editions.

— *J. Kirk Howard, President*

The publisher is not responsible for websites or their content unless they are owned by the publisher.

Printed and bound in Canada.

VISIT US AT

dundurn.com | @dundurnpress | dundurnpress | dundurnpress

Dundurn
3 Church Street, Suite 500
Toronto, Ontario, Canada
M5E 1M2

To my son, Ethan,

for putting up with my eccentricities

FOREWORD

Writing the foreword for another's memoir is an interesting process. To read, reflect, and summarize one's thoughts on another person's character and journey so far — their version of history, to the best of their knowledge — is both rewarding and challenging.

The 4 Year Olympian is a catchy title, yet somewhat incomplete, as it focuses our attention on what Jeremiah did, rather than who he is, who he has become. In his vivid way, Jeremiah explores the other side of prestige and, ultimately, idealism. I felt empathy and compassion for him in his darkest days, as he paid the cost for the sacrifices made. I know that road: the self-punishment, the sobbing soul. In his articulate and heartfelt words, I, too, felt heard: life as an athlete, the loneliness of life as a single dad.

I was fascinated by Jeremiah's intimate description of the Olympic men's eight rowing team, the squad dynamics, and ultimately their ability to come together and endure. He dissects and prescribes the lessons learned, and I find myself grateful for the knowledge shared.

I could see legendary coach Mike Spracklen out there on the water, in his ratty tarped coach boat, recruiting every ounce of energy he could procure from his determined crew. These intimately unveiled vignettes shine in their descriptions, as the scenes come alive. I could hear the sounds of the boathouse, the creak of the dock. I sat in the silence of the mist and longed to feel the fog. Persistence is not pretty; it takes grit to interpret and maintain, no matter the discomfort, the mundanity of it. It is his love of skilled attention and competition, of proving himself again and again, that defines Jeremiah, and through this he pays tribute to his family.

The 4 Year Olympian is more than a sport story. You get as much a sense of where Jeremiah is from as you do of his eventual aspiration, and with it, inspiration. Disciplined, yet facing down the all too familiar battalion of self-doubt. I felt sorrow at times, hope at others, and through this I acquired a greater appreciation for the joys of life.

— Simon Whitfield
Four-time Olympian and triathlon Olympic gold and silver medallist

RACING EIGHT

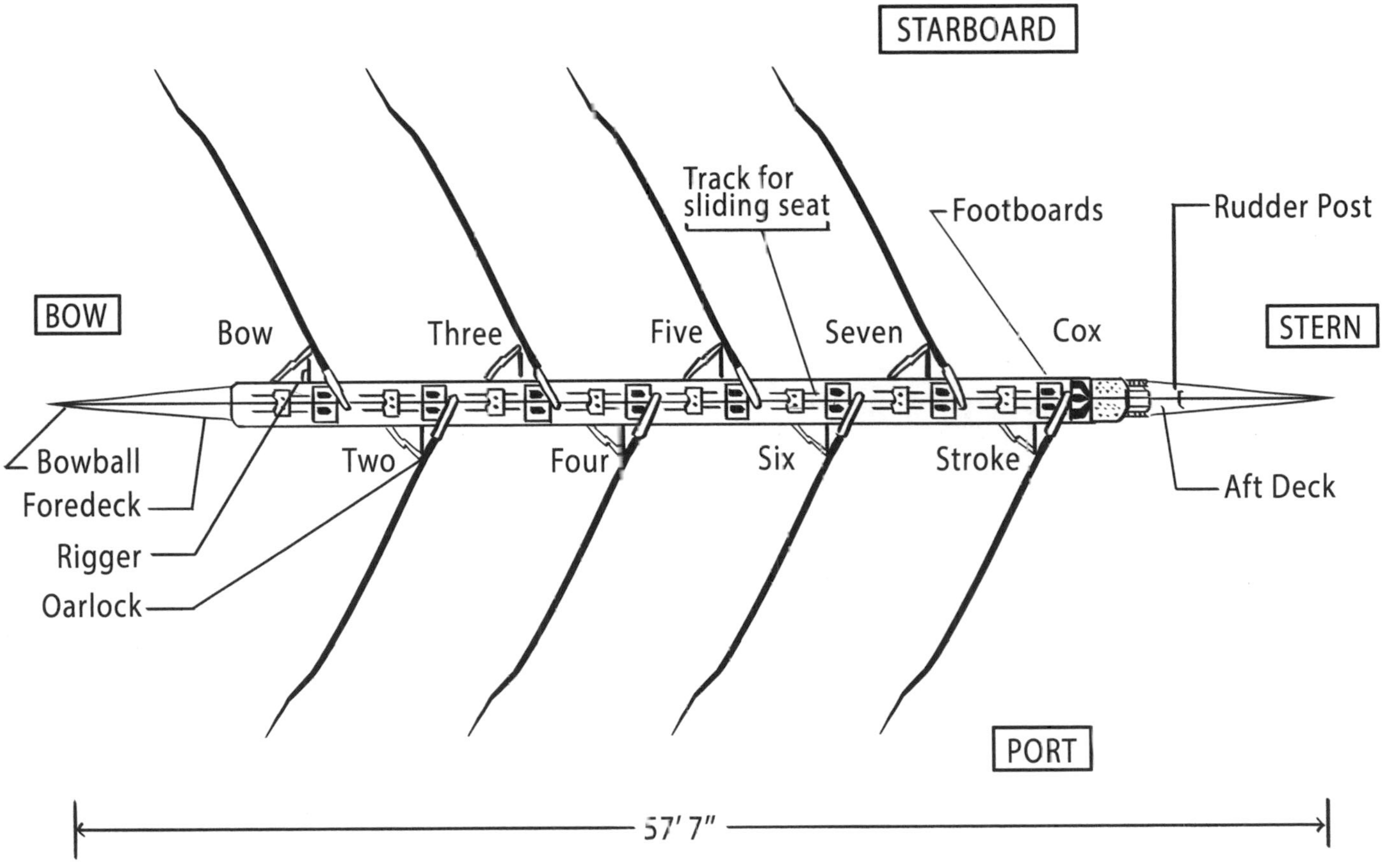

INTRODUCTION

The punch landed just below my eye and jarred me into a new reality — you can get hit. Baron Bradshaw was a skinny bully who walked around town wearing a wife beater and a wallet chain. He had a glazed look in his eyes, the kind that is void of hope. At thirteen years old, he was four years my senior. Sometime early on Baron had determined, it was clear, that he had nothing to lose or gain in life. He defied authority and seemed to revel in his intimidation of other boys in our small town of Port Hope, Ontario.

I had been playing with my neighbour Derek on the stretch of grass that lined the length of the Ganaraska River across the road from our duplex. The park we played in was next to an old file factory that had been shut down since the seventies. It had hundreds of sixteen-pane windows, every one of which we tried to smash with rocks for sport.

Baron had emerged from one side of the shuttered factory. I'd seen some things and heard stories, but until then had managed to stay out of his way. I'm not sure what we did to become targets, perhaps it was because we were the only two boys in the park that day. Perhaps it was because I was big for my age and he took exception to my tall frame.

He came at me, shouting, "You think you're tough? You wanna go?"

I knew by the way he spoke he'd already made up his mind; I was about to get hit. I said everything a nine-year-old kid could think of to try to pacify his aggression, but nothing worked. As he neared striking distance, I started walking backwards, still trying to talk him down. He scuttled at me with a dance in his step like Muhammad Ali and socked me in the eye.

Stunned, I turned and ran to escape, but he wasn't finished and he was fast, running me down the neighbouring vacant parking lot. Derek hung back, worried but glad it wasn't him. I turned back to face Baron and begged him to stop, tears now streaming down my face. His beady eyes were devoid of empathy. He'd proven his point, he was the tough guy, but he wanted more. In quick succession, he punched me three more times in the face before spitting at my feet and sauntering away.

My whole face felt fuzzy and big as a watermelon as I ran across the street to the safety of home. I called my dad, a history teacher who was teaching a summer course at the high school three blocks away, and told him what had happened through choked sobs. I wanted him to come home right away and go beat the shit out of Baron Bradshaw. My dad was not a rash man. He told me he'd talk to me after school.

I went to my room and punched my pillow over and over, angry, scared, alone. I was ashamed of myself for not hitting back, for lacking the courage to defend myself. Behind the tears, I quietly determined I would never let fear impede me ever again. If I found myself in a situation where it came to blows — a common occurrence for boys growing up in small towns — I would stand my ground.

I started doing fifteen push-ups every day and punching the concrete walls in our basement to harden my knuckles.

PART ONE: THE WARM-UP

You have your way. I have my way. As for the right way, the correct way, and the only way, it does not exist.

— Friedrich Nietzsche

1

My little sister, Julia, cried whenever I swore. My older sister, Jenny, dug her nails into my forearms when I bothered her one too many times. I'd look at the purple indents under the smooth skin where the top layer had been raked away and enjoy the burning sensation. The marks and the pain were like a badge of honour.

Sibling skirmishes made up our childhood most days, and perhaps three times in my life led to an ear slap from our German mother, who just couldn't take any more. She'd yell "*Ohrfeige*!" as she jerked her shoulders up and whipped that straightened arm around to connect her palm with the side of my head. It was the same motion as a tennis forehand blasted down the line, and each one landed with brilliant accuracy. Unless severely provoked, my mom, a French immersion teacher, was and always has been a loving mother of three: sweet, kind, and patient. But there was a switch inside her that my troublesome nature always had weight on, like a finger applying slow pressure until I finally flipped off the lights inside her brain.

I inherited the same volatility as my mom, but with a much shorter fuse. Playing board games with me was like walking through a minefield. If I won, everyone would survive. If I was losing, I might explode before the game even ended.

The game Memory was a family favourite. My mom would sit across from me, glancing over wearily while Julia gleefully stacked pair upon pair as if she'd lived every scene on the cards. The German shepherd in the tall grass — may as well have been her first pet; the card with a straight country road lined with poplar trees — as knowable as our own cedar-lined driveway; one of the three pairs of slightly different bouquets of flowers — like she'd just cut and arranged them herself.

Mom knew I was churning inside. Julia's eyes shone brightly above her round cheeks, effortlessly mapping out pairs in anticipation of her next turn. Her memory was too good for me, and it killed me.

Jenny's self-control was equally infuriating. She'd hold her head high and exhibit patience and excessive good sportsmanship until I could not stop myself from flicking her in the ear. Then her upper lip would recede, bearing vampire-like eye teeth, and she'd crush her eyebrows down and together so hard I thought they'd fuse. The sequence was as predictable as a cobra flaring its hood. When she finally struck back, I was ready.

My mom would intervene, sounding like Arnold Schwarzenegger. Stress made her revert to the German accent that revealed her upbringing in post–Second World War West Germany. As the melee grew, my dad would put down his *Globe and Mail* newspaper or whatever book on philosophy he was reading at the time — *Being and Time* by Heidegger, perhaps — and, jarringly pulled back into the reality of a wife and three kids, bark, "What's going on in there?"

Usually a threat of grounding followed, or, if I was being completely unreasonable, the sound of my dad taking off his leather belt, securing it in a loop, and yanking it in and out to make a threatening crack that my sisters and I could hear no matter which nook or cranny of our old house we may have been hiding in. This demonstration was intended to foreshadow the sound of the belt whipping my bare ass in the spanking that would come next. When he finally caught me in his vice grip, I'd buck so hard that my dad could barely keep me belly-down over his knees to deliver a clean strike.

My dad romanticized the great thinkers of the past, letting his lips drop open into a small *o* as he looked through you to a space just behind your head and searched for the perfect quote from antiquity to enlighten you. At dinner he would sit back in his throne, a wooden chair with decoratively lathed legs and back supports, and ponder aloud to three kids who couldn't understand and a wife who had learned not to engage in an argument that would become accusatory and end unresolved anyway. I tried to wrap my young mind around my dad's philosophical dinnertime questions: *What is truth? What is a good life? What is the soul?*

As much as I tried to understand his inner life, my dad was largely a mystery to me growing up. He didn't talk about his past. He had finished master's degrees in both history and political science and had ambitions to pursue a Ph.D., but then three kids and the necessity to provide for his family stymied his academic pursuits. The Ph.D. was a goal that would have stretched him even if he'd had all the time and resources in the world. It was his life challenge, the pursuit that got away. Regret.

When my dad was in grade four, he struggled with reading and writing. On the last day of school that year, he'd walked home and announced to my grandparents that he would be repeating grade four of his own accord. It was one of the few stories from his youth he proudly shared with us. Another came cackling out of my uncle Tim, one of my dad's five brothers, while we were sitting on the screened veranda of the Brown family cottage in Muskoka. I was twelve. He said that when my dad was in his late teens he had been watching his older brother David trying to windsurf with shiny new gear: new wetsuit, new board, and new sail. After several attempts, David gave up, saying the conditions weren't right; there was too much wind (though any windsurfer knows there's no such thing). My dad had been watching David while plastering the boathouse cedar siding with black stain, and my uncle Tim had been re-roofing the red shingles above. When David neared the dock, my dad set down the stain and wiped his hands on his dirty overalls. Then he jumped into the water, mounted the windsurfer, and went cutting across the lake with his rear end skimming the water like a pro. My uncle Tim broke out in laughter recalling the sight of my dad upstaging my uncle David in tar-stained overalls.

This story has been etched into my brain ever since. For better or worse, I think it put it into my head that there is no prerequisite for attempting something in earnest and being successful.

My dad would never be caught telling a flattering story about himself. Self-accolades were vulgar. I had to piece together an understanding of his youth from my mom, uncles, and grandparents.

Over the years, I learned that he'd ridden a bull, hitchhiked across Canada, ridden his bike from Ancaster to Muskoka more than once, and worked in a railyard where he saw a fellow brakeman get crushed between two cars. I concluded that my dad was an interesting man with many talents who'd mostly packed them away and retreated into his own head to consider the Big Questions. This created an urge in me to compete for his attention with all those philosophical concepts taking up room in his head. He'd respond tepidly to my constant attention-seeking antics. Most good news or achievements were greeted with a gently toned "Mmm hmm" or a light "Is that right?" Perhaps because of his own disappointments in life, perhaps because of a recent reading of Nietzsche's attacks on Christianity, he seemed to mute genuine enthusiasm as naturally as wetting his lips.

There is so much I respect about my dad — unfailing honesty and integrity being foremost — but during my teenage years, often catching myself morphing into him, I became determined to avoid the same sense of dissatisfaction. He'd had kids too soon, and three of them were too many.

"Dad, why did you have us?" I once asked, to which he blankly stared back at me, blinking, unable to come up with an answer. He should have finished his Ph.D. and become a university professor. *Then he would be happy,* I thought. Instead, he met my beautiful mom, fell in love, and

The Brown family in their Port Hope duplex in 1995 (Jenny is behind the camera).

couldn't recover in time to resume focus on his academic ambitions. My sisters and I came shortly after — three deep spikes in the coffin of his ambition — and he settled for teaching history to adults who hadn't completed high school.

Marriage is a black hole. I'll never get married, I told myself. *Kids are baggage.* I would do something different, whatever that meant, with my life.

2

When I was seventeen, I got bored at a friend's house party one night during a snowstorm and latched on to someone's crazy idea to rip off a Pita Pit. We ordered twenty-six pitas to a vacant house down the street, and then my friend Dave and I waited in snowdrifts in the middle of February for the delivery man to arrive. We wore balaclavas to hide our identity.

The driver's lights swept the snowy driveway as he pulled in. We were giddy with anticipation — a couple of arrogant, egocentric teens determined to prove to our friends that we had the balls to go through with it (but not enough balls to call the whole thing off).

Approaching on foot, the middle-aged delivery man couldn't see us clearly through the steady curtain of falling snow until he was nearly upon us. Then he paused, looking up from his carefully placed footsteps. His facial expression said, *I'm too old for this shit.*

Dave, short and wiry, making me look like a towering enforcer standing next to him at six feet five inches tall, tried to yank the plastic bin full of pitas out of his hands, but the man wouldn't let go. He turned his hips to leave, yet held on as though his hands refused to give up when the rest of him had. Finally breaking his grip on the third yank, Dave and I ran off behind the house, laughing like hyenas and looping back to the party to the adoration and disbelief of our friends.

The police were called, and it didn't take them long to trace our deep tracks in the snow back to the house. By then, I had started walking home, naively thinking the worst that could happen would be a slap on the wrist and the need to repay Pita Pit for the pitas we stole. After all, I'd only been an accomplice. I hadn't been the one to actually grab the pitas.

The police officer who screeched his car to a halt behind me thought otherwise. I recognized him from my girlfriend's church, not an uncommon occurrence in a town of our size, but all he saw in me was the perp he was after. He slammed me onto the hood of the police car and cuffed me. *Okay*, I thought, *he's teaching me a lesson.*

But he wasn't bluffing.

I spent the night in a jail cell, was woken up at four in the morning to be interrogated, and was then put into a youth detention centre for four days while my parents scrambled to find a lawyer to represent me at my hearing.

The Crown prosecutor recommended an eight-month prison sentence on charges of robbery, assault, and wearing a disguise with the intent to commit a crime.

In an instant, my world had been turned upside down. *Couldn't they see that I was a good kid? That my heart was in the right place?* I'd thought I could talk myself out of it, but I had deluded myself. Actions have consequences, and now one of my stupid pranks had gone too far and the full force of the law was coming down on me.

On the second day of my incarceration at the detention centre before my bail hearing, my parents came during visiting hour. They were greeted as law-abiding citizens. I was treated differently. A burly guard looked through me as he gave me orders. I was stripped naked and ordered to turn around, bend over, and cough before entering the visitation room. The protocol was necessary for a youth penitentiary holding young rapists and murderers amongst its population.

My mom couldn't look at me. This was not her son sitting in front of her in violet-red prison garb. It couldn't be! She radiated disapproval through thin lips pulled into a straight line across her face. She was on the verge of tears. Her upper-middle-class German roots already predisposed her to drawing distinctions between ourselves and lower socio-economic classes, and there I was in prison, the armpit of humanity.

"You're not my son. You're a *criminal*," she said. Her anger came from a place of hurt. Hadn't she raised me better?

My dad was deeply concerned but calm. His thin, receding hair looked thinner than ever. He hadn't slept. His glasses seemed to rest on the creased lines where the tired skin pooled under his eyes. Police officers had shown up on our front doorstep looking for me a few times over the years, mostly for throwing all those rocks through the file factory windows, but this time I'd made a big mistake that might permanently affect my future. Crisis turned my dad into a pragmatic decision-making machine. *Don't do this; don't say that; here are the next steps.* He knew I'd messed up, but it was his duty to help me through.

By my third day there, I had a raw feeling in my chest, like I wouldn't be able to survive this environment for a week, let alone as long as two years. My cinder block cell reeked of urine, and the faded white walls were stained with blood, snot, and shit — walls that closed in on me like a car crusher slowly bearing down by the minute. I welled up while thinking of my impending prison sentence. Eventually distress manifested into anger. I imagined the *real* crimes I would commit if the justice system shut me away in this place.

Months later, I sat in a wooden chair waiting to be sentenced. The court looked like a bank inside, except the teller was a court officer sitting behind bulletproof glass. I was just another deposit to be dealt with and locked away in the vault. All around me sat fellow youth convicts dressed in baggy suits. I thought of what my high school career counsellor had once said in a class presentation: "Dress for where you want to be in five years, not where you are now." I figured my fellow convicts aspired to be used car salesmen. Better than jail. I wore a plain white dress shirt. My white flag. *I give up, you win, please don't put me away.*

"Brown, Jeremiah," a voice buzzed through an intercom speaker, announcing my turn to go into the courtroom.

Justice Morgan was a heavyset, bespectacled, and impatient-looking man. He made wide, sweeping arcs with his arms to clear his black judge gown from resting on his protruding belly. He tilted his chin down and looked at me over his glasses for all of one second. He considered the case details, the recommendation from the Crown for eight months in prison, my lawyer's case for a lenient sentence. The assembly line was moving. More files needed to be sealed and put in the vault.

No, no, no. Slow down, I thought.

"Mr. Brown, will you address the court?" Justice Morgan muttered, the way our reverend glazed over the liturgy in church — tired and disaffected.

It had taken months of lawyer meetings to get to this moment. I'd been forced to change schools to avoid contact with friends who were implicated in the case. I had to drop out of hockey for the same reason. Finally, a chance to talk myself out of a prison sentence and get my life back.

I delivered my prepared speech to Justice Morgan and the court. My words dripped with remorse, partly sincere, partly forced because I was angry at what I felt was an overreaction by the prosecutors, who were throwing the book at me like I was a nasty scourge on society. I had taken a law class in the new high school I was forced to switch to while my case proceeded through the court system. Law makes sense when you read about it in a book, but when it comes down on you, you can't believe how little it captures. Nuance is lost. Your case, your life, is treated like airport baggage. They don't care. How could they, with so many cases to wade through? When you put yourself on the docket, all bets are off.

But I had put myself there. It was my stupid prank that exposed me to an imperfect justice system in the first place. No surprise, though. For me, rules and laws were roadblocks to a more intrepid point of view, one that always challenged convention. I was that little shit teachers dreaded teaching when they woke up in the mornings, because I treated rules like an obstacle course, always thinking of how they could be overcome or skirted.

I finished my plea for leniency, saying I was going to do something with my life. I had immersed myself in my studies at my new school and had an A+ average to show for it. I was going to contribute to society. I wouldn't make such a stupid mistake again.

It was enough.

Justice Morgan lambasted me for five minutes. An eternity for someone with his caseload. He threatened grave consequences were I to screw up again, his cheeks quivering in waves with each soaring sentence.

Then he sentenced me to eighty hours of community service and one year of probation.

Months of foreboding and weight and angst lifted off my chest. I rubbed my hands down my face, looking through my outstretched fingers as if they were the bars of the prison cell I had narrowly escaped. I was *free.*

3

Amy and I started dating in high school, a year before my run-in with the law. I was in grade ten, and she was in grade twelve. She was tall, beautiful, and president of the student council. I was mesmerized by her exotic Siberian eyes that gave away her Russian heritage. I could almost see her decked out in an ornamental reindeer hide and a fur ushanka hat. Teenage emotions and hormones ruled us, and our relationship morphed from lust to young love. The discovery of sex took over my life for the next four years. I was … well, I was sixteen. All I can remember is being between the sheets with Amy, or driving somewhere so I could crawl under the sheets with Amy. Four years in a teenager's life is an eternity. It's enough time to do incredible things — if focused. But I didn't know that yet. What could be as good as being between the sheets with Amy?

Amy endeared herself to everyone she met. She was a connector, she was likeable, but it drove me crazy how important it was for her to please everyone. Whereas my dad trained me to take a point of view and argue it, Amy dealt with difficult conversations about our future, religion, metaphysics — the stuff of my dinnertime conversations growing up — by laughing. On a scale from giggling to buckling at the waist, her laughter increased with the weight of the subject matter, like a baby being thrown up in the air higher and higher, laughing in terror, not joy.

While I finished high school, Amy began a two-year diploma at Niagara College in Welland, Ontario. I drove or hitchhiked the 200 kilometres between us regularly so that we could spend hours fawning over each other. After I graduated from high school in 2003, we both wound up at McMaster University together. My prison scare had been good for my grades, and I was admitted into the business program. By then, Amy had graduated from college and had decided to continue her education at McMaster, pursuing an English degree.

I was eighteen, two weeks into my second year of university, when Amy broke the news to me. We were standing in the kitchen of her student house late one morning when she said, with a rush of breath, "There's something we need to talk about." She searched the ground in front of my feet for the words. Something important was on her mind; she was uncharacteristically sombre. Where was the laughter that came with difficult subjects? Had someone died? *Is she breaking up with me?*

I took her hands and asked her what was going on. When she met my gaze, I saw her pupils were dilating, as if she'd been cast into darkness. The morning sun streamed in through the kitchen window, illuminating bits of dust that hung in the air, as if sharing in my suspense. Four years together, and I'd never seen her like this. She inhaled the breath she would use to deliver the news. Her hands began to quiver.

"I'm pregnant."

The words hung in the air with the dust momentarily, then circled me faster and faster, until my hopes and dreams started spinning in a nauseating whirlwind of future plans adjusting, correcting, and vanishing altogether.

I was nineteen, and I was going to be a father.

But wait, did she take multiple tests? Was she sure? Had she seen the doctor yet? *No? Okay, Okay. A glimmer of hope.*

"Jeremiah, I'm pregnant. This is happening."

An atomic bomb blasted through my ambitions, my future … *our* future. The feeling was like anticipating being behind bars, only this was much worse. This was a life sentence.

And then out of the centre of the blast radius, a rising plume of smoke. I drifted back into the present. There were two of us — no, three of us — to consider now. I took Amy in my arms and cradled her. I swayed my hips gently, and we began slow dancing around the kitchen.

"Everything's going to be okay," I murmured.

I would be there for her. We were in this together.

We lay together, made love, talked about how our families would react. *My dad! Fuck …*

A few hours later, I walked out Amy's front door and everything was different. An inescapable foreboding hung over me. Fall, my favourite season, no longer glowed with red, amber, and golden leaves. Now the leaves simply wilted — wet, tired, and waiting for winter.

For two months Amy and I kept her pregnancy private. The levee of secrecy finally broke during a visit back home in November. I sat in the living room on my parents' blue family sofa, twisting the piping trim on the pillows between my thumb and fingers. My mom sat diagonally across from me on a cushioned rocking chair, reading. Inherited from my great-grandma Dory, the old floral-patterned chair creaked and groaned on four old springs every time my mom shifted her weight. I bore a hole in the wall in front of me with a fixated stare. Every few minutes, beyond my peripheral vision, I sensed my mom gazing at me over her book. She would be psychoanalyzing me the same way she always did when me and my sisters were growing up, like subjects of a social science experiment.

"What's the matter?" she finally asked.

"Nothing."

"Jeremiah." My mom paused. "Is Amy pregnant?"

Of course she would figure it out that quickly.

"Yes," I responded immediately.

My mom put down her book and sighed. She cast me a whisper of a smile, a mixture of pity, empathy, and a touch of pride at her sleuthing prowess. And then came the questions: How long? Does anyone else know? When are you going to tell your father?

"I'll tell Dad tomorrow," I said.

She must have calculated that the best way for my dad to find out about my latest blunder, the biggest yet, would be with her preparation. She told him the news in bed late that night so that I wouldn't be subject to his initial shell-shocked response.

In the morning, while my dad pretended to read the *Globe and Mail,* I squirmed to find the words again.

"Dad, Amy's pregnant."

He calmly folded the paper and lowered it onto the coffee table to his right, letting it drop the last six inches with a perfunctory *thwap.*

"*Smart.* You're real *smart*, aren't you?" he said, his head bobbing up and down with sneering sarcasm. But then his tone grew softer. He'd thought things through already. The dad who became steadfast in times of crisis took over, only occasionally scowling in distain for my and Amy's recklessness. We discussed next steps and considered the options.

Amy and I had already discussed all the options. Abortion was never one of them. I had floated the idea of adoption and then immediately regretted it. Amy was having this baby with or without me, she'd said. The declaration had stung me to my core. Without me was not an option; we were in this together, and we would have *our* baby together. It was my duty, and I would be a damn good father!

The idea that I would be labelled as just another teen who got his girlfriend pregnant was revolting. I took it as another challenge to my character, another reason to write me off. I imagined Justice Morgan scoffing, "Humph! Surprise, surprise," along with others who had questioned my integrity over the years. My perception of these character attacks stemmed from repeated run-ins with authority, and people who at one time or another had predicted my future failure.

4

Amy's pregnancy happened during my latest ambitious project: trying to make the varsity football team. I had never played football before, and two months into my sophomore year I was still struggling to adapt to the new sport. I'd grown up playing hockey, but McMaster didn't have a varsity hockey team, so I'd decided to try out for football as a walk-on.

Clueless and competing against talented recruits from across the country, I'd shown up at training camp two weeks before classes began and hurled every inch of my tall, lean frame into my blocks. At one point the head coach, Greg Marshall, blew his shrill whistle to stop all eighty players so that he could praise my effort during a one-on-one blocking drill against a heavier opponent. "That's the level of intensity we need!" he said. "Now get yer --cking asses in gear." (He only ever articulated the tail end of the F-word: *--cking pick up the pace, what were you --cking thinking?*) That one moment was enough to motivate me for the whole year, and Coach Marshall saw enough in my effort and intensity to keep me around.

Each week on Thursday — the day before the day before game day — Coach Marshall posted a list outside his office and some eighty players would stream through the McMaster athletic centre to see who would dress for the Saturday game. There were only forty-five spots on the roster, and I wasn't in the running, but I'd go read the list to see who was last on the depth chart for my position and then set a goal to outwork them in practice every day the following week.

Coach Marshall had called me into his office before Thanksgiving that first year and had chuckled, saying, "Jerry, make sure you eat two turkeys this weekend."

I took the comment to heart, packing forty pounds of muscle onto my wiry frame over the next eight months, creeping up toward 255 pounds from 210.

I spent my second year making the most of my opportunity on service team offence (the guys who got beat on by the starting defence), or on service team defence (the guys who got beat on by the starting offence). Either way, it was a bleak existence. You got trampled by a herd of buffalo every day, and a roster spot seemed a distant world away. But I took pride in my role. I imagined I was a starting player on defence — an equal — lunging, swimming, ripping, and bull rushing my way through the starting offensive line. I hit the blocking sled as hard as I could hundreds of times until the sound of the springs bottoming out rang in my head the rest of the day.

At football practice the desire to quit plagued me daily. For all my eating, lifting weights, and studying the offensive playbook — in addition to a full academic course load — I couldn't learn the game fast enough as a tight end. Most practices saw me running incorrect routes and smashing into our starting receivers, or getting steamrolled by a defensive end while trying to remember my blocking assignment mid-play. Purple-faced coaches lit into me regularly.

But I wasn't wired to quit. Instead, I began a program of self-loathing. Wanting to quit was a form of self-pity. Self-pity, I thought, meant I was a pussy, and the more self-pity I felt, the more compelled I became to succeed at football.

This had been my reality for my entire freshman year. With Amy now pregnant, my second year of football brought anger and frustration as I doubled down and determined not to let the news make me feel sorry for myself. I would not quit football.

My teammates saw that something was bothering me. They started saying encouraging things more than usual: "Keep at it, Jer. You're putting things together; you're real close!" They saw despair stitched on my face, which they thought was entirely due to how shitty a football player I was. *I'm not just a shitty football player, I'm a shitty football player who knocked up his girlfriend!* I thought, biting my tongue.

I finally found my place within the football team's offensive line unit as an offensive tackle. The o-line was a group of young men led by Coach

Riley, a former Canadian Football League offensive lineman who commanded a special kind of respect from the rest of the team. A bull and a panda bear all in one, Riley could rip into you until your confidence was buried six feet under and then turn around and tell you how proud he was of your effort and improvement. Without a good offensive line, there would be no holes for the running back to run through or enough time for the quarterback to make spectacular touchdown passes. We were the heart of the offence, and I was the runt of the litter.

Every day I drank protein shakes made with five raw eggs and consumed a vegan-shocking amount of chicken, fish, and beef as I tried to pack weight onto my limber six-foot-five frame. At one point my 315-pound teammate Kyle Koch printed out blue T-shirts for the offensive line that read "Chubby Buddies" in big white block letters. When he reluctantly handed me a shirt, it was the first time I'd felt a longing to trade in my lean physique for a bulging barrel chest and no neck so that I could be a true Chubby Buddy.

I decided to tell Coach Riley about my secret after a gruelling evening practice one night under the floodlights of McMaster's back forty field. My teammates jogged through the rain to the locker rooms, where catered hot pasta waited to be devoured before they broke down film of the last game. I asked Coach Riley to hang back so that we could talk for a second in private. As the last players jogged by, sweat evaporating into small clouds over their shoulder pads and helmets, a lump formed in my throat.

"What is it, Jer?" Coach Riley asked.

I told him my news, then immediately made it clear that I wasn't quitting football. Coach Riley put on his panda demeanour. He said I could talk to him any time, and I did. I was nineteen, and the thought of becoming a father scared the hell out of me. Riley checked in with me often after practices, standing close and speaking softly from underneath the Tilley hat he wore every day. Being able to talk to someone about becoming a father lifted much of the burden. I no longer had a big secret. I could move on to thinking about what kind of father I wanted to be and not worry about what others thought.

A week after telling Coach Riley, I told a few other teammates. Thirty seconds later, the whole team knew, and then everybody knew. My best friend, Chris, let out a sigh of understanding when he found out. I'd been acting odd for months and now he knew why. He went through a process I had become accustomed to: shock; an empathetic phrase like "Wow, man! That's *tough*!"; then him imagining himself getting his girlfriend pregnant; followed by more shock; followed by even more empathy.

5

Amy went into labour on May 16, 2005. As we entered the hospital, my sense of smell was heightened as if *I* was pregnant; it smelled like cornmeal mixed with necrotic tissue. Where was it coming from? Amy's room was mostly white, with pastel-blue curtains and blankets. The floor was polished clean of the pools of blood that must have repeatedly splattered it, like in a Jackson Pollock painting. What the heck was that huge stainless steel bowl doing in the corner of the room? Was it for making pancakes the next morning?

"It's where we put the placenta," the nurse said.

For the life of me, I couldn't remember what a placenta was.

The contractions began, and Amy's rapid "oh" breaths preceded a thirty-second death grip on my hand. I reminded her to keep breathing deeply like we'd been taught in prenatal class.

"Shutttt uppppp!" she groaned.

So I shut up. Then I tried to caress her arm, standing helplessly beside her.

"Don't touch me!" she puffed between breaths.

It was startling to watch my always kind and patient girlfriend transform into an assertive drill sergeant.

As the baby crowned, I couldn't help but think of our receiver coach creating the same oval shape with his thumb and index finger while demonstrating a proper catch. When Ethan was finally born, I gave a quick yelp of joy. Having hoped for a boy all along, I'd never been so happy to see a penis. My biological duty had been carried out. My genes would continue, and I had a head start on most other nineteen-year-old man-boys — even this life event could be framed as a competition! As I cut the rubbery umbilical cord with scissors, I experienced a primal (if somewhat grossed-out) satisfaction.

Ethan's eyes were two slits resting on puffy cheeks. His little bluish-pink body was put together like the Michelin Man, and his tiny fingers gaped and clasped onto air, trying to find balance in a new atmosphere void of amniotic fluid.

I went into the waiting room and told our collection of family and friends it was a boy, giving a fist pump like I'd scored a touchdown. Despite all the foreboding and angst leading up to that moment, I was genuinely happy. Mom and baby were healthy, and we could now start the real journey into parenthood.

Our parents were the first to meet their new grandson. My mom had that grin on her face that hid her true feelings. I wondered what myriad thoughts were going through her head. My dad smiled reservedly. He disapproved of the circumstances, but he loves kids and he didn't yet know that he was staring at the baby who would grow into his little best friend.

Amy's mom was ecstatic, as she had been all along. She'd been congratulatory when we'd first told her Amy was pregnant on the couch of her log cabin home. I'd wondered then what kind of crack she'd been smoking — had she forgotten how young we were, how unplanned it was?

Finally, Amy's dad shook my hand in congratulations. He had the patience and empathy of ten men — the complete opposite of me — and though I didn't understand his gifts, I respected him.

The biggest mental adjustment after Ethan's birth was accepting the perpetuity of the change. Ethan was in our lives forever, and along with all the love and wonder came the dissolution of my individuality. It was like I'd stepped out of my own private room and been locked out forever.

6

While Ethan slept, I would go to the YMCA and work out, still desperate to gain strength and muscle mass before training camp in August of 2005. Something about becoming a father hardened my work ethic. Football wouldn't pay the bills, but I felt as though my success in football was linked to the well-being of my son. During camp, I made an impression on the coaches. Every training camp was a tryout; your one opportunity to show the coaches your gains in strength and skill from off-season training. I was now strong enough to withstand a bull rush from the biggest defensive players on the team. I finally graduated from the practice roster, earning a spot in the starting lineup as offensive tackle. At six feet five inches tall, I weighed 255 pounds and I could bench press 225 pounds eleven times — modest for an offensive lineman, but as big and as strong as I'd ever be.

Amy brought Ethan to my football games dressed in a mini homemade McMaster Marauders football T-shirt. At five months old, he recognized me and Amy but probably had no true allegiance to the stenciled Marauder collecting drool on his shirt. After each game at the Ivor Wynne Stadium in Hamilton, Amy would pass Ethan to me from the stands and I'd be circled by a group of offensive linemen resembling a troop of gorillas. Their grim game faces would curl into grins, and they'd gingerly pat Ethan on the head with large, taped-up sausage fingers, worried one of their gigantic limbs might crush him.

Throughout my third season, my fatigue built to a point where I was having trouble staying sharp in the classroom and on the football field. My relationship with Amy was one of existence and not much more. During

Amy, me, and Ethan after a football game.

group work with fellow commerce students, I would nod off in the middle of someone asking me a question, jolting my head back up after realizing, too late, that I'd fallen asleep again.

I was desperate to get Ethan into a routine, but he wouldn't sleep through the night for the first eight months of his life. I tried to convince Amy to let him cry it out, at one point sitting with her in the living room while Ethan wailed away in his crib. Fifteen minutes passed, then thirty. After an hour and a half, he was still crying with the same gusto as at the beginning of the ordeal. Amy pleaded with me, and I finally gave in. She went into his room, picked him up, and brought him out into the living room. He peered over her shoulder at me with glassy eyes and a look that said, *You're mine now, sucker.*

The period of time between September 2005 and May 2006 felt like one long, dreamy coma. Never quite asleep or awake, Amy and I trudged back and forth to our classes, taking shifts with Ethan. I would be alone with him, tired, playing games of distraction, eventually getting bored and counting down the minutes until Amy returned to take her shift. As soon as I'd leave, I could only think about how much I looked forward to seeing Ethan again. That's what babies do; they exhaust you and fill you up at the same time.

Despite new responsibilities, I was having a breakout year as a football player, playing well in games and getting positive feedback from our coaches during film sessions. But I just *couldn't* get the sleep I needed. Every crunching block in my zombie state felt so jarring, like I was being shaken awake just when I wanted to sleep. It made me lash out in anger more than usual, earning me the nickname Angry Dad.

Halfway into the 2005 football season, I tore the labrum in my right shoulder while attempting to block a roid-raging bull of a defensive end in a game against Laurier University. I tried to play through the injury and wound up needing arthroscopic surgery on my shoulder at the end of the season. Rehabilitation took eight months. With my arm in a sling, muscle seemed to evaporate off my frame, and every pound I lost, Ethan gained. He weighed as much as a heavy sack of potatoes now, so I switched to carrying him around in my left arm to avoid tearing the scar tissue in my shoulder. I wasn't cleared to lift heavy weights again until just two months before training camp in 2006, and by then I had lost twenty pounds of muscle. While most people who step on the scale hope to see their weight go down, I was desperate to gain weight. Every time the scale registered under 250 pounds, a pang of disgust resonated inside me. *Weak. Pathetic.*

The role of starting offensive tackle was still mine to lose going into my fourth and final year. I did the best I could to keep my edge, but my confidence was shaken. I'd earned my starting position through relentless physical aggression, and now I was conscious of my shoulder on every play. A millisecond of hesitation before contact is all it takes to get blown up by a defensive end, and I wound up spending much of my last season trying to block them with my head and one arm.

The only dream I'd had was possibly getting a sniff at the CFL draft as a tight end, and that dream was now out of reach. It hadn't yet occurred to me that there was life beyond football, that the greatest challenge of my life was still in front of me.

7

It was in the middle of that frustrating final football season that I began thinking about other sports and recalled a memory from childhood. When I was eight, I saw a huge spread in the *Toronto Star* about Derek Porter, the Canadian world champion in single sculls rowing. The article touted him as the favourite to win gold at the Atlanta Olympics in 1996.

There was a big picture of Porter sitting dockside in his single. Strands of taught, ropy muscle hung off the broadest shoulders and longest arms I'd ever seen. His shins looked like swords.

I thought, *That's what an athlete looks like.*

The memory struck me again when, while walking through the atrium of the McMaster student centre one day, I came across a fundraiser being put on by the university's rowing team. Several unassuming rowers — slight in build, with generous, smiling faces — were challenging students to a 250-metre race on rowing ergometers. It cost ten dollars to race, and if you won they'd double your money. They looked like easy prey. I sat down on the ergometer and pulled a few strokes to see how the pull would affect my shoulder.

No pain. Okay, game on.

On the ergometer beside me the team's best male rower, Aubrey Olsen, sat down on the sliding seat, dropped his feet into the heel cups of the Concept 2 ergometer, and strapped them securely to the footboards. He smiled at me, confident but wary that he was going to have to go hard against me (I didn't have an intimidating build for an offensive lineman, but I did for a rower). Aubrey's right brow rose slightly higher than his left, giving him a permanent look of curiosity. He had an average build, but his legs looked powerful through his spandex unisuit. He was nowhere near as big as our linebackers. *I can beat this guy*, I thought. We set the rowing machine monitors for 500 metres and then rolled forward on the seats for the start.

"Attention … row!" yelled another rower.

I clenched my forearms, contracted my biceps, and thrust my upper body backwards. Aubrey pressed his legs down with smooth power and acceleration, keeping his back in a strong, slightly forward-angled position. I lurched forward for my second stroke. The chain attached to the handle rattled loudly, oscillating wildly and out of control. Aubrey's hands accelerated to and from his chest with quick, athletic motions. His chain purred. His body relaxed and slackened as he rolled forward on his seat for each new stroke. While Aubrey used the full range of the long metal track under his seat, I pivoted on the spot in a seizure. *If only the damn seat didn't move so much, I could use my strength to beat him.*

With 50 metres to go my arms seized up, but it was close and I still had a chance. I threw my head backward, using my shoulders and upper body to take the load for the remaining eight strokes.

Aubrey beat me by two seconds. The whole experience lasted about a minute thirty. My mouth was dry from sucking air, and I panted to catch my breath. This rowing business was harder than it looked. My curiosity was piqued, but only a little. I'd participated in a random fundraiser, a test of brute strength. It might as well have been the high striker game at a travelling carnival.

After shaking hands with Aubrey, I left the student centre to meet Amy and get Ethan before her next class. I never thought I'd sit on a rowing machine again.

8

It's etched into my brain: Laurier University football fans, their faces and bodies painted purple and gold, rushing past us to join their players, some turning back to taunt us. We were gutted. I scanned the field. Our team stood or kneeled, staring silently at the victors. Our football season had ended at the hands of the Wilfrid Laurier Golden Hawks in the provincial semifinal. Our quarterback, Adam Archibald, stood gazing into the end zone, where his final Hail Mary pass had been batted away by a Laurier defensive back just moments before. The scoreboard clock showed 00:00.00. We'd played our last game at the highest level of sport most of us would ever know. A handful of players would have a chance to continue playing in the Canadian Football League, but for most of us it was the end of a major chapter in our lives.

9

It started out as a fleeting thought: *Maybe there is another sport I could still do at a high level?* My shoulder was a problem, but there were plenty of sports that wouldn't put the same stress on it that football had. While Ethan and I watched Amy play hockey for McMaster that winter, I thought about trying out for a Junior C hockey team in Hamilton. Too risky — shoulder. *Javelin?* No. *Kayaking?* I'd seen Adam van Koeverden, Olympic champ in kayaking and also a McMaster student, working out at the McMaster athletics centre a couple of times. *No, I'm too tall.* I thought about the erg competition against Aubrey. *Rowing? Rowing … hmm.* More research revealed that the Canadian men's eight were the current world champions. *Interesting.*

I remembered Aubrey from the erg fundraiser and dug up his number. It was August 2007. I told him I wanted to try rowing a real boat, and he agreed to meet me at the Leander Boat Club in Hamilton. The next Saturday morning, I rode my bike over to the club — a simple, rectangular building with twin exterior staircases leading up to the second storey. Adjacent to the club, sailboats bobbed in the breeze. The sun shone fully that day. I felt relaxed and optimistic, taking the stairs four steps at a time. Inside was a banquet room. It smelled historic. The interior walls were clad with knotty wood panelling. Red leather banquet chairs stood scattered around tables as if a group of people had just left in a hurry. Aubrey stood against a wooden bar at the front of the room, leaning back with an air of pride about him. There was an air of pride about him. His body partially framed the Leander Boat Club insignia mounted on the front of the bar. Behind him, the club's rowing history adorned the walls. Framed black-and-white pictures of rowing crews had started to yellow with age.

Several plaques shaped like shields were mounted onto the wood panels to display the victories of Leander crews in decades past. Aubrey clearly had a reverence for his sport.

"How's it going?" I said.

"Good!" he chirped. He was an exceedingly friendly character. "So, what brings you down here now?"

"I want to go to the Olympics and win a gold medal in rowing," I said, dead serious.

He smiled and looked down to gather himself. "Uh, okay, well ..."

We talked rowing — the physical demands, Canada's success in the sport, his uncle who had rowed internationally.

He sized me up and said I'd probably need to get leaner and lose some of the muscle mass I had worked so hard to pack onto my frame. Trimmed down, he said, I'd be the perfect size for rowing: tall, lean, and strong. After a few minutes, he suggested we go downstairs to the boathouse to try some rowing in the tank before heading out on the water for an introductory row.

The boathouse's ground level housed long, sleek rowing shells resting upside down on wooden racks. Aluminum riggers flared out from the middle of the boats. Small fins mounted near the stern interrupted the smooth, polished carbon fibre grain, poking out like shark fins. The boats were beautiful streamlined missiles. Some shells hung from slings attached to the ceiling, raised and lowered by a rope pulley system. Oars hung down from high wooden racks, resembling a giant kelp forest with thick stalks rising from the ocean floor. The floor of the boathouse was gravel, and the stones crunched loudly underfoot as Aubrey showed me to the change room.

I went inside to change into my favourite pair of loose basketball shorts and my lucky long-sleeved maroon Under Armour compression shirt. A few high school rowers were milling about in spandex that clung to their bodies. *There's no way I'm wearing one of those ridiculous unisuits,* I thought.

I went out and met Aubrey at the rowing tank beside the boat bays.

"Hi, I'm Alan," he said.

He quickly recognized the look of confusion on my face, a common occurrence in his life.

"I'm Aubrey's brother. We're identical twins."

Aubrey emerged to our right, smiling. From that point on, I couldn't differentiate between the two of them.

The rowing tank was made up of two giant basins of water, each three feet deep, with oarlocks mounted on the sides. In between the two basins, rowing seats were fixed on tracks, much like in a rowing shell. You could slide back and forth and row with oars extending into the tank water.

Aubrey sat down on one of the seats and instructed me to strap my feet into the seat position behind him. He demonstrated several strokes while Alan commented on his technique and explained the elements of each stroke: the catch, the drive, the finish, and the recovery. As Alan spoke, I put my oar in the water and joined Aubrey. I wasn't really listening. I wanted to get this fake rowing over with so that I could get on the water in a real boat.

After a few more minutes of Alan's coaching, we stopped and cajoled three junior rowers into taking me out for a row in a four-man sweep boat. *Sweeping*, I learned, was what you called rowing with both hands on one longer oar, while *sculling* was rowing with a smaller oar in each hand.

The three volunteer rowers were half my size. We slid a gleaming four-person sweep boat off the racks and onto our shoulders. The boat dug into my shoulder, which was several inches higher than the shoulders of my pimply faced crew. We walked unsteadily to the dock, swung the boat down to our hips, and then placed it on the water. Alan adjusted the inboard of an oar for me while the three boys unscrewed their oarlock gates and set their oars in place. Alan passed me my oar. It made a zipper sound, increasing in pitch as the carbon threads slid across the hard plastic of the oarlock, stopping with a clunk when the oar collar struck the oarlock. I snapped the gate pin shut and screwed it tight, securing my oar in place. We stepped in.

"Not there!" Alan warned. "The carbon fibre is weak between the slides. Place your foot farther up."

He worried my weight would put my foot right through the carbon deck. It was strange to hear someone worry about being too heavy. Every pound was to be coveted in my mind.

"Ready … shove," said the boy in the seat position nearest to the stern of the boat — the stroke seat. He would attempt to lead our timing and rhythm.

We pushed off the dock. I immediately lost my balance, shifting my hips and arching my shoulders against the sloping boat. The idea behind putting me in a four for my first row was so I could feel more stable with the help of the other rowers. Alan must have miscalculated; the boat was not stable. We rowed with arms only, making our way out of the sheltered harbour. Alan, meanwhile, climbed aboard one of the aluminum coach boats, brought the outboard engine to life with one pull of the cord, and followed us out into the rougher waters of the open bay.

"Okay, Jerry, we're going to start rowing at half-slide," he yelled over the drone of the boat motor.

I didn't know what *half-slide* meant, and I couldn't make sense of the sequence of movements. My oar kept getting sucked into the water when I under or over-rotated the blade at the start of each stroke. "That's called 'catching a crab,'" the boy behind me said, after I took one such stroke and had the oar force me back into his lap.

I sat travelling backwards, third from the front of the boat, floundering helplessly. It was too much. I couldn't manage one single stroke in time with the others. My oar clapped along the top of the water, showering them with cold spray.

After less than a kilometre of rowing, all five of us had had enough. I ran out of things to say to make light of the situation, and we fell silent until we reached the dock. I apologized to my young crewmates for nearly capsizing the boat several times. We lifted the boat out of the water and swung it overhead, drenching ourselves with the lake water I'd splashed into the boat. I apologized again. As soon as the boat and oars were returned to the boathouse, I thanked Alan — or was it Aubrey? — and rode my bike home.

Fuck this sport, I thought.

PART TWO: THE CATCH

Eight, good; eight, good; nine, better; eight, good; nine, better. Very good, Andrew.... Three, no; one [silence]; four, better; two, no; one, no. Don't tear the water, Jerry. Find your stake, and then pull the boat past the stake.

— Mike Spracklen, rating each stroke out of ten

10

After graduating from McMaster in 2007 with a business degree, I immediately began worrying about finding a job. Amy and I had moved in together after Ethan was born, along with her previous roommate and friend, Nicole, who was training to be a nurse and didn't mind living with a newborn. To help pay the bills, we somehow managed to convince two other girls from the university to move in with a baby prone to 2:00 a.m. cries.

I'd renovated the single-car garage behind our house into a recording studio and tried to make it a viable business. It never got off the ground, but the studio came in handy whenever Ethan chose to demonstrate his impressive lungs with a prolonged cry. By the time he'd worked himself up to maximum decibels, I would be bounding down the back steps of the house, often in my socks through a foot of snow, with Ethan in my arms, his crying muffled in a bundle of blankets. Nicole was our friend and knew what to expect, but I worried about losing the other two girls as tenants if they felt they couldn't study or sleep with Ethan around.

Whenever Ethan had a fit, I'd go through the motions: offer a bottle of formula, rock up and down on my toes, speak soothingly, speak firmly, distract him with objects, make weird faces, and finally give up. No one warns new parents about having to endure a cranky baby with no apparent solution. As an individual, I could always at least act on my problem, no matter how frustrating it was. With my infant son, I was forced to accept the frustration, beaten by his sheer helplessness.

Amy and I often sat for long stretches of silence staring at Ethan as he played. It was incredible to watch him learn and grow and giggle, but it made it easy to ignore our own relationship, which was developing into a doormat for our exalted child. We'd become business partners in a joint venture, and so long as each partner contributed to the development of the child — our flagship product — everything would be okay. The idea of investing in each other didn't occur to us (less so to me, to be fair). The idea of *working* at my relationship with Amy was not something I understood. I did my duty; I was manning up. Wasn't that good enough? Couldn't she see?

Our love for Ethan shrouded the fact that we were drifting apart. I'd made no promises about ever getting married. I was a high-risk proposition, and that caused Amy to feel uncertain about the future. I insisted that my commitment was the only thing that mattered, that I didn't need to validate it with marriage.

After Amy finished her degree in May 2008, we moved back home. Her mom, T.J., owned waterfront property on nearby Rice Lake, from which she ferried customers to an island she owned and used to operate a small ecotourism business. We spent the summer working for T.J., digging outhouse holes, spraying poison ivy, or building things. Ethan had just turned three, and followed us around everywhere, always wearing a lifejacket that beefed him up and gave him the stature of a mini Danny DeVito. I spent my days helping Amy's brother, Jeremy, build two eco-cabins on either end of the island. Bare-chested in the sun, sweaty forearms caked in sawdust, the random whine of the table saw and the sweet smell of freshly cut barnboard — it was a satisfying existence.

Living on Rice Lake meant long drives to visit our families in Cobourg, forty-five minutes away. Long drives meant lots of time to think. The transition from university life to the resigned state of the-rest-of-your-life was underwhelming. I was a fiery twenty-two-year-old without a passion, an unlit fuse, craving a challenge and unwilling to settle. My father often said his university days were the best of his life, that he'd never again experience the joy of pursuing a true liberal arts education. My dad had studied philosophy and political science, subjects that were supposed to teach you how to live. I'd studied a more pragmatic business degree — learning how to gather more of the world's scarce resources for myself or my company. My dad's lofty world of ideas naturally set me on an opposing course of concrete action. And at twenty-two years old, I knew I was not done with competitive sport. I supposed I'd take another look at rowing.

I searched rowing videos on YouTube and came across two Kiwi rowers, Rob Waddell and Mahé Drysdale, in a head-to-head race to see who would represent New Zealand at the 2008 Olympics. Waddell, gold medallist in the single sculls at the 2000 Sydney Olympics, had come out of retirement to make a bid for Beijing against his fellow countryman, Drysdale, who had won the World Championships in the single sculls the previous three years in a row.

A little more research, and I learned that Waddell also held the indoor world record for 2,000 metres on the same Concept 2 rowing machine Aubrey and I had raced on at the McMaster rowing fundraiser. His time was 5:36.6, a record he'd set earlier that year.

After an hour of watching Olympic rowing footage, I decided I was ready to give rowing another shot.

11

The closest rowing club was in Peterborough, a city north of Rice Lake. I drove to the club on a warm Sunday afternoon in July. The club was deserted, quiet. I walked around to the front of the boathouse, which faced the calm waters of the Otonabee River. Nobody was there. Both boat bay doors were closed, but I found an unlocked door on the side of the building. I entered into dingy darkness, a smell of musk, scrambling to find the light switch.

"Hello?" I called out.

Silence.

My eyes adjusted with the help of daylight creeping through the cracks of the boat bay doors. I found the light switch, flipped it up. Cold white light shuttered, then solidified, illuminating the bays. So many shells! I scanned them, unsure of what I was looking for, wondering which one I might be able to use.

Near the front of the boat bays, I came across five Concept 2 ergometers lined up in a row. I remembered Waddell's world record time, 5:36.6. *Let's see how close I can get,* I thought.

Wearing jeans, steel-toed boots, and a T-shirt, I hopped on the erg casually, set it for 2,000 metres, and went as hard as I could for about a minute. And then I held on for dear life for another five and a half minutes — a textbook fly-and-die rowing race profile. It's a good way to break in new jeans.

The time of that first test was 6:38 — a full minute slower than the world record. Okay, so there was work to be done. I was more curious about how my time stacked up against male heavyweight rowers in general.

At six foot five and 230 pounds, I was the same size as Waddell, but clearly inferior in training and physiology.

That evening I emailed the club, asking if I could rent a single shell. A club coordinator named Geneve responded the next day with good news: a Trent University rower had agreed to rent me his boat for a small fee.

I drove back to the club the next day and met Geneve. She showed me to the boat and helped me select oars.

"Have you rowed before?" she asked.

"No. Well, once. In a four," I said.

"Usually, we require new rowers to take our learn-to-row class before we rent them equipment."

"It's not necessary. Watch."

I was impatient, arrogant. I scooped the loaned single shell off the top rack in the boat bay and struggled to balance it. Geneve grabbed the stern just before it hit the floor. "Oops," I smiled.

The boat was twenty-seven feet long and only eighteen inches wide. I walked it fifty feet to the dock held lengthwise across my body, like a giant tightrope walker's balancing pole. I set the boat in the water, placed the oars in the oarlocks, snapped down the gates and screwed them shut, and placed my foot in the boat.

"Don't step there," Geneve warned.

Right, like Aubrey had said.

She grabbed the aluminum rigger to stabilize the boat while I got in and slipped my feet into the shoes mounted on the footboard.

"Okay, I'm ready!" I said.

She looked skeptical. I tried to row out of her line of sight with arms only. She stood on the dock staring until, not knowing what to make of me, she turned and walked away, shaking her head.

The water of the Otonabee River was calm and clear. You could see the bottom to a depth of twelve feet before slabs of rock turned green, then disappeared into blackness. I thought of the many hours I'd spent in my grandpa's red canvas canoe in Muskoka, with its leaky cedar rib-and-plank construction. The rowing shell I now sat in was one quarter the wetted surface and tippy as hell.

It was time to try my legs. I unlocked my knees and slid forward on the seat, getting no more than halfway up the slide before rolling hard to port. I stuck out my left hand, helplessly bracing against water, pausing for a moment, then tumbling in with my feet still stuck in the shoes. I scrambled underwater to pull at the laces attached to the Velcro straps on my shoes to release myself, only now understanding they were there to prevent newbies like me from drowning.

I tried to get back into the boat. Impossible. The oars swung in different directions, as if magnetically opposed to their proper positions. At last, I decided to swim the boat 2,000 metres back to the dock.

Geneve was waiting for me, arms crossed.

"This boat will do fine, thanks!" I said, pulling myself out of the water.

Before leaving I asked her, "Is 6:38 a good two-hundred-metre ergometer time?"

I was hoping her eyes would light up, followed by something like, *Oh wow! That's amazing for your first erg test!*

Instead, she seemed unimpressed: "It's not bad for a college-level heavyweight rower … I guess."

I strapped the boat to the roof rack on my car and escaped back to Rice Lake, away from the watchful eye of Geneve. I looked forward to figuring out the sport once and for all, on my own.

I spent one week with the boat on Rice Lake, each day walking down the boat ramp, wading through weeds until I was thigh-deep in water, then propping myself unsteadily on the rolling seat. I stayed close to shore so that I could quickly get back in the boat each time I capsized, which was at every attempted stroke initially.

I thought of the story my uncle Tim had told me about my dad jumping on my uncle David's windsurfer and flying across the lake. I'd imagined learning how to row would be just as effortless. Not so.

Ethan watched me curiously from shore in his diaper for a few minutes before losing interest.

Make a fool out of yourself, Dad. Just don't go too far.

I didn't think I needed a coach. I had the equipment, the lake, and YouTube. On my last day with the boat, I discovered I'd had the oarlocks backwards the entire time. This meant I'd been rowing with no clearance for my hands at the finish of the stroke. No wonder my hands were getting stuck against my body.

Despite my ignorant, stubborn approach, there were moments of insight, like a portal into another world where, for two or three strokes, all the rigidity and frustration would melt away and I'd glide freely across the water. Once I'd managed four or five full strokes in a row without falling in, I told Amy and Ethan to come watch, only to fall in once more. It was the beginning of chasing an elusive state of perfection between man, vessel, and water.

12

I Superman-launched myself onto my parents' basement couch, flipped on the TV, and started mashing ketchup chips into my face with my palm. I'd returned the rowing shell to the Peterborough club after failing to figure out how to row for the second time. All together, I had six days of rowing experience with nothing to show for it. I thought rowing would be like riding a bike, difficult at first, but leading to that aha moment, where everything fell into place.

It was Sunday, August 17, 2008, and the Olympics were on TV. I channel surfed, looking for replays of events that had taken place earlier in Beijing. The familiar CBC logo with Olympic rings came on the screen. I paused. The elevated pitch of an announcer's voice was calling a race, excited, worried: Would the Canadians be able to hold on? The Canadian men's eight rowing crew was rowing for gold, and I'd joined the broadcast with 500 metres left in the race. I set the converter down on the coffee table in front of me. The Canadians had a three-quarter-length lead on the rest of the field, but the British and Americans were charging back in the late stages. I stood up.

The broadcast zoomed in on the Canadian crew, their faces etched with pain, teeth bared at the end of each stroke. The long shot camera footage hid their pain when the camera zoomed back out. It made rowing look effortless, smooth, *easy.* I'd fallen for that illusion.

The British and Americans kept closing, with only 100 metres to go. The bows of the boats heaved back and forth, straining forward, slipping back. After each stroke, the Canadians' lead seemed to melt away. I started jumping up and down. Come on! *Come on!*

They did it. They were Olympic champions!

I watched them celebrate with envy. The rower seated second from the stern — seven-seat position, in rowing terms — climbed toward the back of the boat to hug his teammates. Most of them bowed their heads in exhaustion but still managed to raise their limp arms in victory. Nestled in the stern of the boat, facing the eight rowers, sat the coxswain. It was his role to guide the rowers through their race plan, steer the boat, and motivate the crew — a commanding presence in a diminutive body no larger than a horse jockey. He ripped off his headset microphone, splashed water in the air, and shouted praise at the completely spent men in front of him. Later, all eight rowers, clad in red-and-white spandex with the maple leaf on their chests, lined up shoulder to shoulder to receive their gold medals. One of them belted out our anthem at the top of his lungs.

I burned for that moment. *I will be on that podium one day*, I thought to myself. What did they have that I didn't? I shared the same body type: lean and tall. It was easy to picture myself standing alongside them. I still didn't know much about the physiological demands, but the path seemed clear: The only thing between me and a moment like that was a mountain of hard work. An Everest-sized mountain of hard work.

I had to find a way to get to Victoria, home to the men's national rowing team. But how? How could I get there, and how could I make it work? I needed time to train, time to raise my son properly, a job to support myself, and had a girlfriend to keep interested. I couldn't see a path forward. Then, with hope fading, I came across a TD Bank job opening in Victoria and things took a serendipitous turn.

"And you are aware that the job is very technical and analytical?" The woman warned, her voice bearing the weariness that comes from a long career in human resources at a major bank. She was screening me for an entry-level associate position with TD Commercial Bank — this was my ticket to Victoria.

"I'm aware," I told the woman.

Long days without a fixed goal had me restless. Hours spent sitting on the kitchen floor with Ethan stacking soup cans to make a tower gave me time to wonder whether the story of the rest of my life had already been written:

kid, marriage, job, mortgage, car payments, more kids, bigger mortgage. If life is a roller coaster, it looked like I'd be riding the merry-go-round. But I didn't want to know every twist and turn that lay ahead. These thoughts drove me toward an existential crisis — I felt like I had something to prove. What or to whom, I didn't know. Mostly to myself, I think.

"Can you tell me about a time you used analytical skills in a financial context?" the woman asked.

I stammered, caught off guard by the question. My mind went blank. I started speaking, hoping my brain would catch up with my mouth. It didn't.

"Uh, sorry, can you repeat the question?" I asked.

The woman repeated herself, softening her tone and switching to the encouraging voice of someone with years of experience dealing with nervous candidates.

"Uh, right, analytical skills in a financial context." I repeated her repeated question and made up something plausible — more indicative of creative thinking ability than financial acumen. My response was satisfactory. She set up a second phone interview with a VP in Vancouver the following day at noon.

I took the call in half a suit. The plan was to be fully dressed, but I'd lost track of time reviewing accounting principles from old textbooks all morning in my parents' basement. Where were my pants? I couldn't find them. The phone rang.

"Hi, may I speak with Jeremiah Brown, please?" said a baritone voice.

"This is Jeremiah," I said.

"Hi, Jeremiah, this is Mauro Manzi, district vice-president."

We talked football for the first five minutes. I got the impression he was as much concerned with making sure I had half a personality as with sussing out my analytical skills. Too many Type A personalities in his office, perhaps.

We found some common ground, laughed hard together, and then Mr. Manzi got down to business.

"Okay, I need to ask you some finance questions now. Do you have the sample financial statements I emailed you?" he asked.

"I do." I squirmed in front of my computer, my calculator shaking in my free hand. There were a hundred business grads interviewing in person in Vancouver that day, and me on the phone in my underwear in Ontario. Single-digit addition was hard to think about in my state, let alone the myriad of advanced financial questions Mr. Manzi could ask me about the statements on my computer.

"Can you discuss what you think about this company's balance sheet in general financial terms? Any red flags?"

Shit. *Buy time.*

"Well, without knowing the industry, liquidity looks okay. Decent capitalization, not overleveraged. Umm …"

What was the catch? I didn't see it. I was sunk.

"Yeah, looks pretty straightforward to me. Nothing to note, really," Mr. Manzi interjected.

I exhaled a quiet breath of relief.

Next, he asked me to look at the income statement and calculate the company's true cash flow for the year. I knew the intent of the question — would I forget to add back amortization, a non-cash expense? I did the math three times, just to be sure, and gave him my answer.

"Okay, Jeremiah. I think that's all I need from you for now. Thanks. We'll be in touch."

I hung up, let out a whoop, and hopped around the basement in celebration. I'd gotten the job. I knew it in my gut.

Right away, I phoned Amy. "Congratulations!" she said uncertainly. She didn't want to leave Ontario. She'd grown up helping out with the family business. Her Russian immigrant grandfather had built it from one cottage into a sprawling resort that was popular with American tourists. Now her mom was developing her new eco-cabin resort business, and Amy, who had grown up believing she would continue the family business, wanted to help build it with her mom. And I was trying to pull her across the continent for my first real career opportunity. My compromise was that we could come back. After two or three years of experience, I could get transferred back to Ontario, somewhere close to her family and her mom's business. She eventually, hesitantly, agreed.

Somehow I'd forgotten — during the interviews, the congratulatory phone call, and the offer letter that came in the mail — about my criminal record. A harpoon pierced my excitement when, in the last paragraph of the offer letter, I read: *conditional on satisfactory criminal record check.* It had been five years since my run-in with the law. Even though I was a youth when convicted, criminal records last five years for indictable offences.

Criminal record checks did not produce a paragraph of context under each conviction. Robbery was robbery, whether you pistol-whipped a bank teller and stole thousands, or you stood beside your friend as he grabbed a tray of pitas from the delivery man. I felt raw, old feelings of persecution returning.

The bank needed to fly me out to Vancouver to sign job offer documents and attend an orientation. I would go and try to explain my criminal record. They would reject me. They'd practically gone over my university transcript with a magnifying glass; there was no way they'd let a criminal record slide. I worried the whole plane ride from Toronto to Vancouver. In the taxi from the airport to the hotel, the jovial driver peppered me with questions. My answers were short, the conversation giving way to silence.

The next day, feeling sorry for myself, I wrapped a blue tie around my neck into a double Windsor knot. *Why didn't you bring a green one, idiot?* Then I walked to the soaring TD Tower at 700 West Georgia Street in downtown Vancouver. Its black glass facing gave the impression it housed a government secret service agency. I gathered in the waiting area of TD's human resources offices with twelve other new hires, waiting to be found out.

A woman named Lisa welcomed us and asked to be followed to a boardroom. She wore tailored black pants with sharp creases, a matching black blazer over a colourful floral blouse, and, completing her careful choices, TD-green nail polish and a TD lapel pin. We filed into the room and around a long boardroom table, excessively deferential to one another in taking our seats. Lisa took us through a dossier welcome package and then asked us if we had any questions. She was sweet. I did not look forward to telling her I was a robber.

The meeting wrapped up in fifteen minutes. As the others said their thanks and left, I remained seated in my tall-backed boardroom chair, waiting patiently. Lisa smiled. "Jeremiah, is there something I can help you with?"

"Can we speak privately for a minute?" I asked.

"Of course!"

She said goodbye to the last two hires to exit the room, then closed the door.

I took a big breath. “So ... about this criminal record check. Something happened a long time ago, five years ago, when I was seventeen, but if you get my record, I think it’ll still show up.”

She stopped straightening some papers in her hands, leaned forward, and tilted her head to the side. “What did you *do*?” she asked, more curious than alarmed.

“I robbed a Pita Pit, but it’s not as bad as it sounds!” I said. She sat motionless as the whole story poured out of me. Finally, I came to the end and prepared for Lisa to retract the job offer.

“Oh! Ha, ha, ha ... too funny!” she laughed. “Don’t worry about it, Jeremiah. You’re fine.” More laughter.

I couldn’t believe it. She dropped her head and kept on laughing. I started laughing with her — too hard. My life was back on track.

13

Amy and Ethan stayed behind in Ontario while I flew to Victoria in November 2008 to begin my new job. We arranged for them to join me in Victoria in the new year, as soon as I'd found a suitable place for us to live. In the meantime, the bank put me up in a temporary condo rental near the office. It was my first extended time away since Ethan's birth, and I spent my evenings walking the streets to collect my thoughts about the future.

Within days of my arrival, I started working out again at the YMCA, having not lifted weights since football had ended the year before. I used to warm up with two forty-five-pound plates on the bar for squats. Now I could barely get through six reps at that weight. My strength had atrophied over the past year more than I'd realized. I spent a few weeks reawakening my muscles and eating like a football player again, my self-esteem perking up after devouring a massive chicken stir-fry and seeing my weight a pound higher on the scale.

Before flying back to Ontario to be with Amy and Ethan for Christmas, I attended the TD Bank employee Christmas party in Victoria. I mingled, drifting from group to group to introduce myself to my new colleagues. I met a guy named Mike who gave off a relaxed vibe, like we already knew each other. We shared particulars.

"So, what do you do with your free time while the family is still back in Ontario?" he asked.

"Well, truth is, I came out here to learn how to row and go to the Olympics." I smiled, expecting him to laugh. He didn't.

"You've certainly got the height for it," he said. "You need to give

Doug White a call. He coaches for the Victoria City Rowing Club. He'll get you going."

It turned out Mike had spent some time rowing on the national team years prior as a lightweight. It was my good fortune to run into him by chance.

Doug White. I wrote the name down. The next day I found his phone number through the Victoria City Rowing Club's website. I called him and told him I wanted to learn to row. He didn't say much, just to meet him at the Howard Johnson hotel restaurant six kilometres north of the city at nine in the morning on the following Saturday.

Upon some Google researching, I discovered Doug had coached Canadian under-twenty-three crews to international medals, had coached several national teams internationally, and had even coached at the Olympic level. My stubborn arrogance was tempered by my two false starts in rowing. I needed a coach, and I hoped Doug was my guy.

The "HoJo," as I later found out local rowers called it, was just off Highway 17, en route to Elk Lake. I rode my bicycle there and arrived to find Doug sitting in a booth, cradling a cup of steaming coffee. He stood, and we shook hands. He had a thick crop of hair on top of a weather-worn face, taut, pulled-in lips, and kind, twinkling eyes. I filled him in on my life: football, Ethan, injuries, what had brought me to Victoria. He chuckled when I talked about my attempt to master rowing on Rice Lake on my own, and even more when I told him the oarlocks had been backwards all along.

Doug didn't say much. He listened and allowed the silence to hang whenever I paused for a moment. He was considering me carefully, mulling over my potential. My tone grew more confident as I spoke. An intensity was building. *Tell me I can't do it. I dare you.* By the end of my exposition on why I had what it took to become an elite rower, I was rocking back and forth on my seat.

I paused. His turn to respond. He interlaced his fingers and looked me in the eye.

"Jerry, what exactly are your ambitions? What do you intend to do in this sport?" he asked.

"I want to go to the next Olympics and win a gold medal," I said.

He didn't smile. He didn't look away. He didn't even blink.

"Okay," he said. "We'd better get to work. We don't have a lot of time." He made a few calculations in his head. "We'd need to get you on the national team, training full-time, by 2011 at the latest. It'll be tight, but it's possible."

Doug believed in me from the moment we met. I saw it in his eyes — the desire of a coach hungry to bring out the best in an athlete. He saw that I had good size to work with, but more importantly, he understood my determination. For the first time, someone credible validated my desire to compete at the highest level, and just like that, the quest was officially born. I was going to try to become an Olympic rower in the next three and a half years, in time to compete at the 2012 London Olympics.

14

My first workout with Doug began with a trip to Elk Lake at the ungodly hour of 4:30 a.m. My alarm clock jerked me out of a deep sleep, and staring blurry-eyed at the red digits, I decided that all rowers were fools. I pulled off my blanket quickly and mumbled some obscenities while walking across the cold hardwood floor on the sides of my feet. The smooth surfaces of my rented condo reflected the pale, yellow glow of a street light outside. I munched on a bagel in the kitchen in silence, still half asleep, my lower lip hanging and my eyes squinting to adjust to the kitchen lights. I wasn't a morning person. This was going to suck every time.

Doug coached the senior program at the Victoria City Rowing Club (VCRC), which had gone off the water until February. So I would have to wait until the new year to get on the water, but in the meantime Doug had invited me to train indoors with VCRC in the mornings before work.

The Elk Lake basin sat eleven kilometres north of the city. A single yellow light mounted on the corner of the building marked the Elk Lake boathouse. It was made up of four gable-roofed boat bays sandwiched together, with offices and an indoor rowing space located in the loft of the first bay.

The men's change room was rundown: cracked ceramic tiles, sagging benches, the floor nothing more than human-tramped dirt. The communal shower had six fixtures. A few, missing their shower heads, shot out sharp jets of water like pressure washers. I was surprised. The Elk Lake boathouse was home to the Victoria City Rowing Club and the University of Victoria rowing teams, but it was also the designated training centre of the Canadian men's national rowing team — Olympic champions, no less. I had expected more.

I changed into shorts and a T-shirt and then went back into the hall to find Doug waiting with an insulated portable mug in his hands. He smiled and said hello, then led me up some steep narrow stairs to the loft above the second boat bay. Ergometers were nestled in against the sloping walls of the triangular room.

Four more rowers joined us, making up the entire senior club team for VCRC — Trish, a junior rower still in high school; Greg and Jesse, two guys who had rowed competitively in the past but seemed now to be rowing for recreation (which made no sense to me at 5:20 a.m.); and Camille, an experienced rower who was dating one of the gold medallists from the men's eight, Andrew Byrnes.

We mumbled hello to each other in the bitter morning cold, then started the workout together, rowing side by side on ergometers in one half of the room. Doug stood behind me and talked me through the whole workout.

"Keep your arms straight. Drive with your legs first, then open up your body, and finish with your arms.

"No.

"No.

"No.

"That's better."

He picked me apart like a surgeon, repeating instructions until my body complied. There was nothing intuitive about the rowing motion. It was a sequence of three drive phases, starting with legs, then body, and then arms — separate, but overlapping and flowing together. After every stroke, Doug reminded me to slow down during the recovery. I wanted to zip forward on my rolling seat to begin the next stroke as quickly as possible.

"Whoa, you'll go slow *and* exhaust yourself doing that," Doug said, speaking like a horse whisperer to his new colt. "Now make sure you hold your legs down long enough for your upper body to swing forward and for your hands to clear your knees."

Our five bodies heated the small space into a steamy sauna. By the end of the session, I at least knew generally how I was supposed to row, though there is a cavernous gap between knowing and doing. Doug seemed pleased with my effort, and chuckled in his quiet way as I bombarded him with questions.

"See you tomorrow morning," he said.

15

On the plane back to Ontario for Christmas, I reflected on the beginnings of the next phase of my life. I had a challenging banking career ahead of me, rowing had become a real opportunity to realize my athletic potential, and I'd been away from Ethan for almost two months. I was shocked at how much he'd grown when he came running into my arms at the airport. Had it been two months, or two years? He was taller, with less baby pudge, smarter and more aware; even his eyes tracked faster. I realized not all of my stress had been job-related. Part of it was due to how badly I missed my son. He was three years old and growing fast.

Amy smiled while I attacked Ethan with kisses and squeezes. Then I hugged her and we kissed; she smelled like home. But there was some distance between us — more than the usual boredom of our relationship.

Amy was tired of the uncertainty around our future. I didn't see it, but it was the beginning of our relationship's unravelling over the coming months. It probably didn't help that Beyoncé's hit single "Single Ladies (Put a Ring on It)" was burning up the charts at the time. Another reminder of the lack of ultimate commitment in our relationship.

Amy and I were going through a phase. I figured she was just nervous about moving across the country, and that we'd be fine once the three of us were all living together again. She'd see how great Victoria was — cherry blossoms in February! After a few months we'd be back to normal, even if our normal was a bit boring.

I flew back to Victoria eager to continue my training with Doug and the rest of the VCRC senior team. Our plan was to have me train twice per day — one ergometer workout at the boathouse before dawn, and a second session on my own during my lunch hour. I did my workouts at the local YMCA, a five-minute walk up the street from where I worked.

After three weeks of this routine, the left side of my back started to get sore, my butt ached, and I'd become thoroughly disillusioned with rowing. One day, my back seized up and I stopped in the middle of an ergometer workout. The ergs were set up against the far wall of the YMCA, facing the cardio zone; rows of stationary bikes, treadmills, and, closest to me, elliptical machines. I stared at the people bouncing around on their ellipticals, second-guessing my decision to pursue rowing seriously and contemplating quitting for the first of many times to come.

The negative self-talk was crippling, and I had hardly begun. *Shit, this sport isn't right for you after all. You're not flexible enough. You have back issues. It'll only get worse. Quit, quit, quit.*

I began thinking of my entire athletic life: a series of almost-got-there results. I'd won a few most improved awards as a young minor hockey player. The same happened when I was a football player: I won the *Carpe Diem* Award for most improved offensive player the year before I injured my shoulder.

Always "getting there" or "almost made it."

Never "I did it."

I blamed myself for giving up too easily in the past. I felt like I'd never truly given something everything I was capable of, and I was tormented by the pattern of rational thinking I used to justify when and why things hadn't gone to plan.

I'd grown up going to an Anglican church every Sunday with my family, and even though I'd refused to go to confirmation at the age of thirteen (more to defy my parents than to make a statement about my beliefs), I had a residual sense of fate, or even worse, determinism. It was like nothing I did mattered because some god, mind, or meddling supernatural being was pulling all the strings. I was sick of my passiveness, that stench of weakness that coated my expectations on a daily basis. I loathed it like a cancer that had invaded my mind gradually over the years. *Fuck you, God,* I thought. *I am in control. I decide, not you.*

I wasn't exorcising God from my mind. I was challenging him, or whatever faint notion of a higher being I had left from childhood. I reframed my rowing quest as an exercise in discipline. It became bigger than rowing. It became a test of my resolve. My will.

For the first time in my life, I wholeheartedly rejected rational thinking about how things were going — that habit of assessing progress in life from moment to moment — and resolved to see my rowing journey through to the bitter end, whether that end involved standing on the Olympic podium or still falling in the water every few strokes when the Olympic team was announced.

I'm going for it, no matter what, I thought from the YMCA's floor, rolling out my seized-up back on a foam roller.

Nothing was going to stop me.

16

On a cold Saturday morning in February 2009, I showed up at the Elk Lake boathouse to begin on-water training. On Saturdays rowers slept in until 7:00 a.m. It was the first time I'd arrived at the club in the light of dawn. I had started to enjoy the darkness, like it was in cahoots with me in my covert mission to sneak up on the rowing world.

Organized chaos: high school rowers in brightly coloured, hip bone–clinging spandex bustled about, getting their boat assignments from coaches and taking them down from the boat bay racks. Boats travelled upside down on the pavilion, with skinny legs moving underneath like centipedes. Shouts and laughter rang out under wisps of morning fog. I found myself sidestepping and ducking away from the unyielding march of boats down to the dock.

Doug instructed me to take a single down to the water before heading off to get some pontoons to help keep me afloat. I grabbed the single a little off-centre, and the bow smacked into the floor. Then I overcorrected my grip in the other direction and smashed the stern into the ceiling while walking out of the boathouse.

It wasn't a great start.

Kids whizzed around me with competence while I fumbled around in this new world I intended to dominate. I felt stupid and self-conscious standing beside my boat on the dock, waiting for Doug. I squirmed, scratched my neck, fiddled with the oar. My cheeks flushed with embarrassment. I thought I was done with those kinds of feelings. I was twenty-three, a father, and had started a career, and yet I was back at square one and vulnerable, as if it was my first day of football training camp in my freshman year at McMaster. I tried to focus on Doug's instructions for mounting pontoons onto my single shell, but all I could think about was how pathetic I looked as I fumbled around trying to get my bearings.

Doug held the boat so that I could get in without flipping it, and at last I was ready to escape the curious glances from other rowers.

Well, not quite.

As I pushed off the dock, I immediately lost my balance and leaned hard onto the outside pontoon. Doug pushed the butt end of my port-side blade clear of the dock, whereupon I promptly lost my balance and shifted hard onto the opposite pontoon. The two stabilizing pontoons were mounted across the deck in front of my feet. They prevented me from fully capsizing, but not much more. I was like a child riding a bike with training wheels set too high, leaning hard on one side and then the other.

After twenty attempted strokes, I hadn't gone more than twenty metres. The other rowers' curious glances transformed into amused gazes. I wondered how anyone was supposed to control such ridiculously long oars. Frustration began to combine with my mounting embarrassment.

This was different than floundering around with Aubrey's juniors that day in the four, or managing a few consecutive strokes in the single on Rice Lake. I was fully vested now. I had talked a big game, and now, a month into dryland training, it was my first day on the water and I was a world away from my goal. I instantly regretted the smug proclamation that I was going to become an Olympian; I hadn't given myself leeway to gracefully bow out.

Doug gave me instructions: *Tap down on the oars with even pressure; keep your left hand slightly in front of your right so that you can keep both handles at the same height; feather the blade parallel to the water with your fingers, not your arms and wrists.*

A million mistakes each stroke — each different, like an interpretive dance on water.

I was trying, but feelings of helplessness invaded my concentration. Every botched stroke was accompanied with self-talk: *You can't do this. You're living in a delusional dream world. You had your chance in sport; the window of opportunity has passed.*

I wondered if it was my temperament, if I couldn't help but bite off more than I could chew. The self-doubt was familiar. Every sport I'd tried,

I'd started later than others my age. I was in a familiar position, and I recognized what the future held. But I didn't want to catch up. I wanted to excel. I wanted rowing to be the sport that was so well-suited to my body type and athletic ability that I would naturally rise to the top ranks of rowers in Canada. In short, I wanted rowing to be different. It wouldn't be. The only thing I could do differently this time was persist.

Outwardly I tried to remain enthusiastic and process what Doug was telling me as best I could. One thousand metres later, on the other side of the bay, my negativity began to subside and I started to really hear Doug. I couldn't quite manage the entire sequence of the stroke while staying balanced, but I started to grasp the individual movements. I started to relax a little. The less I fought against losing my balance, the easier it became to stay centred in the shell for a few metres at a time. Despite my floundering and embarrassment, I enjoyed the pull of the oar through the water, the vague sense of possibility.

Doug was patient as I leaned on the pontoons. Most of the high school coaches on the lake that day followed their crews closely and barked instructions at every stroke through a loudspeaker, but Doug only told me something once every few minutes. He knew not to overload me.

As I hacked my way back to the dock at the end of our first session, any remaining arrogance in me was gone. The more I learned what it was going to take to become an Olympic rower in time for the 2012 Olympics, the more I realized how far-fetched an idea it had been to begin with, and yet the more determined I became to continue.

Sometimes the only difference between a clumsy fool and a future Olympian is the determination to continue. Every other rower must have gone through what I was going through. I felt I could create a mental foothold by setting my sights on an Olympic medal from day one. I had the physical tools. But would I be up to the task of compressing the necessary learning into the next three and a half years until the Olympic Games?

It would require an ability to endure as much uncertainty as physical and mental suffering.

17

Most rows that first year on the water were scenes overlapping each other. Winters in Victoria don't freeze the earth and water like in the rest of Canada, but there is a cold dampness that permeates your bones to the core, the kind of cold that stays with you long after you've left it. Five thirty a.m. starts were insulting from the moment you threw your blanket off your warm body in the morning to the lonely crunch of gravel underfoot while walking to the boathouse. Every session began with a few of us huddling around Doug in the boat bay in the darkness of pre-dawn, Doug squinting to make out the condition of the water. We mounted LED lights on the bows and sterns of our boats. In the darkness, red and white dots of light would float their way down to the docks like sparks dancing from a fire. On the frosted docks, boats rolled from shoulder down to waist, down to water. Nobody spoke, leaving only the sounds of rowing: plastic water bottles bumping and rattling against carbon fibre decks and aluminum riggers; the tearing and retightening of Velcro straps on the shoes mounted inside the boat; some soft curses from half-asleep rowers whose feet got soaked while stepping out of their flip-flops and into their boats.

Once on the water, the darkness added to the challenge of staying balanced. A neon-orange light mounted on the boathouse gave me my horizon as I slipped off into the pre-dawn night. The boat's gentle, ebbing wake gurgled and disappeared in the moonlight. The glug of my oars catching, pulling, slinging the boat forward with each stroke put me in a trance; searching for the perfect extraction of blades from water, flicking fingers forward from the second knuckle to rotate the blade onto the feather, cutting into the cold wind at my back. The water, pooling in front of my blade, resembled a smooth oil slick. My oars swept the air in a giant arc, like the upper half of a snow angel. Gliding smoothly forward for each stroke, I tried but failed to embody the finesse and intention of a ballet dancer, leaning on either port or starboard oar to maintain balance. After 1,000 metres, my damp fingers and toes equalized with the temperature and went numb, lost for the time being.

Many giant buoys, like floating bowling pins, needed to be avoided while rowing to the north end of the lake. They were placed like road signs in the middle of a highway, indicating speed limits for motorboats. Gliding backwards in a boat gives you the feeling of perpetual danger. At any moment, our sharp bows, deadly as spears, could impale a fisherman floating in his inflatable dingy. Usually, a warning of "Watch the fuck where you're going!" would give us plenty of time to avoid disaster, but our heads were always on a swivel.

The real danger was other rowers. Especially inexperienced rowers like me. The story of Canadian Olympic rower Silken Laumann's calf being almost completely sheared off in a collision with another rowing boat before a 1992 World Cup race in Essen, Germany, is Canadian rowing folklore. Now boats have rubber bow balls to reduce the risk of freak accidents like Silken's, but the ball is smaller than a tennis ball, and I wondered if it would just make a bigger hole in someone's body.

We started every workout with a warm-up of increasing pressure, from rowing light, to half, to three-quarter, and then full pressure. Doug took to following me closely in his aluminum coach boat, sitting at the back with an arm stretched behind him, steering the outboard motor. I imagined his spine must have been permanently twisted from the hours he spent sitting in that position.

The rowing course on Elk Lake has two lanes of traffic, north and south, and is shaped like a banana. My teammates Jesse and Greg said it was that way because disgruntled fishermen kept dragging around the red buoys marking the course — payback for having to constantly avoid getting impaled by rowing boats. Whatever the reason, the bendy course caused me a lot of trouble. I tended to drift to the centre line as if pulled by an equatorial current. Sometimes, if Doug left me for a moment to coach the others, I would unknowingly drift so far across the centre line that I'd be rowing into oncoming rowers on their starboard side. This would confuse the University of Victoria and VCRC masters rowing crews sharing the lake with us. My margin of error was so great they lost confidence in their own course. Seeing me, breathing hard, they'd look around bewildered before returning evil eyes at me, the chump 50 metres off course.

Initially, staying upright in my boat once the stabilizing pontoons were removed was the biggest challenge. It was extraordinary to me how easily some high school single scullers navigated their boats. How did they do it? Turning on a dime, taking off from a start, backing into starting position (*backing* meaning rowing forward in the direction you're facing).

Rowing has a steep learning curve because of how difficult the basics are. Imagine learning to ride a bicycle with the ground moving underneath. A rower is most stable when both oars are floating flat on the water at a ninety-degree angle to the boat — akin to a cyclist having two feet resting on the ground. The cyclist will push off firm ground to gain momentum; the rower has only their balance to begin with. My tendency was to roll up to the start, lose my balance on the way to full leg compression, and then careen over into the water as if shot by a sniper hiding in the treeline.

I wanted to force the proper technique into my muscle memory, but that's not how rowing works. The trick to sitting at the catch, the tipsiest position, is to keep your shoulders and arms loose so that the submerged blade of the oar can find its natural resting position, the upper edge floating just under the surface of the water. If sufficiently relaxed, you can stabilize yourself with this subtle ballast.

The first time Doug told me this, I looked to port to see if my oar was submerged, and before I knew it, I was submerged. Next, Doug told me not to look at my oars. Instead, I was told, I should rely on the feel of the balance in my loose grip. This looseness in my upper body was completely opposite to the bracing for impact I was used to as a football player. Football requires raw aggression — punching chests, smashing helmets — but rowing requires moulding all that aggression into one smooth ribbon of power through the water.

From a fully compressed starting position, managing the first stroke in a single shell is half the battle in learning how to row. It's like gripping a fish by its body without letting it slip away; the blade of the oar wants to break the surface of the water or dive deep as you try to lock on.

After a few failed attempts to learn this — each time ending up submerged in freezing water — I concluded February was not the time to learn how to row from a standing start. But, as with any new endeavour, the first hurdles can be more discouraging than the hardest challenges that come later in the journey. Early progress is like watching a plant grow: you can't see it, but it's happening. Slowly, roots grow, a foundation takes shape, and progress becomes visible. The key is not to get discouraged in that time before your progress reveals itself.

18

In February 2009, Amy and Ethan joined me in Victoria. I soaked in the morning sun reflecting off the ocean strait to the east as I drove up the highway. Another airport reunion. They never get old when kids are involved. I lifted Ethan off his feet and squeezed the breath out of him. I hugged Amy and held on a bit longer, thankful that she'd made the trip. It was a huge change for her to move across the country. It took courage.

I'd rented a cottage on a lake in Langford, a suburb twenty minutes from Victoria's downtown core, putting me in a near-equidistant triangle between home, Elk Lake, and work. It was twelve kilometres to the lake from where I lived, and another eleven to the office. It would have been great training to do thirty-five kilometres of bike riding every day on top of my rowing routine, but I didn't have the time for it. Instead, I bought an electric motor conversion kit and transformed my mountain bike into a zippy battery-powered scooter.

Spring starts in February in Victoria, so my plan was to bundle up and ride my souped-up electric bike to Elk Lake, and from Elk Lake to my office after the row. I put my wrinkle-resistant dress shirt and pants in my backpack to change into. Just in case the rain got through my cycling rain suit, I also kept extra pants and a dress shirt at my office. I thought my plan was bulletproof, and it gave me a general sense of winning, like I had creatively solved a problem in a way most wouldn't be willing to do. But my solution was unsustainable. I had to get up at 4:30 a.m. to accommodate a morning workout, tiptoeing around the cottage so that Ethan wouldn't wake, and it was tight getting to work on time.

At one point, my jovial boss, Rob, made a not-so-jovial comment that I should make sure — especially as a new associate — that I wasn't the last one in the office in the mornings. I had to dial it back. The Olympics would be a marathon effort, not a sprint. I stopped doing on-water workouts with Doug and the VCRC seniors in the morning and focused on lunchtime workouts at the YMCA for the time being.

My job wasn't getting any easier. Expectations rose as time went on, and my head spun by the end of each day, trying to keep track of the various deals going on within my portfolio. Lunchtime workouts at the Y became entirely a stress reliever from work. I put all my frustration into the rowing machine, shocking our office secretary, Donna, when I came back sweating through my dress shirt, with beads of sweat still trickling down from my temples.

The honeymoon period began to wear off from that moment at the Y when, with a strained back, I had cursed God and affirmed (in what deserves capital letters) The Decision. Some days I missed workouts. I didn't yet operate with the discipline it was going to take to become an elite rower. Doug wanted me to train twice on Saturdays, but sometimes I'd forgo any training at all on the weekend. I just wanted to relax and spend time with Amy and Ethan. Besides, I was still improving. I did a 2-kilometre ergometer test in March 2009 in a time of six minutes, twenty-three seconds — already thirteen seconds faster than my first 2-kilometre test. I was happy to believe that I would go on shaving seconds off my time at that rate until I'd broken Rob Waddell's world record.

It was wishful thinking. I was experiencing the huge gains that come at the beginning of any new endeavour. But the gains get smaller and more difficult to come by as time goes on. The law of diminishing returns applies to all athletes who try to test their limits. It would be another nine months before I would find my par — that point where you stop enjoying gains in speed and start scraping and clawing to shave a second off your time. No, I was not yet training like a future Olympian.

On a Sunday in March, after I'd missed both training sessions the day before, Doug emailed out the training program for the following week. I read the email while bouncing Ethan on my knee. Underneath the program, he wrote:

> This is the time of year to train hard to get the seconds you'll need in summer racing. Training is about eliminating excuses.

It stuck in my head the rest of the afternoon: *Training is about eliminating excuses.*

19

I didn't see it coming. I was so caught up in trying to balance my new career with my attempt to become a world-class rower that I lost sight of everything else. It's a necessary ingredient, selfishness. But Amy had her own dreams. She wanted to start her own tourism business, have a big family. She cared deeply for everyone in her life, yet somehow found herself shackled to a boyfriend who was increasingly swept away by his ambition, pulling her away from the relationships that were deeply woven into the fabric of her life. In the months after moving out West, Amy's voice grew timid, her eyes distant. Always one to celebrate the little joys in life — with gifts, treats, crafty homemade cards for loved ones — she now had to muster effort for these things. They still happened. I came home from work at least once per week to find Amy and Ethan grinning about the surprise dessert that lay in wait for me. Only for Amy, the acts of kindness came from the groove of habit and must have felt hollow compared to Ethan's unbridled joy. A small-town girl uprooted and displaced, she was the settler to my nomad. And I left her on her own, far from family and friends, with only our three-year-old for company nine hours a day.

If there are make-or-break moments in a relationship, when one of you needs to go more than halfway to keep it alive, this was one of those times. But I wouldn't do it and I couldn't do it, in that order. Wouldn't, because I was just as uncertain about our future together as Amy was. I saw the end of the relationship on the horizon, but I didn't have the maturity to sort out my feelings and make a decision. Amy and I had both made mistakes as teenagers that had caused trust issues between us. I thought with time they'd go away, but trust is something you have to keep working at once it's been compromised. I wasn't working anymore.

Amy had moved across Canada for *my* opportunity, and she was lonely in our cottage, cooped up by herself with Ethan. No amount of willow trees, lakefront, or any other natural beauty was going to fill the emptiness she must have felt. So, I understand now what happened next.

"I'm going downtown tonight to watch a friend's band play," she said one night. "You remember my friend Owen, right?"

I did.

"Oh right. Okay, yeah, have a fun time," I said.

She had makeup on for the first time in months.

"You look hot," I said.

She rolled her eyes.

I was thankful this friend's band had rolled into Victoria for a show. It was just what Amy needed — some time to herself to let loose and hang out with another adult who wasn't me.

"It might go late, so don't wait up for me," she said.

Then she opened the door and slipped out of my life.

It turned out the friend was more than a friend, and so began months of our relationship unwinding. I refused to sleep in the same bed. I swore I'd never make physical contact with her again. Somewhere under all my indifference, I had been stung awake. I thought, *Jesus, what is the point of building a life with someone when it can all vanish so quickly?*

Lunchtime workouts at the Y turned into ground zero for my mental state. I was a cocktail of pride, jealousy, and rage. Every moment anyone had doubted me in my life flashed across my mind's eye like an old View-Master. Mostly my heart was heavy, punctuated with spikes of anger and determination. But out of this state, a whisper sounded inside me. *Nothing will break my will.* I took sadistic pleasure in the negative emotions that had overcome me. A quiet, little voice told me that if this didn't break me, nothing could. Amy had moved on because I hadn't put any effort into our relationship. Well, I would show her and others what I was capable of when I put all my focus and effort into something. It would be something bigger than her. An accomplishment so distinguished that she'd look the fool for drifting away from what we'd had.

Stupid. Fucking. Pride.

Sometimes in the weeks that followed, I would slide back and forth on the ergometer, back and forth, back and forth, my mind swan diving into the abyss until hitting an emotional rock bottom. Instead of stopping, I enjoyed it. You can push off rock bottom. There's freedom there. I'd lost my girlfriend of eight years, had just let her go — the mother of my child. A cacophony of disastrous futures lay in wait, and I rolled them over in my mind like bitter pills on the tongue.

My reflexive instinct was to push back. I'd had the same experience of working from despair in my second year of university, when I was a shitty football player trying to get better and got rocked by Amy's pregnancy. It was that feeling of not seeing a way forward, not seeing how it would work out, but then to continue anyway.

I didn't have any friends in Victoria after six months of living and working there. Instead of friends, I had my dad. He was my confidant, the voice of reason and understanding. I would call him from work at the end of the day to unload. He would absorb my toxicity over the phone so that no one else would have to. He'd summon his calm-in-the-storm voice: "Okay, Son. Look, here's what you do ..." We shared the same temperament; I could sense him working to stay calm. Ours was a relationship of bonding through tough times.

Life doesn't slow down when you're down. It carries on insensitively, just when you'd like a pause to gather yourself. Within two weeks Amy and I had found our new normal for the near future. The emotion died down for the most part. Our communication was cold, businesslike — my doing. I started jogging around the small lake we lived on after work, running until thoughts about me and Amy gave way to the immediacy of the effort.

At the lake, training under Doug continued.

"Will she and Ethan move back to Ontario?" he asked me one morning.

It was one possible scenario I hadn't seriously entertained, and it caught me off guard. To think that Ethan would live away from me at all, let alone for an extended period in another province, crushed me.

"Not a chance!" I said. Ethan's last name was Brown. He was my son, and I would die before letting him be taken away from me.

Shortly after Amy and I broke up, I started looking for a place to live in Victoria. I wanted to be closer to the lake and to the office so that I could be more consistent with early morning training. Even after breaking up, there was no realistic option other than continuing to live together in the short term. We wanted the best for Ethan and it gutted both of us thinking about how to explain things in a way he could understand. There is a gradient involved in moving on after eight years together. It would take time.

Emotion that had been nonexistent while we were together now came flowing out of me in torrents. Whenever we were in the same room, I felt clutched with anger, regret, and disappointment. I *did* care about her, but there was no doubt in my mind we were through. It was liberating to be decisive. The whole problem was a lack of choosing. I hadn't chosen to actively work at our relationship, and had ultimately faced a pointed question: Are you in, or are you out?

I was out.

Searching real estate listings online, I came across a small one-bedroom condo for sale. Perfect. It was just across the blue Johnson Street Bridge on the west shore of the harbour — a ten-minute walk to work and fifteen-minute drive to the lake. That day I met the seller for a showing, and committed to buying it on the spot. Then I called my dad and told him I had an investment opportunity.

The condo cost $235,000. I could have carried the mortgage based on my salary, but it would have been a stretch. To get to the Olympics I needed a financial plan — even Canada's top Olympic rowers made less than $20,000 per year. I needed to put myself in a position where my cash flow wasn't under pressure, so I asked my dad to invest 30 percent in the property while I carried the mortgage on the remaining 70 percent. This would set me up with a low monthly mortgage payment, essentially buying me more training time with every dollar of savings once I quit my job to row full-time. After making the team, it would take a year to be considered for the highest level of funding the federal government awarded Olympic-bound athletes. The best I could hope for during my first year on the team would be a development funding stipend, which amounted to $10,000 per year. So, as I continued learning how to row, I started saving every penny I could. My cost of living, including Ethan's daycare, was going to be roughly $22,000 per year, meaning I needed to save at least $12,000 to cover the deficit between my expenses and the development card funding.

I explained all this to my dad, and he agreed to go in on the condo with me. As much as I had in front of me as an athlete, my whole plan would hinge on the support of others. In Doug, I was getting the coaching I needed, and in my dad, I had a confidant and partner. Within the 575 square feet of our new home, Ethan, Amy, and I would remain together for the time being. And though I didn't know it at the time, Amy would become my most reliable and crucial pillar of support over the coming months.

20

The spring of 2009 turned to summer, and with the change in seasons my skill in the single shell improved. I went from slapping my blades along the water, resembling a Canada goose batting the water with its wings before lifting off, to executing consecutive strokes clear of the water. Strokes with oars perfectly balanced above the water are the rower's version of a climber taking in a breathtaking view, a tennis player's joy in a perfectly placed volley, a ski jumper's exit into thin air. The allure of precision of motion, of flow, of near perfection.

The uniqueness of rowing compared to other racing sports is the fact that we face backward. Humans are bad enough at estimating distances over water when looking forward; if you're sitting in a boat looking backward, it's near impossible — only the aid of buoys marking off common increments allow a rower to calculate distances.

Doug staggered the starts of everyone on the VCRC senior team, giving the slowest boats a one-minute head start. The idea was to have us all arrive at the other end of the lake together. This made me fixate on the other crews I trained with. I never did develop a sense of where I was on a 2,000-metre racecourse, but the resulting disorientation had me frothing when the crews behind me entered my peripheral vision. The first half of each run of the lake was all about self-motivation, knowing each stroke brought me closer to the other crews. Then a snaking fold in the water would appear beside my stern, twisting in the moonlight, and the hunt was on. The meandering slip of water turned into a steady, rippling wake. Then Jesse and Greg's double would appear with the flash of blades exiting the water and twisting onto the feather. As I passed the double, renewed motivation would sling me onward and past the rest of the group before reaching the other end of the lake. There I'd rest behind the small island in the dimness of dawn, listening to the rising chatter of vultures in the trees until Doug puttered into view, blinding me with his headlamp, saying, "I'll give the double forty-five seconds this time."

By the fall of 2009, I had developed enough technique in the single to start thinking about competition. I thought I was pretty fast, beating up on the double in the mornings, but it wasn't really the case because Jesse and Greg were rowing more for recreation than for competition. I was improving quickly, but I wasn't as fast as I thought.

In early October 2009, I competed in my first time trial in windy and cold conditions on Elk Lake. The time trial was to see which athletes would be invited to represent British Columbia at the National Championships a few weeks later. I came in fourth overall out of a pool of mostly lightweight rowers who were younger than me. It was good enough to earn an invitation to represent British Columbia in the heavyweight single sculls event.

A week later I was on an airplane flying back to Ontario to compete at Nationals. The regatta was held in London, Ontario, during a cold snap. It snowed the first day I went to the course, to find the racing schedule. I met Chuck, the British Columbia athlete development manager. Greeting me as if unsure whether he'd see me again, he led me down to a field of overturned boats in the wet snow. "We arranged for you to borrow this Hudson single for the regatta," he said, pointing to a sleek new shell on stretchers. "Let me know if you need anything." And with that, he turned and walked back up the bank to the clubhouse.

I sensed this was my moment. I would show the Canadian national team that I was the next big talent to come along.

As I tinkered with my boat, I saw Ben Rutledge walking a pair (a two-man sweep boat) down to the water with his partner. Ben had rowed in the two-seat position in the gold-medal-winning eight at the 2008 Beijing Olympics. I'd read everything I could find on each of the Olympic champs from that boat. I recognized him like someone I used to know, even though we'd never met. He was bald with a menacing forehead and a strong, lean physique — the kind of guy it would hurt to tackle. I watched him with concealed awe. *What was it about him that made him an Olympic champion? Was it his physical gifts, his determination, his skill? In what combination? And most important, how could I beat him?*

Over fifty rowers had entered the men's heavyweight single scull category, necessitating a time trial to whittle the field down to thirty-two boats. I looked at the starting order posted on the side of the boathouse; it served us an unofficial ranking of the top athletes. At the top of the list was Malcolm Howard. I instantly recognized the name — another athlete from the Beijing gold medal eight. I'd heard other rowers talk about him in passing.

"No one will touch Malcolm."

"He'll beat everyone by at least ten seconds."

"I heard he's planning on racing the single in the next Olympics."

On and on it went about Malcolm Howard.

On the morning of the time trial, I shared a van to the course with a few other athletes who were staying at the same hotel. A large group of rowers gathered around the regatta marshal to hear the announcements before heading out on the water. The marshal emphasized the different flow patterns — the racecourse, the warm up course, the dock traffic. My eyes glazed over like they did when my football coaches had written up drills on whiteboards.

Once bobbing in my shiny new Hudson racing shell 50 metres from the dock, I realized I'd forgotten to bring a watch in the boat with me. I was mostly worried about missing my start time, so instead of warming up properly, I did a few hard strokes on the way to the top of the course and left it at that. I was still of the mentality that I should conserve my energy for the race, but without a warm-up I was only ensuring the race would be more painful.

I collected behind the starting line with the other single scullers, strung out like logs in a log pond. Wisps of vapour rose from the glassy calm of the water, burnt off by the sun. Every fifteen seconds the starting umpire shouted, "Next!" Then, "Go!" I saw Malcolm Howard, the athlete on the tip of everyone's tongue, take off first in his single. I remember how big his cheeks puffed out before he exhaled each breath; you could have stoked a bonfire with those breaths.

When it was my turn, I took off hard and settled into twenty-eight strokes per minute — still my upper limit at the time. Most of the other rowers would be at thirty-two to thirty-four strokes per minute, but if I attempted that rate I knew an oar would fly out of my grip and land me, with a splash, in the water.

There was an eerie juxtaposition between the intensity of my effort and the quiet of my surroundings. The shoreline drifted by on my starboard side, the peaceful morning song of birds the only sound. At 500 metres in, the rowers congregating near the starting buoys looked like tiny water spiders crawling around, and I began to feel the effects of my insufficient warm-up. The grottiness crept through my body slowly, my blood vessels forcefully dilating to accommodate the demands of my pumping heart.

In isolation, I found it easy to think about stopping. No one was watching; no one cared. Similar thoughts had struck me while training alone on Elk Lake. What kept rowers honest in the middle of a lake with no one to hold them accountable?

My thoughts were quickly drowned out by the sounds of my hoarse, panting breath and my oars cutting into the water. I felt like no matter how hard I pulled, I was slipping back. The time trial format sets up a punishing cycle of self-doubt: *Okay, I'm on my pace. Shit, get it back. Okay, that's better. Damn it, you lazy bastard! Okay, that's better. Shit, get it back....*

At 1,250 metres, cursing like a sailor, the self-loathing was all-consuming. A hatred with no external object to ground it. There's no physical outlet for this form of anger because your technique demands constant focus. For this reason, rowing is the ultimate attack on the human psyche, best suited for the determined *and* masochistic.

Momentarily, in the last 500 metres, the pain felt less foreign and I wondered if I'd finally warmed up. At last, the lane buoys on either side of me changed from white to red, indicating 250 metres until the finish line. The final sprint felt like a million jellyfish stinging my body all at once. How much longer could I starve myself of oxygen? How much pain could I endure?

Crossing the finish line, I wobbled and fell forward onto my oars like a marathon runner collapsing through the red tape, only this debilitating fatigue had been packed into seven and a half minutes. The rower after me finished strongly, beat my time, and maintained his composure. Like I had with Ben Rutledge, I wondered about the possibilities: Was he fitter, technically better, more naturally gifted, or some combination of the three? I wondered how much hard work could make up for genetic differences — could it make up for a litre less in lung capacity, say? I doubted myself.

The next day of racing was called off due to inclement weather. A storm front had moved in and brought with it strong gusts of wind and sideways freezing rain. I emailed Doug to tell him I had come fourteenth overall in the time trial. He would be happy with that preliminary result.

The next race was the A/B semifinal. The wind died down enough to allow racing to resume, but there was a 100-metre wide channel of water perpendicular to the main course that joined it about 500 metres from the start. The wind billowed down through this channel and created two-foot crosswind swells in the middle of the warm-up loop, making me feel more like a tightrope walker than a rower.

In my preoccupation with sizing up the rowers around me, I forgot how precarious the situation was for my rudimentary skills in those conditions. The whitecaps were bad enough for me to catch a blade on a wave while coming up to the catch, sending me tumbling into the dark water. The falling in part wasn't so bad — I'd had a lot of practice getting back into my boat — but in the near-freezing water temperature, and dressed in nothing but a few layers of spandex, my limbs were paralyzed by the cold water. Safety might be the primary concern, but all I could think about was the loss of credibility I'd just suffered in the eyes of my competition. It took me almost two minutes to get back into my single, including once getting upright only to flip back into the water on the other side. So much for any intimidation I might have been able to work up as the unknown new guy.

An umpire approached in his launch and asked if I still intended to race. Yes, I did! I raced 1,250 metres to the start line to arrive just in time, shivering and hypothermic in two-degree Celsius biting wind. I couldn't feel my arms or legs while sitting at attention in the starting gates. At the starting horn, my competitors surged out of the start, quickly leaving me in their wake. As much as I tried to hold a reasonable twenty-eight strokes per minute, it turned into working very hard at twenty-four and moving along at trawling speed. Even had I not fallen in and frozen to the bone, it was obvious the top single scullers were much faster than me. They skipped across the water as if one with their boats — part amphibian, part human — while I picked my way through the course, fading with each sloppy stroke. I came in last, destined for the C final. The only consolation came when one of the stronger scullers, Mike Braithwaite, rowed by me on his way back to the dock and said, "That took balls to finish the race after falling in like that."

I appreciated his sportsmanship, though my testicles were shrivelled up like walnuts.

In the C final, I was outworked by another sculler in the last 500 metres and came in second; fourteenth overall for the regatta. My fairy-tale entry into competitive rowing was dashed.

Racing at that level erased all vain hope that maybe I was just naturally gifted enough to break onto the team. Even if I did have some aerobic capacity and long arms and legs, it was still going to take a couple of years to put things together on the water.

21

A few months later, in January 2010, I participated in the University of Victoria's annual Monster Erg event. It was one of several indoor rowing races held concurrently across Canada that made up the Canadian Indoor Rowing Championships.

Thirty ergometers were set up in a long row in the university gym, and I found myself flanked by the top varsity athletes from the University of Victoria rowing team. Luckily, there were no national team athletes present that year. I had two goals for the event: win it, and break through the six-minute barrier.

Two months earlier, I had pulled a 2-kilometre erg score of 6:08 on an erg in my condo's gym. I was so excited I jumped off the erg, pushed through the glass doors of the gym, and strutted around the block with a huge smile on my face, adrenaline and endorphins coursing through my body. Six minutes over 2 kilometres on the ergometer was the unofficial minimum standard required to train with the men's heavyweight national team. The national team was within reach, and I could see the top of the mountain (a false peak, really, as the law of diminishing returns would soon take effect).

There weren't many people outside at that time of night, but when I did cross someone's path, I would think, *I'm going to do something great, and you don't have a clue.* Ambition swept up in arrogance. They didn't care. Most of the general public doesn't even know what rowing is — canoeing, kayaking, rowing, it's all the same to them. But rowing was fast becoming my whole world. *How could they* not *know about our sport?* It felt as if the world was standing still while I was moving closer to becoming an Olympian.

The two athletes on either side of me at Monster Erg were my competition for future spots on the national team. I wanted them to know they were behind me in the queue. The goal of breaking six minutes was a stretch, but I went for it. After seven hard strokes off the start, I locked my pace onto the split time that would put me just under: 1:29 per 500 metres.

It was always a relief to pass the halfway point during these brutal tests, when the distance remaining on the ergometer screen switched from thousands to hundreds of metres. But with 600 metres to go, I started slipping off my target split time. It would float up to 1:32 per 500 metres momentarily before I forced it back down. I knew that each time I drifted, it would be much harder to make up the lost time. The pain unravelled my focus as my split time began oscillating up and down. I started to lose good form. In the final 300 metres, the various parts of my face twisted into a look of horror as I lost connection with my body. It was no longer about technique; it was about sheer will. The university guys on either side maintained good form. In contrast, my body heaved, my arms dipped at the catch, my head was thrown backwards and angled to the side — I looked like I was riding a bronco.

With six strokes left to go, I knew all of them needed to count to break six minutes. Confusion. The last seconds of an erg test or on-water race, if you've truly committed, scramble your mind. How long can you hold your hand over a flame? How much longer can you hold your breath under water? Rowing competitions are to a great degree a comparison of how many times each athlete has put themselves into this darkness. To hell with technique. I was going for it.

After the last stroke was over, I bucked and shuddered with pain, nearly collapsing to the floor. I looked up — 5:59.8 showed on the screen. Mission accomplished, barely. It wasn't the best time I'd ever do, but it was one of the greatest efforts I've ever given.

Your effort is the only thing you can control. The path to the Olympics would be paved by stacking these efforts side by side, one after another. Relativity — comparing yourself to some outside standard — is bullshit. At every level in an athlete's development there is only what they are truly capable of in the moment, based on all their preparation up until that moment. All that matters is the athlete's commitment to reach their current potential. What one is capable of and what one does — the gap between these two things is where all the self-doubt and questioning comes in. As you approach the blurry line of physical limit, the gains are miniscule. How far are you willing to go for so very, very little? This is the question that I needed to ask myself over and over and over again.

22

By 2010, when my second year of training rolled around, rowing had become no more than an exercise in discipline. The previous year had seemed like a series of cold showers on my dream. There were so many guys faster than me. Mountains seem more climbable at a distance than when you're huffing up one; the more I worked toward my goal of getting to the 2012 Olympics, the more clearly it appeared out of reach.

I let the uncertainty affect my training plan. In the winter months, I was happy to get off the water and back into the weight room. I hit the weights hard and put on a few more pounds of muscle mass. The problem with the added muscle mass and strength on exercises like the bench press was that none of it was sport-specific. The world's best rowers have stringy bands of muscle hanging off their frames, not bulging pecs and biceps. I wasn't playing football anymore, and yet I was building upper body mass that was going to slow me down on the water.

Sure enough, in early spring 2010 I suffered a rude awakening on the water when a male lightweight rower beat me in the single sculls in the Duelling Over a Grand regatta in Victoria. At 1,000 metres, it was half the usual race distance. It should have been perfect for me; I could rely on my strength to blast through the shorter distance. The $1,000 prize would be a helpful addition to my savings. But I felt lethargic, as though all my gains in strength had sucked the agility of movement out of my body. My upper body mass was inefficient, wasting precious aerobic resources. I finished the race nearly blowing a gasket, while my opponent, the victor, pivoted and paddled away briskly to begin his cool-down. I sat exhausted, a heavy swell in my biceps, chest, and shoulders. The sensation was like swimming with clothes on. I needed to get leaner.

Trying hard would not be enough. I'd fooled myself into thinking that I was making progress just because I had been working hard, but I'd actually taken a step backwards because my effort wasn't focused on the right elements of training. To correct course, I spent much of the first half of 2010 doing more work on the water in the single and less on the erg and in the weight room, gradually leaning out in the process.

My rowing didn't improve in a linear fashion as time went on. After the winter break, the oars felt foreign in my hands, my movements jagged. It was like stepping on the ice for the first skate of hockey season, except my hockey legs always came back within a few laps of the rink, while my boat feel took a week.

I became obsessive about technique in the single. Doug challenged me to row a full length of the lake without once allowing my blades to skim the water on the recovery. *Impossible,* I thought. I was cheating, scraping my blades across the top of the water on the recovery to stabilize myself. "You'll find the set when you exit cleanly at the finish and move your hands away level," Doug would repeat ad nauseam.

There were so many movements to execute in smooth analog, but I could concentrate on only one thing at a time. It was a small victory if I managed to extract my blades cleanly without washing out the end of the stroke. By the time I thought about level hands, I'd have already lost balance and slapped my blade on the water to prevent falling in.

Keeping your balance in a skinny single requires finesse subtler than the small steering wheel adjustments you make to keep your car straight on the highway. Headwinds are a gift for the developing sculler. A strong headwind cradles you like an invisible helping hand, stabilizing the boat. Tailwinds are more challenging, accentuating small mistakes and pushing you off balance. Crosswinds are infuriating; each broadside wave makes balance twice as difficult.

I prayed for straight headwind or tailwind conditions before every practice. Elk Lake had a nasty habit of giving you a little bit of everything in the same session — tail, cross, head, tail-cross, head-cross. It reminded me of a football drill we used to do, squatting on a half stability ball while a teammate circled, giving you little pushes to knock you off balance. The football drill lasted only thirty seconds. One length of Elk Lake took roughly eight minutes to row. Eight minutes of feeling off balance in a rowing shell is enough time to make you consider heading for shore at ramming speed, grabbing your boat, and smashing it against a tree.

Finding the balance was hard enough without anyone watching me. When Doug followed me, all I could think was, *I'm bad, but I'm not this bad.* It reminded me of piano lessons growing up; I could polish a piece of music to the point of nailing it four out of five times, but when I played it under the watchful eye of my teacher, Mrs. Bickle, I'd screw it up four out of five times.

I tended to develop a bad habit in one part of my stroke while focusing on another.

"You're collapsing your body too much at the finish," Doug said during a row. "Don't collapse; stay tall at the finish." He repeated this every day for a month until I shook the habit, jumping on me if he saw it creep back in.

"Doug, I think I'm wasting energy doing it like that," I'd say.

"No, you're not," he'd say. And that would be the end of it.

Doug and I were a good match in temperament. He was like a martial arts sensei, guiding my energy back into the task at hand whenever my frustration hit a boiling point. I could spend a whole practice welling up into a rage. As an outlet, all I could do was slap my blades up and down on the water — hardly as satisfying as smashing into a defensive end, and ineffective in dissipating my anger. Doug would putter up slowly to offer advice in his quiet, undulating voice, a voice that was unintelligible much of the time under the burping and growling of the boat motor, but whose cadence rolled over me in soothing tones: "Okay, Jerry, it's coming. It'll take time, but you'll get it."

On a Saturday in May 2010, I stood in the boat bay with Doug and asked for a progress report. "We need to get you in the mix with the national team as soon as possible," Doug said. He was friends with Mike Spracklen, the head coach of the men's national team. Most Saturdays he would meet Mike for coffee after the team's 11:00 a.m. row. "I'll ask

Mike if it would be all right for you to participate in their Saturday morning time trial," Doug said. Every Saturday the national team would row four timed 2,000-metre pieces.

Later that week, I got an email from Doug saying that Mike had given his approval — finally, a chance to get in the mix with the top rowers in Canada.

23

I hadn't met Mike Spracklen yet. I'd seen his boat buzzing up and down the lake, but never the man in the boat. To me, Mike *was* his boat, like a giant Wizard-of-Oz head floating across the water. The national team rowers referred to Mike's boat as the popemobile because his cockpit was enclosed with canvas and plastic zip-up windows, completely protected from the elements. At seventy-three, slightly stooped and balding, Mike also bore a slight resemblance to Pope Benedict XVI.

His boat enclosure sat atop two long pontoons. Two loudspeakers mounted on either side of the boat sent Mike's crackling voice across the lake like an AM radio broadcast. Mounted from above, a single wiper cleared a swath of windshield free of rain, sleet, and sometimes even snow. Blue canvas and plastic side windows enclosed the boat in a toasty cabin. The popemobile was made complete by a small Canadian flag, mounted atop a skinny six-foot pole, flapping in the wind like a sprinting fish.

The north and south ends of Elk Lake were called Point One and Point Two, respectively. I rowed to Point One to join the team for the start of the time trial, excited and nervous. As I neared the red buoy marking the start of the course, I could make out the silhouette of Mike's head perched on sloping shoulders through the foggy plastic window of the popemobile. He had anchored himself to the starting buoy and was calling out the starting order for the time trial.

"If you are not ready to go, we will not wait for you," he warned. "It will be a running start, as usual. Use the strokes available to you before the line, so that you are at full power when you cross it," he said, pronouncing "power" like "pow-wah" in his British accent.

He had a handheld talkback mic wired to the inside of the boat, which he held in front of him with his thumb cocked, like someone about to activate a detonation. He had a habit of pressing the button on his intercom system while he thought, giving a prelude of buzzing white noise to what he was about to say.

"Howard … Ready, go!"

"Bergen … Ready, go!"

"O'Farrell … Ready, go!"

Each *go* was followed shortly by another as each athlete passed through the start line where Mike noted their time of departure. At the other end of the lake, another coach did the same with a watch synced to Mike's, marking the finish and capture times.

I was last. "Okay, you may go now," Mike said. I don't think he remembered my name. *He will after this,* I thought.

"Ready, go!"

Oars bending, flexing under my strength, I shot through the start line, a man on a mission. I stared down at my stroke coach — a rowing computer displaying speed and stroke rate — determined to maintain thirty strokes per minute.

Mike had a reputation that preceded him. He was one of the most successful rowing coaches in the world, with over thirty-eight World Championship or Olympic medals won by crews he'd coached over the previous three decades. He began his coaching career in his native England, coaching the Great Britain double to silver at the 1976 Montreal Olympics, then continuing to coach the greatest oarsman of all time, five-time gold medallist Sir Steve Redgrave, to his first two Olympic gold medals: one at Los Angeles in 1984 in the coxed four, and one at Seoul in 1988 in the coxless pair.

In 1992, Mike coached Canada to its second gold medal in the men's eight. But along with Mike's coaching success came a reputation for subjecting his athletes to gruelling training loads. He eventually returned to Great Britain to coach the women's program. In 2000, despite winning a silver medal in the women's quad — the first ever Olympic medal for a British women's crew — the British rowing team decided to part ways with Mike due to athlete complaints about his brutal training program.

As Mike's boat shrunk into a glimmering piece of fibreglass in the distance, all I knew was that Mike was the man who'd coached the 2008 Canadian men's eight to gold in Beijing, and I needed to earn his confidence.

Just as this conviction was forming resolutely in my mind, I smashed into one of the large white buoys floating on the centre line of the course. I was so focused on the speed and stroke rate digits displayed on my Stroke Coach monitor that I'd lost track of my course. The impact knocked my port oar out of my right hand, *Not again!* I thought, as I rolled overboard. But by that time, I was probably one of the fastest in Canada at getting back into my boat after falling out. Determined to continue, I held the oar handles together in my right hand and dolphin-kicked my way back into the boat. Within fifteen seconds, I had my feet strapped back into the shoes and was rowing furiously again, my boat half full of water.

I wondered what was worse: the embarrassment of falling in, or getting back into my boat so quickly that Mike might assume I was fifteen seconds slower than I actually was, lacking the potential to develop into an Olympic rower.

It was only May so the water was still frigid, but I finished the first run at a good clip, enough to keep my body from losing tactile control from the cold. I rowed around the island at Point Two and floated idly at the back of the pack, dripping wet. A few national team guys cast me amused looks. I wished I knew them, so that I could crack a joke and ease my embarrassment. Instead, I pretended like nothing had happened and got ready for the next piece.

This time I zigzagged down the course, looking over my shoulder every five strokes, overcorrecting my steering one way, then the other.

"Mind your course!" Mike called out over the PA.

I was bearing down on his boat in the last 50 metres.

"Down!" Mike shouted.

I finished the second piece on a forty-five-degree angle toward shore. Luckily the piece ended before I ran aground.

By the third 2,000-metre piece, I relaxed. I was halfway through, and the novelty of rowing alongside the national team had worn off. The first two pieces probably could not have gone worse, but they were over. I submerged my port oar and picked at the water with my right oar, turning my twenty-seven-foot single shell around for another run of the lake.

"O-kay," Mike said, with a downward inflection on *kay*, running out of patience, "are you ready?"

I wondered what he thought about me. Had he written me off?

"Ready … row!"

Each time I blasted off the start, I felt untouchable, like no one in the world could keep up with me. Twenty-five strokes in, I felt like I was going to self-combust if I had to row twenty-five more (with 200 to go). Each 2-kilometre timed piece was 10 percent motivating — *I'm the next champ; I will destroy world champion Mahé Drysdale in the Olympics in the single sculls event* — and 90 percent soul-crushing — *this is not physically possible; this sport is sadistic; what the hell am I doing out here?*

I limped through the fourth piece to complete the workout. I was completely cooked, despondent with how it had gone. Was anyone truly capable of rowing 2 kilometres, all out, four times in a row?

A saving grace awaited me back at the boathouse after I put my boat away. An assistant coach had posted the times for the time trials, giving me my first chance to compare times with the top heavyweights since the 2009 National Championships. I looked past the first time — meaningless, since I'd fallen in — to the second, third, and fourth times. My second time put me right in the mix with the others. I was fifth fastest out of sixteen national team scullers. But my third and fourth times had faded massively compared to the others. Still, I latched onto that second time as an indicator that I was within striking distance of the team.

The guys on the national team may have felt some pressure from my decent second time. More likely, they would have dismissed me as some punk who had picked one piece to go hard on and cruised on the others.

Later, I, too, would scoff at people who did what I was doing: jumping in comparatively fresh and laying down fast times on the first one or two pieces, only to fade by the fourth piece. The national team athletes understood that the Saturday morning 4 × 2,000-metre time trial was a measure of fitness, that your average time across all four was what counted, not your single fastest time. Even splitting (maintaining a consistent speed) for each piece would have been the logical approach, but I had it stuck in my head that all this training was for one day when I'd be on the Olympic start line with *one* 2,000-metre race for medals.

As I walked toward the parking lot, I crossed paths with Doug on his way to coach the VCRC team for their second session.

"How'd it go?" he asked.

"I hit a buoy on the first run and fell in," I said.

"Oh. Shit," he said. Then he smiled. "It's good that you kept going."

24

Despite progress on the water, my living arrangement at home wasn't sustainable. The condo was becoming a morgue holding the corpse of my relationship with Amy, rotting, festering. We did our best to cohabitate in a common living space about the size of a shipping container, but it wasn't working. We put on a good show for Ethan — God, we loved that kid so much — anything to carry on the appearance of a happy union between Mom and Dad. Polite hellos and a cordial, "How was your day today, Mommy?" To which Amy would respond, "Good. How was your day, Daddy?"

Finally, we agreed it was time to part ways. A friend's vacant bed and breakfast across town gave Amy a temporary place to go. She made a few trips to move her stuff, and then got Ethan ready for his first night in their new place. I walked out of the condo to say goodbye to them under the potted tree that Ethan ran circles around whenever we'd leave to go somewhere.

Amy and I each died a little, standing on the patio stones outside the condo, as we tried to explain to our five-year-old what was happening, how things would work going forward, when we weren't even sure ourselves.

"Mommy and Daddy are going to be living in different houses now," Amy said. "Mommy and Daddy are really, really good friends, but we need to have our own houses now."

She looked like she might cry if she didn't leave soon. I felt numb, my Adam's apple rising, swelling. Ethan looked at the ground, tracing his hand along the concrete bench surrounding the tree, walking in circles as he so often did, trying to understand.

"So me, Mommy, and Daddy will live at Mommy's house for three days, and then at Daddy's house for three days?" he asked. He couldn't conceive that the three of us would not always be together. We'd already moved several times in his young life; he thought this was just another temporary arrangement, like when I'd moved out to Victoria alone to start working.

"No, Daddy and Mommy are going to have our own houses now, and you will spend some of the time at Mommy's and some of the time at Daddy's," I said, taking over for Amy — she was fighting hard now to hold back the tears, her eyes glassy.

Ethan looked confused. It didn't make sense. Confusion turned to anger. "I don't want to do that!" he said, defiant. "I want us to live *together.*"

The lump in my throat felt ready to burst, like someone was crushing my trachea in a headlock.

"It's time to go," I said. There was nothing more to say now. We couldn't explain away what was happening.

"No!" Ethan said, breaking off, running down the sidewalk past the neighbouring cedar-facade townhomes.

I chased him down and scooped him up in my arms. He writhed against my hold, knowing it was impossible to escape, but bending, jerking, and stretching all the same. I put him in the back seat of Amy's car, holding him in his booster seat with my left hand and wrapping the seat belt around him with my right. Amy was in the driver's seat now, looking dead ahead.

Ethan's anger gave way to tears. "I want you to come. I want you to come," he choked between sobs.

"I'll see you really soon, Ethan," I said. I tried to sound as casual as possible, like what was happening was no big deal — a necessary arrangement that would change nothing between us — just as my world was turning upside down. It would change everything. "Love ya, buddy." I closed the door. Amy didn't look back. She couldn't — she was crying noiselessly to herself, her shoulders trembling.

She pulled out of the semi-circular driveway onto the street and drove away with Ethan crying and crying in the backseat, peering at me through the window. My heart broke into a million fucking pieces.

As soon as Ethan was out of sight, I turned and made a brisk path to the condo entrance. I couldn't leave the scene fast enough. *Move, just move.* I got to the elevator, pushed the up button, and waited, thoughts racing, guilt washing over me. The elevator opened; I got in. The elevator accelerated upwards, adding to the sinking feeling in my gut. I watched the red LED lights flick — two, three, four, then five. I was in a trance. The doors opened. My sweet neighbour Barbara appeared. She was in her seventies, whip-smart, and we were friends.

"Oh hi, Jeremiah. How are you?" she asked.

"Fine, thanks. Where are you off to?" I smiled the fakest smile ever to grace my face.

She was going for a walk to exercise her ailing knee. I got the progress report. I nodded. Finally, the elevator started buzzing loudly, angry at being held open too long. I said goodbye.

I walked the ten steps to my door, pushed through, collapsed onto my kitchen island, and cried in big convulsing sobs like I hadn't experienced since I was a kid.

A few days later, while Ethan was at kindergarten, Amy and I met at her new temporary home to go over a parenting agreement we found on the internet and had modified for our purposes. She gave me a tour. The house was decorated with floral wallpaper, brown buttoned couches, and elaborate lamps and coffee tables. Ethan shared a room upstairs with Amy. His bed had a wrought iron frame painted white. It was tucked into an enclave that used to be a closet in the side of the room. I sat on it, and the springs sagged loudly. *He'll never fall asleep on this thing.*

We went downstairs, through the living room, and sat across from each other at the dark cherrywood dining room table. I passed Amy her copy of the parenting agreement and then started talking through the clauses the same way I would explain a loan agreement to a client at the bank. Neither of us could bear the thought of being away from Ethan for long, so we agreed on a custody schedule that split the weeks in half. Ethan would be with me Sunday until Tuesday, and with Amy from Wednesday until Saturday. Every week we would alternate who got the extra day. We crossed out all the clauses about division of property and income and left in the important parts: We would share custody fifty-fifty, and neither of us would move Ethan from Victoria without the other's consent.

When I went through the agreement, Amy started crying. I tried to harden myself, as was my typical reaction when Amy cried.

"I just feel like we're failing, like we've failed," she said.

"I know," I said, breathless.

Our relationship wasn't salvageable, but we had done well raising Ethan together, and we would find a way to keep doing it together even while pulling apart.

We witnessed each other's agreements. Then I left.

There is only decision and action. Everything else is a wasteland, I thought, as I walked to my car.

25

I spent every other day on the phone with my dad in the following weeks, his voice something familiar I could latch on to. We had conversations punctuated with long silences, me taking big breaths and exhaling into the receiver, and him offering advice when he could.

Work also helped me after the breakup. Things had been improving, and I began to feel more competent. Learning my job was like learning a new language; I had imprinted all the processes and freed up mental resources for applying judgment, for considering, weighing, recommending loan facilities, new deals — all the things I was hired to do. I had been promoted to work as an analyst on my own portfolio, and I knew my clients well. I could defend my work in a team huddle in Rob's corner office with the credit VPs on speakerphone, hashing out the salient issues of a new deal. It felt like I had finally arrived, and a lingering confidence followed me out of the office at the end of each day.

Those good feelings lasted on days when Ethan was with me after work, but when he was with Amy I sat at my kitchen island, eating my dinner alone in unusual silence. I had always growled at Ethan during dinner when he leaned his head on my arm or when he playfully bumped me while we sat side by side on bar stools. "You wouldn't poke a bear while he was eating, would you?" I always warned. Now I missed his daily pokes. I missed tousling his hair at any given moment, grabbing him in my arms and squeezing his little skeleton until he let out a breathless "Okayyyyy."

To escape the depression caused by the absence of Ethan and Amy, I committed myself even more to rowing. It's a wonderful sport for someone feeling a certain kind of emptiness. It's technical enough to stop running thoughts, and repetitive enough to lose yourself in it. You can just *be.*

October 2010 passed by in three scenes: working, training, and missing Ethan half the time. Doug had me pushing hard for the National Championships, to be held in Victoria that year. I wasn't falling in anymore, but I still had trouble staying straight within the buoyed lanes of a racecourse.

We worked on racing starts. A good start depends on several factors: pressing the quads down with a relaxed upper body, drawing the oars evenly, blades at the same depth, exiting at the same time. Me, I was like an old Cessna taking off a dirt runway strip. My oars were like wings, bobbing, rolling slightly after takeoff, then stabilizing with speed. A good start felt like flying.

"Quicker with the hands around the finish," Doug repeated, ad nauseam (everything ad nauseam). "Stay tall, drive the legs."

We did five-stroke starts, then ten-stroke starts, then twenty-five-stroke starts into race pace. When done well, my blades cut into the water like bullets shot through a silencer.

Two weeks before the Nationals, Doug prescribed race pace workouts: 1,500 metres, 2 × 1,250 metres, 750 metres, and 4 × 500 metres. There was little consolation in racing less than 2,000 metres. I did the math: I would be at race pace for over 6 kilometres. How the hell was I supposed to go all-out for that distance, even with a break between pieces? I just wanted to hit it and quit it: one 2,000-metre race, and done. Doug knew what he was doing, but I still had much to learn about becoming a fast rower.

As the Nationals approached, I sensed my opportunity. The earth spun, people got on with their lives, plans changed and they adapted, but not me. I had a one-track focus on becoming an Olympic rower, and the Nationals were a make-or-break moment along the journey.

The regatta began in the last week of September. Young rowers gathered in Victoria from across the country. Clouds blotted out the sun, as they did every year during the Nationals, but the water was as smooth as glass. The national team athletes would not participate this year due to final preparations for the World Championships in New Zealand, which was being held unusually late in the year. Malcolm Howard wouldn't be there. Neither would at least a few other rowers who were likely faster than me at the time. I had to finish in the top three to be considered for a development funding card, which would give me $900 a month during the following year, or I would have to delay the jump to full-time training from 2011 until the next year, 2012 — just months away from the Olympic Games and far too late to challenge for an Olympic seat. Amy was eager to return to Ontario, Ethan was growing up fast, and I was at risk of having the bank transfer me to another city, as was the norm after two years on the job. No, it was now or never. I had saved the $10,000 I needed to cover half my living expenses the following year, and the D-card would cover the remaining half.

"Lane six, tap it up; lane three, back it down; lane three, hold; lane two, tap it up."

The starting announcer did his best to align our boats for the final of the national championships. A crosswind kept pushing us into the side of our lanes. It was an impossible task to get everyone level for a fair start. He gave up.

"Attention. Go!"

After the semi-final, I'd gathered around the results bulletin board that was mounted on the side of the boathouse to compare my winning time with the other semifinal race. Mike Braithwaite had won, but his time was a second slower than my winning time. Braithwaite — the guy who had medalled behind Malcolm Howard at the 2009 Nationals and the rower who had given me props for racing despite falling in during the warm-up — was a world under-23 bronze medallist in the single. He was shorter than me, with a body like an ape walking upright: strong, hairy forearms, and a deep chest. He was a smug son of a bitch too, soft-spoken, but with beady little eyes that flashed a perpetual inner intensity. Pale skin, weather-worn like a sailor's, tough like a hide. Braithwaite. *Is that Old English? Yes, he is descendant from Norse Vikings who won't give up, damn him.* I hated when I couldn't know an opponent from looking him in the eye.

I stumbled out of the start, driving my oars too deep and losing balance. I recovered on the second stroke, then overcompensated by strong-arming the next ten strokes until I had a length on Braithwaite and the rest of the field. All six rowers moved across the water like a navy fleet heading for a beach landing.

The chop in the middle of the lake destabilized my boat. The water tossed me, teased me. I cursed the conditions. Braithwaite kept coming at me, like the Energizer Bunny, relentless. I cursed him, too. My forearms stiffened, already tight from my muscled start. Kevin Kowalyk, another strong sculler in the mix, was pushing hard on my port, but where Braithwaite showed no signs of fatigue, Kowalyk's body language revealed pain.

After 1,300 metres, Braithwaite bumped his rate up two beats per minute and started attacking me. Sparring on water in a single scull is infuriating. I'd rather be punched in the face than watch an opponent break me down inch by inch in a rowing race. Braithwaite was beating me with patience. His speed had been steady from the start. I had spent too much energy early on, and now I was fading. Each stroke brings a moment of hope; the surge in boat speed at the finish of the stroke, a moment of calibration — have you gained, stuck, or lost water to your opponent? A moment of strengthening resolve or crumbling despair follows — do you work harder when the heat is on, or do you wilt? It's the tsunami of race psychology, the struggle to stay ahead of the wave of doubt chasing you, looming larger every second. It's that fucking panic that I hadn't yet learned how to manage.

Braithwaite moved through me steadily, sawing the water with his oars. He took a foot of water each stroke. I had no answer. He won the race with 400 metres left in it. I turned my focus onto Kowalyk. Something was wrong with him — a cracked rib, maybe. Whatever Kowalyk's injury was, it had taken the fight out of him. With 200 metres left in the race, I knew I had come in second.

After the race, I stood on the podium with Braithwaite and Kowalyk. As we received our medals, I scanned the crowd for Peter Cookson, the national team's high-performance director. I wanted confirmation that I'd made the team. I saw him standing to the side of the boat landing near the outdoor boat racks.

"Here you go, Jerry," he said as I jogged over to him. He passed me a cheque in an envelope for $500 — the prize money for second place — and then turned to leave.

"Peter" — I stopped him — "what's the next step with D-card funding and joining the team?"

"Well, Jerry, we'll have to wait and see. You had a good result today, but there are some stipulations around erg performance that we'll also have to look —"

"I pulled 5:57 on my last 2k and 19:36 on my 6k," I interrupted. "I met the erg standards for a D-card. What's left to decide?"

"Jerry, I can't give you an answer right now. The coaches and I will look at all the data for all athletes and come to a collaborative decision through due process."

What the fuck? I thought. He sounded like a risk manager in the bank, giving me the runaround about policy instead of talking about the deal. Why was he giving me lip service? How was it so clear to me what I was going to do but so lost on the people who were supposed to be helping me get there?

"Look, Peter," I said, "I've been preparing for this moment for over a year. I'm leaving my job. I'm doing this." I looked him straight in the eyes. "But I need that D-card money to make it work."

Forget going into debt. I didn't need that hanging over my head when I was all in.

Peter broke my gaze, searching the ground for what to say next like a pressed politician in a media scrum. "We'll go through the process, and we'll let you know," he said.

26

The following Monday morning I sat in the boardroom with my bank colleagues for our biweekly meeting. Rob went over the usual stuff: new borrower numbers, deposit and credit volumes, referrals.

At the end of the meeting, he said, "And before we wrap up, I have a special announcement to make. Our very own Jerry Brown placed second in the men's heavy single sculls.... Do I have that right, Jerry?" — I nodded — "At the national rowing championships held at Elk Lake on the weekend."

Everyone lit up. Some interesting news at the end of a boring meeting. Rob had read my name in the *Times Colonist* newspaper and caught me off guard with the recognition.

One of my colleagues questioned me: "So, does that mean ... are you ... could you make the Olympic team?" she asked.

"You never know," I said.

It was true, I didn't know.

Two weeks later, I received an email from the national team development coordinator. All athletes being considered for national team selection and development funding were required to do a battery of ergometer tests: a 2k, a 6k, a one-hour test (which sounded like torture), a three-stroke max watt test, a one-minute max effort test (brief, but still torture), and a ten-stroke max watt test.

It all felt like a colour-by-numbers approach to talent identification. How much data did they really need? They had no test that would show them what was in my heart, how fucking determined I was. Even in the bank, we analysts were taught to look beyond the financial data. The three *Cs* in commercial lending were character, capacity, and collateral. Character came first.

Finding faults with the system was easy, but I was making the same mistake thousands of other promising young athletes make: I was overestimating my stock. Just because I was in the middle of a quick rise in the rowing world didn't mean I'd done anything yet. For one thing, consistency in testing says a lot about an athlete's training. My personal best time of 5:57 on the ergometer wasn't the whole story. Six weeks after winning Monster Erg, I sat down to my second 2-kilometre erg test of the year at 5:45 a.m. It was an unthinkable time to attempt a 2k, but Doug worked most evenings managing a liquor store and it was the only time everyone on the VCRC senior team could do it together. I took five hard strokes and settled into my pace of 1:29 per 500 metres. But 250 metres in, I started burning up as if it was the third quarter of the distance. My body was still asleep, the back of my throat was caked dry from sucking air, and I didn't have the benefit of ignorance anymore — I knew how much pain was in store for me. I stopped rowing. Doug gave me a questioning look. He'd never seen me quit. "I'll try again in the evening," I said. I walked out of the boathouse, utterly defeated.

When I returned that evening I acted like a prima donna, obsessed with conditions not being perfect before the test. I hadn't eaten my yam two hours before. I was mentally fatigued from work. Excuses, excuses. *Suck it up, pussy.* I finished the test with a time of 6:04. For the first time, I had taken a step backwards. Yet, what I saw as failure was only the very beginning of progress. I had no idea just how much the coming months would be riddled with it. I would soon learn that seeking failure every day would be the only true path to the Olympic Games.

27

One day in October 2010 I had my third encounter with Mike Spracklen while putting my boat away. We made eye contact. He opened his mouth as if to say something, then closed it.

"Hello, Mike," I said, seeing he might talk to me.

He straightened his posture. "What is your plan?" he asked.

"My plan?"

"Yes. Doug tells me you have a plan to join the team. What is it?"

"I need to work until the end of the year to save enough money before switching to full-time training. I'm aiming for January 1, 2011," I said.

"Hmmmm …" he said, with that many *m*'s. "If you're serious about this, you need to increase your training volume *now*. You *should* have started months ago." He locked his thumbs behind him and rolled back onto his heels in disapproval.

"It's the earliest I can do it," I said. "I don't have the money. I don't even know if I'll get a D-card."

Mike looked past me across Elk Lake. He started nodding his head, more of a tremble, really. I wondered if he had Parkinson's. He was in his seventies. No, it was just a mannerism, as if to confirm the thought he hadn't yet put words to. He shot me a sly, squinting look. "We'll see what we can do about that," he said.

Soon after this brief exchange, I got an email from Peter Cookson congratulating me on being selected for the national team and receiving a development funding card. It was a watershed moment for me. I called my parents. My dad was encouraging in his modest way.

"That's good, son. That's very good." He said "son" in sentences only when showing affection; "son" equals *I'm proud of you.* One syllable, and it rolled over me like warm molasses.

My mom's reaction was predictably German: "Are you sure you're comfortable leaving your job, your *career*, to do this sport?"

"It's the *only* thing I'm sure about right now!" I said.

I never thought I'd think twice about leaving the bank, but my mom's caution made me reflect. What if I failed and lost my funding, would I have a job to go back to? My competency at work had mirrored my progress on the water; after two years, I was good at it. I liked my co-workers, the rhythm of the workweek. Heck, I even had an office with a view of the Olympic Mountains across the Juan de Fuca Strait. Was I throwing it all away for a pipe dream?

I wasn't sure how Rob would react when I told him I was leaving. It was a Friday. I had decided to ask for a one-year leave of absence — the maximum allowable under bank policy. If my request wasn't approved, I would quit.

I walked to his office nervously, my pulse pounding in my ears. My hands were cold and sweaty. I hate how easily I get nervous. As soon as Rob shook my clammy hand, he'd know something was up. I rubbed them on my pants one final time before knocking on his office door. He looked up at me through the frosted bands of privacy glass and ushered me in. I crossed his expansive corner office and took a seat in front of his desk. "I'll be with you in one moment," he said, adding his comments to a deal that needed to go to Toronto for final approval.

I caught myself analyzing him. Supple skin, a bulbous nose, pinstripe pants, a starched white shirt with stiff collar stays cradling a perfect Windsor-knotted tie, his hair so sharply manicured at the neck I thought he must start each morning with a haircut.

Finally, he swung away from his computer to face me. "Sorry about that, Jerry. So, what's up?"

I filled him in, ending with "… and so, I'd like to request a leave of absence." He smiled and chuckled in a way that could have meant *You're out of your mind* just as easily as *Of course we'll support you.* I hung in suspense.

"Jerry, that's fantastic. I figured you'd bring this up sooner or later after coming second at Nationals." Relief washed over me. "Of course you have my full support. I'll give my recommendation to HR, and I'm sure they'll be onside."

God bless you, Rob.

PART THREE: THE DRIVE

Listen for a bell tone at the catch; that's when you know you've locked on. If your catch is slow, you'll waste the first quarter of the stroke.

— Mike Spracklen, coaching the catch

28

I equate the time between making the team and actually beginning full-time training to walking up the side of a volcano that was about to blow — I was ignorant and simply happy to take in the view. I'd worked so hard to make the team — balancing work, fatherhood, a failed relationship — that I momentarily became happy just to have made the cut. I relished the opportunity to compete, and I was proud of myself.

Through November and December, I trained hard — a young man working with a strengthened sense of purpose. I churned the water with my oars and stretched the erg chain. The flywheel of the ergometer sounded like music whirring in my ears.

Doug knew the real journey was just beginning. He gave me warnings: "The hard part will be surviving the first few months of Mike's training program. He won't wait for you." It was a passing of the baton from Doug, who had made me into a rower from raw ingredients, to Mike Spracklen, who would pull more out of me than I knew existed.

As the days grew darker into December, I knew there was one missing piece of the puzzle that would make or break me. It was Amy.

I remember waking up one morning to the ascending marimba ring tone on my iPhone and sitting up on the edge of my bed. I always took a minute, sometimes several, to convince myself not to quit rowing and roll back into the body heat that had not yet escaped my rumpled blanket. I stood up. It was pitch black. I had covered the window with tinfoil so Ethan and I could get to sleep in our bunk beds while it was still light out. I navigated the bedroom floor with my toe, feeling for obstacles like a soldier sweeping a minefield with a metal detector; Hot Wheels and Lego were the principal offenders. I lost my balance. *Crunch.* I stepped on the half-built Lego dungeon Ethan and I had worked on for an hour before bed. "Shit," I muttered. Ethan would be furious.

I sat at my kitchen island and munched on my toasted bagel with peanut butter and honey, staring at the sleeping world through the wall of windows endcapping my shoebox condo. After pulling on three layers of spandex and cursing silently during the struggle, it was time to extricate Ethan from the top bunk. I wished there was some way to keep him sleeping, like a miniature coffin with ventilation and wheels. As soon as I'd forklift my arms under his sleeping body, he would stretch out and stiffen into a plank, pointing his toes and arching his back. It became very much like taking my boat off the racks. "Time to go, buddy," I whispered. I cradled him as gently as I could, trying to maintain balance while stepping down the cold steel steps of the bunk bed ladder. At the bottom, he shifted, wrapping his arms around my neck and his legs around my waist, and burying his face into my neck like a baby chimp clinging to its parent. With my free hand I slung my backpack onto my left shoulder, grabbed a few blankets, and left.

Outside, I could see my breath in the cold. It was a typical West Coast morning: overcast, with a lingering dampness that kept the pavement dark even though it hadn't rained. I mummified Ethan with the blankets before shuffle-jogging my way to the car parked out front. He squirmed, shifting his head under my chin, melding into my body. I put him into the back seat of my 1991 Toyota Corolla. The car was pink on top and red on the sides, like a tie-dyed T-shirt, worn down from the sun. I'd bought it off a college student for $500, and talked it into starting each morning.

I twisted the key in the ignition and waited the customary three seconds before the engine coughed to life. *Atta girl.* I drove through the city, a string of green lights, my private highway in the dark pre-dawn. Ethan sat sleeping in his booster seat like a sack of potatoes, his head flopped to one side at an angle that made me wince. When we got to Amy's, her porch light flicked on. Disrupting Ethan's sleep for the second time, I collected him out of the back seat. I took the porch stairs three at a time and met Amy. She was tired, slow-blinking, but happy as always to see her son. I unwrapped Ethan from my chest, and he twisted into his mom's arms like a magnet suddenly reversing polarity. I wanted to wrap my arms around both of them.

My drive to the lake was marred with guilt. There was no way our temporary arrangement could last. Ethan was in kindergarten now, and routine was more important than ever. Rowing had taught me to cherish routine; consistency in training meant everything. And Ethan had taught me in his first five years that kids need the same thing. I couldn't go on carting him back and forth like a UPS priority package.

I pulled into the Elk Lake driveway a few minutes late. My usual parking spot had been taken, forcing me to circle back to the upper lot. I stepped out of my car into a biting crosswind that cleared the sky. Douglas firs bent plaintively beyond the boathouse. The moon was still out, turning silver the remaining leaves bravely clinging to the maple trees lining the lot. It was a morning when, had I been early, I might have rowed to Point One at the north end of the lake, laid back onto my bow, and gazed at a million stars until the sound of Doug's encroaching outboard motor switched me into work mode.

But this morning I was late. I plopped my boat into the water, weaved around the big white buoys, and cut across the middle of the lake to fall in with Doug and the rest of the senior VCRC team.

Thoughts of Ethan and Amy distracted me. How does anyone get shit done in the wake of a breakup involving kids? I pulled my oars as hard as I could, felt my lungs expand, felt the flaccid muscle in my quads flex into place. Uncertainty around my family life gnawed at me. It was all I could think about — a spiral of dissecting my relationship with Amy: *What had gone wrong? Could it be repaired?* No, it wasn't something to be repaired. We were fundamentally incompatible. When Ethan came along, he was a gift. Amy and I had taken turns being selfish over the years, and Ethan was a chance for both of us to put someone before ourselves.

I thought of my dad not quite achieving his Ph.D., stopping to work and support his three kids. When I was a teenager, we'd drive two hours to my hockey games in silence. Was he mulling over Plato's *Republic*? Tired from work? Wishing he was somewhere else, living a different life? It seemed like he was living a self-imposed sentence to do his duty as a father. The death of his scholarly ambitions had saddled him with a melancholic boredom.

I'd studied him in those silences, imagining what choices I would make differently to avoid a similar fate.

Now I was faced with a life-defining choice. Would I let myself drift apart from Ethan over the next two years while I chased my Olympic dream, turning into one of the millions of part-time dads who got their fathering in when they could on weekends and around work schedules? I knew the stakes. I wouldn't be able to fool myself into thinking I had no choice, that circumstances had prevented me from being a present father. Bullshit. It's always a choice. And I wouldn't be able to choose my ambition over Ethan. Only Amy could make it so that I didn't have to choose between Ethan and the Olympics. I needed to convince her to move back in with me.

I don't remember how the conversation went, only that Amy agreed. I made no appeal to save our relationship; it was purely a selfish request to move in with me and begin a platonic relationship that would keep our little family together for the time being. Keeping the family together meant keeping *me* together. It was a short-term strategy that gave me a brief window of time to chase the Olympic dream.

29

On January 1, 2011, I fell into rank with the national rowing team. All athletes were required to report to the Pacific Institute for Sport Excellence (PISE) in Victoria for benchmark testing. The training season had begun without me at the start of December, but everyone else was returning from a one-week Christmas break, so I had the sense we were starting together.

PISE was a gleaming new sporting complex — the product of government investment in high-performance sport in Canada. I pulled into the parking lot and walked up a steep embankment to an expansive square-paved front entrance. A bronze statue of a diver, arms outstretched, ready to spring, seemed to beckon for a high-five. I walked along floor-to-ceiling tinted windows plastered with life-sized posters of Canadian Olympians: Simon Whitfield, Adam Van Koeverden, Jake Wetzel. It was incredible to think I would now be training at their level.

Ahead of me three national team rowers, whom I recognized but didn't know, caught each other up on their Christmas travels. I recognized the dialect of camaraderie from my football days. They walked through giant automatic sliding doors and up a concrete stairwell to the second floor. I followed. Inside it smelled strongly of freshly recycled rubber flooring. Perforated sheets of red steel were bolted into the concrete walls. Sharp lines, cold concrete — this was a futuristic high-performance facility that called upon hardened, cold-blooded athletes to make use of it.

About twenty-five heavyweight and lightweight male athletes moved among three stations: anthropomorphic measurements in the sport science and technology lab, a core strength assessment in a lecture room, and a flexibility test in a group fitness studio. None of these things would hurt, yet my heart pounded as I shuffled into line.

A wiry woman of about forty with a high ponytail read my name from a clipboard. I stepped forward. "Please remove your shirt and pants," she said. I had a flashback to prisoner intake at the youth penitentiary. She grabbed at my body like a farmer inspecting livestock, pinching as much skin and fat from above my hip as possible before measuring me with a body fat caliper. The shiny steel instrument had parabolic measurement markings that reminded me of the protractor I'd used in grade eleven trigonometry.

Next, she found a fingerful of skin and fat under my triceps that I didn't know existed. I started to feel self-conscious: too skinny to fit in with offensive linemen, and too fat to fit in with rowers — I couldn't win.

The woman pulled out a black permanent marker and a neatly wound measuring tape, which she held above her head and let unravel to the floor. She drew small *X*s on my pecs, biceps, back, lower abdomen, upper thighs, and calves. *X, X, X,* like a teacher marking an exam that my body had failed. She instructed me to bend my arms at ninety degrees, now straight out, now down at my sides, as she darted from measurement to measurement like a hummingbird. The tape felt cold against my skin. When she stooped to measure my upper quad, I tensed briefly. *Please, God, do not let me get an erection.* The last time that happened I was thirteen in a swimming lesson, and I'd jumped into the water. There was no pool in the sports science lab.

"You're all done," she said. "Next!"

I moved on to the core strength test — a side plank where you're elevated on your elbow, keeping your body perfectly straight, and extending your opposite arm above you. Sort of like a sideways Usain Bolt pose. I managed about a minute and a half on each side before collapsing. The next athlete was a much shorter lightweight rower who looked like he could hold it for an hour. (Tall people don't get credit for the extra leverage sapping our strength on these kinds of tests.) He was still holding the same side when I left a few minutes later.

The next station was a sit-and-reach test, requiring you to sit with legs flat on the floor and stretch as far past your toes as possible. I'd done the same test during football training camp, and our strength and conditioning coach had found my lack of flexibility amusing. "That's it?" he'd asked.

Now I stretched forward as far as I could, still two inches short of my toes.

"That's it?" asked the physiologist.

After the tests I milled about, waiting for the most important test of the day: a 6-kilometre ergometer test. This was the big one, the one I had been working towards for the previous two months. I hadn't broken nineteen minutes (the unofficial minimum standard for the 6-kilometre distance, like breaking six minutes over 2 kilometres), but I was determined to do it that day. I wanted to send a message to the national team guys who'd been ignoring me: I was coming for them. All of them were hungry to secure a seat in a boat. The sight of me, no matter how small a threat at that point, was unwelcome.

Two rows of ergometers were set up in the gymnasium, a cavernous space that dwarfed the tall rowers busy choosing ergs. Someone had propped open an emergency exit door, creating a steady draft of cold, wet air. With it, a pool of daylight spilled onto the polished hardwood floor, reflecting into our faces — solemn faces, preparing for pain.

"Ten minutes to start time," yelled Brian Price. At 5'4" and 120 pounds, Brian was a commanding presence in a small package. A thirteen-year veteran of the national team as coxswain of the men's eight, including coxing the boat to gold in Beijing, he had as much swagger as any of the athletes. *Little fucker*, I thought.

I took a seat in the second row of ergs, near the open door. In front of me, with their ergs pushed against the blue gym pads on the front wall, were faces I recognized from seeing them in passing at the boathouse. Malcolm Howard was in the middle of the first row, flanked by Rob Gibson, a University of Washington rower. Rob's upper body was built like a defensive end. He was the first rower I'd met that I might not want to run into during a football game. He wore earbuds and an iPod was strapped to his arm; he was focused, transported to another world by his music. In my row, I recognized Andrew Byrnes, also from the Beijing eight. He cast his eyes downward with minutes until the start, carefully screwing down his water bottle lid and placing it beside his erg. He took deep breaths. Further down the line sat Doug Csima, a fellow McMaster University grad. Doug's girlfriend had actually been my roommate in university one year, and he and I had crossed paths occasionally. When I'd passed by him in the VCRC boathouse earlier that summer, we'd picked up where we'd left off, acting less like we had anything in common and more like two men trying to fill one Olympic seat. I was still the football player. This was his world, and I was intruding. He sat on his erg with both feet planted on the floor. Thick black eyebrows hung low over his dark eyes, exuding intensity.

"One minute!" Brian hollered. My surroundings fell away like slabs of glacier ice sliding into the sea. Now it was just me and the erg again. *Loosey-goosey, stay relaxed, find your rhythm.*

"Sitting up."

We sat poised with legs bent and arms outstretched.

"Ready, go!" Brian released us.

The familiar whir of the ergometers came to life, like the sound of waves crashing and churning toward shore.

The start of a 6-kilometre erg test doesn't have the urgency of a 2-kilometre distance. It's more marathon than sprint, like you're setting off on a long journey that you're not sure you'll survive. I let myself drift into a dreamlike state. I settled on twenty-eight strokes per minute and locked my eyes on the computer monitor displaying 1:35 per 500 metres — a pace that would give me a time of nineteen minutes. During every stroke in the first 3,000 metres I am a flight engineer checking all systems: *Have I gone out too hard? Do I have enough fuel to continue this pace? Is my body withstanding the pressure? Fuck it, override, continue, continue.* With 2,000 metres to go, I know what kind of fight I'm in for; it's either a courageous push to the finish or a desperate attempt at damage control as I slip off my pace. This day, I wasn't sure.

Occasionally Brian's voice appeared behind me: "Keep it there," and "Hold it, don't slip," and "Come on, big guy."

As lactic acid usurped all thought, I lost connection with my body. I was thrashing at the chain. I didn't want to pull anymore; I wanted to smash the machine to bits with an axe. Red anger bubbled inside me like lava. In the last 500 metres, I knew I should attack if I wanted to break nineteen minutes. I increased my rate to thirty strokes per minute, adding more slop to my deteriorating technique. The metres passed faster, flicking from triple digits to double digits: ninety, seventy-eight, sixty-two, forty-four … At zero, I collapsed forward, letting go of the handle, reeling. I'd done it: 18:59. I continued writhing in pain. It always took several seconds after finishing for the lactic acid's paralyzing effect to let go. Then I came back to reality.

I looked around to see who was still rowing. Malcolm had finished first by a wide margin, and Rob had finished a second before me. I was third fastest in the field. Athletes stopped rowing all around me, stopping abruptly like seized pistons, gulping drafts of fresh air flowing in from the open door. Pants, moans, and a few fucks echoed into the exposed steel framing of the ceiling.

Mike emerged from the rear of the gym, saying, "Well done," his soft voice barely audible.

I walked out of PISE to my ol' Corolla, humming with endorphins — that sweet chemical high athletes live for. Day one was complete. I had been pinched and measured, stretched and stiffened into planks, and had met my target on the ergometer test. I drove home happy with my first day on the new job.

Things were about to get much more difficult.

30

The next morning, I drove over the Bay Street Bridge on my way to Elk Lake. I looked past the harbour to the Victoria cityscape, to my old office. The TD sign, glowing green, poked above the pyramid roofs on the corners of the Bay Centre. It felt good seeing it fade in the rear-view mirror as I drove north, opposite the rush of commuter traffic heading into the city. Unimpeded, free, I was going against the grain again, diverging from the common path, and this gave me a deep, quiet pleasure.

The national team began its first training session at 7:30 a.m., a welcome change from the merciless 5:30 a.m. starts with Doug. There was no grand welcome at the boathouse when I arrived. No media scrum, no banners proclaiming "Welcome Jerry!" It was business as usual. Rowers took oars down to the dock in orderly fashion. The zeal of the Olympic pursuit lay buried somewhere in the backs of their minds.

Mike's popemobile purred away from the dock, leaving a trail of small eddies folding over each other in the water. At Point One, a long line of men in single shells spread across the lake, like a cavalry of centaurs with long, sleek carbon fibre racing shells for lower bodies.

After 6 kilometres of warm-up, we were ready to work. We spread out in a long line, over twenty of Canada's top rowers. Everyone looked to their port side to align themselves with the next guy, paddling then holding, reversing then holding. Like drag racers inching to the start line. Mike's PA crackled: "Pyramid twenty-two, starting at rate eighteen, ready … *Go!*"

The sound of oars snapping firm against oarlocks echoed across the lake, and the mass of rowing centaurs lurched away, leaving me half a boat length behind after the first stroke. In two seconds, I learned that each training run was an all-out race within the confines of Mike's dictated stroke rates. I mashed my feet into my footboards, trying to make up the lost ground, but the line swallowed up the gap where I had been. I was relegated to the second tier with a few other stragglers, a shameful position. We rowed unsteadily in the wake of the first group that had surged ahead. *Fuck.*

On the second run, I was ready. "Straight rate twenty-two," Mike said. "Ready … *Go!*" This time I drove my oars deep and hauled as hard as I could, throwing my body into the bow — an Olympic hang clean, all power. Second stroke: more of the same. I surged ahead with the leaders. Halfway through, someone yelled something at me. I couldn't make it out. At the end of the run, the rower repeated it: "I don't care if you beat me at twenty-two, but you were overrating the whole fucking way, buddy." I said nothing. He was right, I hadn't looked at my stroke coach once during the piece. Overrating is cheating in the context of group training. At the same length and power, a higher stroke rate means you're going faster. The rower was Will Crothers. He had buzzed red hair and bright blue eyes. Freckles covered his body uniformly. Will had done his college rowing at the University of Washington, where he'd stroked the varsity eight. It was his second year training full-time with the team and he was desperate to register on Mike's radar as a top athlete.

The second session of the day was an unsupervised 10-kilometre technical row. I put my boat in the water in a light mist, which found its way down the neck of my rowing vest and up the sleeve openings at my wrists. Mike drove his boat to and fro across the lake, coaching the top athletes on their single sculling technique, but not me. You needed to earn his one-on-one coaching.

Once I was 100 metres away from the dock and had graduated to full strokes, I noticed a painful pressure as I pulled on the oar handles. My fingers and palms were laced with puffy blood blisters resembling engorged leeches. Stroke by stroke, they burst like jumbo bubble wrap. The painful pressure turned into a searing sting, and my oar handles grew slippery with blister serum and blood. Ravaged hands are part of the sport, but usually blisters give way to calluses. In my case, the flesh on the inside of my palms and fingers didn't deal well with the damp cold of West Coast winters. The wetness kept my skin malleable and apt to tear open as easily as Play-Doh.

Mike's training program was such a massive step up from the volume and intensity I had been accustomed to that my hands (my whole body, really) would remain an open wound from January until June 2011.

The final session of the day was held at PISE: an hour of weights, followed by a 10-kilometre ergometer workout. After four sets of lifting weights with depleted bodies, we headed upstairs for the 10k. Windows along the side of the room revealed people walking home for the day in the early darkness of winter. For us, 10 kilometres of Greek warship slave rowing lay ahead.

I took a seat on an erg in the third row beside Mike Wilkinson, a Vancouverite whose rugged facial features belied his warm personality. Mike had beaten me easily at the 2009 Nationals. At the 2010 Nationals, he raced the pair instead of the single. Now we sat down together, and, expecting no more than to deflect glances, I was surprised when a big disarming smile spread across his face and he offered me his hand. "Hi! I'm Mike," he said.

"Jerry," I said, with a less certain smile.

Brian set up a fan in the front corner of the room and opened the side windows before taking his place beside Mike at the rear of the room. Brian was Mike's little henchman, standing at his side like an obedient Chihuahua.

Brian put us through a nineteen-minute pressure pyramid warm-up while Mike paced the room, praising good technique and criticizing the bad. The warm-up got our hearts pumping and sweat flowing, and after nineteen minutes I'd already had enough rowing for one day. I followed suit as everyone stripped off their top layer and rolled their unisuits down to the waist. The room was steaming when Mike began talking.

"I know you've heard this from me before; however, it bears repeating why we train the way we do. We train length and power at low rates during the winter so that come racing season we are able to maintain more power and a longer stroke at race pace." He struggled to make his voice heard over the sound of the fan blowing behind him. Brian turned it off. It was hard to imagine how someone so soft-spoken could have a reputation for ruthlessness. One look around the room told me that Mike was revered by his athletes. When he spoke, they leaned in like children listening to a captivating story.

It was a short story.

"Okay, sitting up to start. Straight rate twenty-two," Brian said.

I turned to Mike Wilkinson, my new ally, to ask him what split time he was aiming to hold.

"It's basically balls to the wall for thirty-five minutes," he said.

With Mike Spracklen, there was no such thing as steady-state (low-intensity, long distance training). Months later I would ask him for his definition of steady-state training while standing drenched in sweat after a Wednesday around-the-lake row. His answer: "Steady-state is rowing at 95 percent of maximal effort.... No, 99 percent of maximal effort."

We rowed together, a mass of human flesh connected in rhythm. The row of backs in front of me glistened with sweat. Muscles tightened at the catch of each stroke, rolled and rippled under the skin like bubbling molten mercury, disappearing again during the recovery. I tried to match Mike's split time but kept slipping off it. I was furious with my body for not complying. In the second row, Doug Csima and Rob Gibson rowed beside each other. Doug's face was fixed in the same grimace the whole time, like the pain was present but compartmentalized away somewhere. Rob looked despondent during the drive and confident during the recovery. It was as if each stroke was a one-rep max barely accomplished, yet repeated over a thousand times.

One of the team physiologists had told me it would take eight months to a year just for my body to adapt to Mike's training load. I would have to prove her wrong. I found no consolation in being the new guy, nor did I accept that I shouldn't expect to match my new teammates without years of training at the same volume and intensity. Truthfully, my first 6-kilometre ergometer test had been a misnomer. All it did was show that the sum of all my training in 2010 was equal only to the starting point for a national team athlete. Everyone would get faster — at least, everyone who could endure the training.

Every 1,000 metres in that 10-kilometre erg was a revelation, each second of lost pace a dismantling of my pride, and in its place a cold reality based in fact: physiology, endurance, pain, suffering, persistence. These were the things that would make or break me. Not hope, not good intention, not desire. Just work.

As we approached the final few hundred metres, rowers powered down one by one until the hum of spinning fans gave way to the singular whine of my ergometer. I rowed it out, embarrassed at finishing last. “Atta boy!” Mike Wilkinson said, encouraging me.

At the end of the day, I realized that the level of training required to become an Olympic-calibre rower was far beyond what I had been able to do while working full-time. On paper, my ergometer scores put me in close range, but *close* is sometimes the furthest away you can get. *Close* creeps in like an olive branch, beckoning to your psyche to make peace and be satisfied. It’s the story you’ve heard a hundred times: *He almost made it.*

When I got home I could see Ethan from the street, running and jumping in and out of the frame of our condo window in the heat of an imaginary action-figures battle. I couldn’t wait to go in and collapse on the couch. By the time I exited the elevator and reached our condo, my legs begged me to stop moving. I turned the handle and leaned my shoulder against the heavy door, letting my body weight overcome the resistance of the door closer. Ethan charged at me and jumped into my arms before the door had shut behind me. I braced myself, groaned as he whopped me with his fifty pounds, and collapsed to the floor, with my monkey enjoying the ride.

Day two in the bag. Another 573 days until the Olympic Games.

31

One evening in our second week of training, Peter Cookson called a meeting with all the athletes. We filled a lecture room and loaded up on pasta, salad, and bread that had been catered for the team. Only Donna Atkinson, the CEO of Rowing Canada, and Peter were in the room with us.

In 2010 the men's team had performed poorly at the World Championships in New Zealand. The men's eight came in seventh, and the men's four came in twelfth. After the poor performance, and amidst complaints from some athletes about coaching and the selection process, Rowing Canada had hired Canadian university basketball coach Ken Shields to conduct a review. Though Shields had the pedigree of being the winningest coach in Canadian university basketball history and was former head coach of Canada's national basketball team, Mike later described it as a witch hunt designed by Rowing Canada executives to oust him.

Peter stood at the front of the room, glancing between his watch and the door with the same evasive expression on his face as when I'd asked him about my development funding after Nationals. None of the coaches were present for reasons that became obvious as he began speaking.

"As you know, we conducted a review of our coaching staff that has now concluded. The reason I've asked you all to meet with me and Donna this evening is to get your input and discuss next steps.

"Specifically, numerous concerns about Mike Spracklen have emerged from the report that need to be addressed."

At this point, the room erupted into a heated discussion between athletes for and against Mike. It went back and forth.

Against: "He plays favourites, and the rest of us are fodder."

For: "He coaches to win!"

Against: "He plays mind games and verbally abuses athletes."

For: "Seriously, verbally *abused*? That's ridiculous."

Against: "His selection process is bullshit!"

For: "You're just trying to settle a personal score from Beijing."

On and on it went, much of it a grudge match between Dave Calder and Scott Frandsen, who had won the silver medal in the pair in Beijing, and Andrew Byrnes, Malcolm Howard, and Brian Price, who had won gold in the eight. History had certainly etched itself into these experienced rowers. If the degree of one's wounds correlates with how much one cares about something, it was clear that these guys — whatever their past — cared deeply about how things had gone and how they should be. Scott Frandsen spoke with a raspy shortness of breath in passionate anger. Dave was equally adamant. They wanted Mike fired.

It seemed stupid to hold a town hall meeting with the athletes. There were more of us than available seats in boats. Naturally, the majority of athletes would be gutted from not making the cut and would welcome a change that might offer them a second chance. Were we there to have our feelings coddled, or were we there to *win*?

In the end, Peter announced that the team would be divided into two groups: those who wanted to compete for a seat in the eight, and those who wanted to compete for a seat in the four, the pair, and the double (the pair is a two-person sweep boat, and the double is a two-person sculling boat). Collectively, this became known as the "small boat group," which would train under Terry Paul, the coxswain-turned-coach who had won gold under Mike in the 1992 Olympics.

I was faced with choosing between the two training groups, and it wasn't an easy decision. During the first two weeks in January, all the workouts were either in singles or in doubles and pairs. I had no sweeping experience, so I had teamed up with another sculler named Fraser Berkhout to form a training double.

Fraser was a strong-headed rower who had more confidence than any athlete I'd ever met. He was as tall as me, with a ropy, muscular build and a toss of dirty blond hair. On the water, he was shiftier than a small-town politician and he had more gears than an eighteen-wheel truck. He'd tilt his head from stroke seat mid-training run and utter things like "Just cruise" and "Okay, hit it" and "Crush it at the 750," which didn't meld with my desire to pin it all the time. It was everything I could do just to keep myself in sync with him, never mind executing his audibles on the fly. More concerning, though, was that we were committing an egregious faux pas in Mike's book. There was nothing Mike hated more than athletes who would pick and choose training runs, conserving energy near the back of the group on one run and then surging to the front on the next. Mike expected your best effort from the first stroke through until reaching failure.

Fraser once recounted a story of choosing to race the single internationally one season instead of accepting Mike's offer to join the eight. He told me he'd been blacklisted by Mike ever since. He worked hard to frame Mike as a crazy old buzzard, but I took it in stride. I would draw my own conclusions. In the meantime, we became friends by virtue of one sensing in the other an opportunity to realize his Olympic dream.

In the solitude of my drives to and from Elk Lake, and away from Fraser's strong opinions, I was able to weigh the factors in play. Canada hadn't won an Olympic medal in men's sculling since the 1984 quad won a bronze at the Los Angeles Olympics. Germany, Great Britain, New Zealand, and the United States were the dominant rowing countries, with medal contenders in most boat classes. But while many smaller countries (or countries where rowing is less popular) didn't have the depth to field a medal-contending men's eight crew, they could send their best athletes to compete in the smaller boat classes. Even if Fraser and I could qualify the double for the Olympics, it would be a stretch to make the A final. On the other hand, Mike's men's eight crews had a history of Olympic success … and failure. He'd coached Canada to gold in 1992 and 2008. In 1996, Mike coached the United States men's eight team to a fifth-place finish. In 2004, the Canadian men's eight entered the Olympics as reigning world champions, but collapsed in the final, finishing fifth. Rumours abounded that Mike had pushed the crew too hard in the lead-up to those Games. Mike presented a high-risk, high-reward proposition.

My goal was to get to the Olympics in whatever boat class possible. If there was more than one opportunity, then the goal escalated to getting into the boat with the best chance of winning a medal. If there was more than one medal contender, then the goal escalated to getting into the boat with the best shot at a gold medal. That boat was the eight. The other medal contender was the pair made up by Scott Frandsen and Dave Calder. At times, they were arguably our strongest medal contender. I never rowed with either Scott or Dave, and it would have taken some serious chemistry and obvious improvement from the start to challenge either of them (not to mention, I didn't know how to sweep row at the time). Additionally, the Kiwi Pair of Hamish Bond and Eric Murray was making that event a race for silver or bronze due to their extraordinary dominance over the rest of the field. Germany was dominating the men's eight event, but not by the same margin.

On the Monday following the announcement of the split into two training groups, Mike approached me in the PISE hallway before our 10-kilometre ergometer workout. He asked me to follow him down the hall a ways until we were out of earshot of the rest of the team.

"Jerry, you ought to know this report conducted by Ken Shields is a personal attack on me," he said, pausing with an affirmatory head nod. "I

Legendary rowing coach Mike Spracklen.

want to tell you that your best opportunity lies in training with the eight," he said, lowering his voice.

I looked down and tried to quickly come up with something diplomatic to say. I didn't want to get on Mike's bad side the way Fraser had, but I also didn't trust Mike. There was something Machiavellian about him. His words came out with the pacing of an ominous Shakespearean sonnet, and I couldn't tell — with the voices echoing in my head: *he treats athletes like fodder* — if he was being genuine or if he just wanted another mule to push his top guys.

"Mike, I think my best chance for success is with the small boat group because I don't know how to sweep," I said.

"Jerry, look," he responded, "the eight will need you in London. It is much easier to go from sculling to sweeping than from sweeping to sculling. You'll learn how to sweep, you'll see."

I believed him, but was my hubris deceiving me? I would be subjecting myself to great uncertainty under Mike, and I hated that, but he was my best chance at an Olympic medal, there was no denying it. I made my decision: I would learn how to sweep and try for a seat in the eight. I hoped Mike would be right about me.

32

I kissed Amy for the first time in over a year and a half. She was talking about maybe starting a relationship with a guy she'd met. We were standing in the condo, she by the door and me eight feet away, leaning against the kitchen island. It was evening. Ethan was asleep, and only the ambient lighting of the kitchen pot lights filled the room with a dim glow. I was still attracted to Amy despite eighteen months of avoiding all physical contact. I was familiar with her, I knew her body, and at times I had a tremendous urge to go to her. This was one of those times.

When she mentioned the new guy, Chris, a carnal twisting sensation wrapped my insides, like there was some sick appeal to the thought of her with someone else. Images played in my head against my will. I was forced to watch the worst my imagination could muster. Maybe, in the deep recesses of my mind, I'd thought we'd get back together eventually, once the anger and hurt had scabbed over.

I already knew about Chris. A flirty message had popped up on Amy's cellphone one day while she was in the bathroom getting ready for work. It had transported me back to the emotional nausea of our breakup like it was happening all over again. To end the tortuous thoughts, I walked over and kissed her.

We kept kissing for two weeks. Sneaking them in when Ethan wasn't looking because we weren't sure what we were doing. Probably we both knew it was a lapse and not reconciliation. I'd pull Amy into the tiny laundry room and slide the door shut. "Mommy and Daddy are just doing some laundry together," we'd yell to Ethan.

After a couple of weeks, we were filled up on whatever desire had been pent up over months of separation and the question of where it was leading finally hit me. Where had my untethered passion led me? I chastised myself for how weak I had been after all the careful work to make the difficult transition out of the relationship. How the hell would I become an Olympian if I didn't even have the self-discipline to keep my most basic urges in check?

When I broke it off, Amy was angry. I'm human, I said. I made a mistake, and it would never happen again. *Never.* My decisions needed to be chiselled out of stone, not written on some whiteboard ready to be rubbed out at every bout of second-guessing.

"I don't need to go over everything again," I told her. "Breaking up was the hardest decision of my life, but it was the right decision."

And then I said, "But, I still need your support."

33

January and February of 2011 were the darkest, gloomiest months of my life. Memory paints those early days with blurry strokes of grey. Minutes felt like hours. After our morning slugfest — every morning session was a slugfest — I'd lie down on the change room bench with my spandex rowing clothes for the next practice rolled up and propped under my head. Just as I fell asleep, some retired masters rowers would come in off the lake and fill the room with their endorphin-fuelled chatter, rousing me in a panic, thinking I had slept through our 11:00 a.m. row.

My hands continued to deteriorate. When I took Ethan to his hockey practices, I had to ask other parents to tie up his skate laces. Pink swaths of exposed flesh laced my palms and the insides of my fingers. The skin, supple and wrinkled from near constant rain, flaked away like pastry. I tried wrapping my fingers in electrical tape to reduce the friction against my oar, but the tape only made things worse. After doing some research, I learned that Krazy Glue was initially developed to seal battlefield wounds in the Vietnam War, so I started applying a thick layer of glue on the insides of my fingers and letting it dry before training. But this only delayed the same end result. There seemed to be no solution.

I didn't dare approach Mike. How would that sound? *Are you a pussy, Jerry?* he'd say. (He wouldn't have said that, but I imagined as much.)

At one point in early February, I stood in the boat bay looking out into sheets of rain drumming the dock before our second row of the day. I held my throbbing hands in front of me as if holding two invisible cups of coffee. Allison Dobb, Malcolm Howard's single sculls coach, walked by me and saw the despair etched into my face.

"Jerry, is everything all right?" she asked.

"I don't think I can take another stroke," I said. "My hands are fucked."

"Take the rest of the day off; don't worry about it," she said.

Take the rest of the day off? How could I? I needed every minute of every workout to put myself in contention. But the pain in my hands was psychologically draining. I felt like I was undergoing Pavlovian conditioning, as if someone had studded my oar handles with broken glass and then forced me to row until I associated the sport with pain and suffering. The fatigue, the muscle fever, the sore joints in my back — all that was manageable, but the hands drove me crazy. Until Allison suggested it — so casually, too — I hadn't considered time off as an option, but I listened to her. I went home and fumbled in the kitchen with my injured paws, trying to cook a stir-fry. After eating I flopped on the couch and dozed off with my arms bent up at the elbows, hands still gripping the invisible coffee cups like a corpse with rigor mortis.

Never in my life have I craved sleep more than during winter training under Mike Spracklen. Between our 11:00 a.m. and 3:00 p.m. training sessions, I started going to Fraser's house regularly to warm up, eat hot food, and sleep. Fraser and another national team rower, Will Dean, stayed with a sweet old lady named Elsie who lived in Cordova Bay, five minutes from the lake. Elsie had billeted rowers for years, and had recently begun suffering from Alzheimer's. In exchange for dirt-cheap rent (but mostly out of the goodness of their hearts), Fraser and Will made sure she took her meds on time and drove her to doctors' appointments. They played bridge with her, and hide and seek with her grandchildren when they visited. The first time I visited, Fraser had barely finished saying "She's very affectionate" before Elsie pulled me in tight and planted a red lipstick tattoo on my cheek. "Oh hello, dear," she said.

There was a spare bedroom upstairs with a bed covered in a heavy quilted blanket that I could have stayed wrapped in for days. Less than thirty seconds of staring out the floral-laced curtain of the bedroom window passed before I slipped into a deep sleep, with bacon, eggs, and toast warming my belly.

34

The team often trained at Shawnigan Lake, located a forty-five-minute drive northwest of Victoria. My first row at Shawnigan was a battle royale among sixteen rowers and two coxswains divided into two eights. I had no experience as a sweep rower, but Mike put me in three seat in one of the eights and I was given the warm-up to learn how to sweep, which is to say, I didn't learn.

When Mike gave the command to begin the first length of the lake, everything went to hell. Suddenly I became one eighth of a unit, a Viking warship surging violently toward its enemy. All the finesse and fluidity I had grown accustomed to in my single was replaced with a brute power that I hadn't experienced since being scooped up by my uncles as a kid. We rowed at a steady twenty-two strokes per minute, but even that was too high for me. There was something primitive about sweep rowing, with its long single oar and thick wooden handle. It was like trying to draw a picture with both fists around a giant pencil. One minute I'd been a proficient sculler, and the next it was as if I'd suffered a spinal cord injury and was learning how to walk again. Unlike the symmetrical position sculling requires, sweeping forces you to twist out toward the water to get a good, long stroke. Every time I rolled up and twisted at the catch, I couldn't shake the feeling that the same motion would dunk me if I was rowing my single. But with 2,000 pounds of flesh and carbon fibre and aluminum, it's not possible to flip the eight on your own. After two years of finding my balance alone in my single, I was being introduced to a new concept called *teamwork*. I hated it.

I was a pinball knocking back and forth between two seat and four seat, trying not to plunge my oar into the rower's back in front of me and

avoiding being impaled by the oar behind me. The eight
powerboat speed. For the first kilometre of hammering aw
feet of water at each catch, only sinking my oar by the tin
were halfway through the stroke. Some strokes went so d
have taken the oar out of the oarlock and used it like a ca
fifth stroke was an air stroke; I was so overloaded with
requirements that I'd forget to put my oar in the wate
backwards on my slide from the lack of resistance and
the lap of two seat behind me.

Halfway to the south end of the lake, my body was
to keep up. The rower in two seat saw my predicament an
back off the power by 10 percent and work on your form
thing in response and wondered how the hell he was able
Was he joyriding back there? The intensity of my effort w
had going for me. I'd pass out before becoming dead
With Mike's hawk eyes scanning the crews, I was determi
that, despite my awful technique, I could be counted on

There's something beyond commitment that is har
It's the reason you keep rowing when your sense of co
since died — masochism, perhaps. By the third 7-kil
of the workout, a now-familiar mixture of frustration a
spine. I was being bullied by this fucking miserable
respite, only ceaseless provocation, stroke after stroke

Suck it up, pussy.

Shawnigan rows continued every Tuesday and T
forming in my stomach before each row. *Would* this *rou*
me from the boat? The rowers around me were fluid in
spoke, in their rowing clothes accumulated over years
Harvard crimson, Oxford blue, Cambridge teal, Wash
Cal Bears yellow. They formed small cliques based on
whom in a given year, or who had represented Canada
international regattas. I brought no history or sentim
sport. Only a desire to excel.

In those first weeks I said little and rowed har
of Victoria rower with whom I'd been carpooling t

heaved along at
y, I missed three
e my teammates
ep I may as well
oe paddle. Every
new motor skill
r at all, shooting
nearly falling into

agged from trying
d said, "Dude, just
." I grunted some-
o speak intelligibly.
as the only thing I
weight in the boat.
ned to demonstrate
for my effort.
l to put into words.
mmitment has long
ometre training run
nd rage crept up my
sport. There was no
fter stroke.

hursday, with a knot
see a massive crab eject
rowing, in how they
of college rowing —
ington Husky purple,
who had rowed against
at under-23, or senior
ntality with me to the

d. A strong University
Shawnigan Lake quit

ier than the eight, but also
sation of flying over water.
ur wobbled and listed down
n mark. Anything closer to
n improvement, as far as I

y on. By the end of the day,
Olympic gold and silver
in Light, Scott Frandsen,
y last, desperate to come
these *Olympians.*
ting orders and I found
sima behind me. Now
ile to break the silence
my ear: "Let's go big
outside of a pair, and
own his competitors,
l winning pieces, and
to toe.

35

With my introduction to sweeping complete, Mike decided it was time I switched out of the double and into the last sweeping boat I had yet to row: the pair. Fraser had started training in the small boat group with Mike Wilkinson, so our partnership was over. Mike paired me with Kevin Kowalyk — the guy I'd battled at Nationals a few months before.

Kowalyk was a grinning sarcastic fellow off the water and relentless on it. He described himself as a fat kid from Winnipeg who'd got fed up with being tormented by his peers in high school. He decided to take up kick-boxing to lose weight and defend himself against bullies, and eventually switched to rowing after suffering one too many concussions.

One day we were tossing around a hypothetical question about who would win in a fight. I gave him a playful punch in the shoulder. His expression darkened suddenly, and then his left foot whipped past my nose with a roundhouse kick so close I could feel the breeze. The high school torment had left him with permanently primed defensive mechanisms. I recognized the same aggression that I, too, had pulled along from my youth. He was unpredictable, and I had no interest in being on the receiving end of that vicious kick.

Kowalyk saw in me a strong guy lacking finesse but possessing a desperation to succeed. We formed an unlikely team of two guys late to the sport (Kowalyk, thirty at the time, hadn't started rowing until he was twenty-five). Somehow, we needed to become world-class sweep rowers in a matter of months.

Each of us thought the other could do more to improve the quality of the rowing (which is the default outlook of new sweep rowers). But we knew what we were after: that stretch of the skeleton connecting oar handles to our leg drive, that feeling of oar and shell slicing through air and water for a perfect set, and dropping in with no missed water at the catch. There were issues at first — balance was a big one — but we knew that once sorted, the rest would follow quickly. Until then, the main challenge was keeping up our spirits. If my default reaction was to continue despite feeling defeated, Kowalyk's was to continue despite feeling nihilistic. He was the first rower I paired with who could be more morbid than me. I didn't mind that so much.

I don't recall any specific breakthrough moments, only that after three weeks we had figured out the basics enough to trail within a stone's throw of the pack, and after a couple more weeks we were at the back of the pack. Now that we were generally able to row up and down the lake without our technical shortcomings masking our fitness, Mike decided to switch pair combinations. He put me in bow seat with 2008 gold medallist Kevin Light, a stroke of good fortune for which I'll be forever grateful.

A new partner, a new opportunity. When pair combinations were changed up, it was a chance to demonstrate one's versatility in rowing well with a number of partners. If you had been in the top pair for the previous few weeks, the *coup d'état* would be dominating the group again and, specifically, your previous pair partner's new boat (to show that you were the horse and your former pair partner was the cart).

Kevin seemed so ordinary. He wasn't particularly big or powerful, and he didn't seem to have an outwardly ferocious competitive spirit. He later told me that he'd found it difficult to train with the same fire after winning the gold in 2008. He'd taken most of 2009 off after the Olympics and struggled to regain his drive in 2010, coming twelfth in the coxless four at the World Championships in New Zealand. Just like it had with Kowalyk, a partnership made sense. Kevin could benefit from my raw power and intensity, and I could benefit from Kevin's excellent technique and experience.

During our first row I apologized nearly every stroke for my clumsiness in bow seat: "Sorry, sorry, ah shit, sorry, sorry, fuck, sorry." Lucky for me, Kevin was fast to forgive mistakes. He had patience, and he was relentless.

We started moving our pair faster and faster until we started winning the odd training run and generally holding second position in the group behind Will Crothers and Gabe Bergen.

On May 15, the entire team did a time trial in pairs or singles. By then my cumbersome sweep technique had smoothed out. We'd practised racing starts lurching off the line at thirty-eight strokes per minute. I'd grown familiar with the sensations indicating a fast-moving pair: the instant connection at the catch, the continuity of the stroke, the boat skimming across the water instead of plowing through it. Some countries train their rowers to take time at the finish and then accelerate into the catch. Mike trained us to push our hands away from our ribs and swing over quickly after the finish, then take time decelerating into the next catch to prevent checking the run of the boat. My instinct was to row more like the Germans, feeling the pause at the finish instead of at the catch, but who was I to challenge Mike Spracklen?

Dave Calder and Scott Frandsen started the time trial first. It was clear why they were Olympic silver medallists; they moved together like one fluid body, the smoothest pair rowing I'd ever seen. Their connection at the catch was instant, as if they had locked on even before submerging their blades.

Gabe and Will took off the line, chasing after them. We were next. *Don't blow a tire on the start*, I thought. We tapped our boat up to the invisible start line as directed by Paul, one of the assistant coaches.

"Attention," he said.

My oar suddenly felt foreign in my hands. *Did I remember to square my blade properly, or is it slightly angled?* If it was, I would pull us down hard onto starboard on the first stroke. Why couldn't every start be a running start, so that there wasn't so much pressure to get the first five strokes right?

"Go!" yelled Paul.

The start was smooth and snappy. We propelled the boat up above race pace. "In two, that's one … two … here," I said, signalling the change down into race pace, seeking that perfect rhythm.

It was my job to execute the race calls, and I missed our first two calls.

"Legs down!" Kevin shouted back to me, frustrated.

"Here!" I responded. *Fuck.*

At 750 metres into the race, I couldn't believe we weren't yet halfway. I looked through Kevin's back to some imagined point 2 metres in front of him. We rowed best when I blurred my vision from the granular to the peripheral.

"Swing togethhh . . ." I was panting hard around 1,200 metres. *It shouldn't hurt this much so soon,* I thought. *We went out too hard, we went out too hard, we went out too hard!* My body slipped out of form. I was lunging now.

Kevin took over the race calls: "Sit up! Sit tall!"

Every time I drew the back of my blade across the water on the recovery — leaning so hard to starboard I may as well have been water-skiing on it — Kevin kept on rowing as if an imaginary keel ran right up his ass and fixed him square on his seat. Only with the worst of my gyrations behind him did his shoulders shift to regain balance.

In the last 400 metres, my vision narrowed and little bits of black interrupted my field of view. They swirled before me like little galaxies.

"Yeah?" Kevin said.

"Yeah!" I said.

"Here!"

The language of rowing into a final sprint is composed of single words — sometimes single syllables of words. "Yeah?" from Kevin meant, *Should we take it up two strokes per minute to start our final sprint?* My response, "Yeah!" meant, *Yes, we should do that.* And "Here!" meant, *We're increasing our stroke rate for the next three strokes, then settling for four, and we will repeat this cycle until we cross the finish line or fall unconscious.*

Passing the red buoy indicating 250 metres to go, we managed one last resurrection. Our sprint didn't yield more speed; it only kept us from slowing. The familiar cluster of Douglas firs flowing by us on starboard, the passing of a public dock far off on port, the narrowing of the lake — these all meant we were less than twenty strokes from the finish. We crossed the line, and I collapsed forward over my rigger. I wheezed, "That was the hardest thing I've ever done in my life."

Scott and Dave won the time trial. Will and Gabe were several seconds back in second place, but Kevin and I had come third by only half a second behind them. No one had expected us to do quite that well.

The next morning, I crossed paths with Peter Cookson, who was riding along in Mike's launch that day. "Jerry, well done," he said. "Keep working hard; you're on the right track."

36

During one of our Shawnigan training sessions in March 2011, we boated two supposedly evenly matched coxless fours, but one boat kept beating the other by a huge margin. I was in the boat getting trounced and feared that it was me holding us back. Mike decided to do an experiment, swapping the positions of two athletes into the opposite boats. He manoeuvred his boat in between our oars, and then Will Dean climbed onto the pontoon of the boat and was taxied to the other four, where he traded places with Gabe Bergen. We reset, Mike said "Ready, go!" and immediately our boat pulled ahead of the other four by a huge margin. The difference was exactly the opposite. It looked awful for Will, like losing a seat race by ten seconds. Odd, because Will was generally accepted as one of the strongest athletes competing for a seat in the eight. We all cringed, imagining ourselves in his shoes. It's a rower's worst nightmare to be singled out like that. Maybe he was hiding an injury, or maybe it just wasn't his day, but the damage had been done.

Before that training session it was Will Dean's seat in the eight to lose, and I had been on the outside looking in. By the end of the session, it was mine to lose. A seat race between two rowers is not only a direct comparison — it can also reveal much about the rowers who kept their spots in each boat. Taken in context with the various combinations Mike had created over previous weeks, this particular seat race also demonstrated my ability to go fast in any combination of the team's top rowers.

Mike made no statement to the effect that Will Dean would be replaced by me in the eight. That's not how Mike operated. Instead, it came up unexpectedly. After our morning row at Shawnigan, we steamed up the change room with hot showers, stuffed ourselves with breakfast, and then returned to the boathouse, where we napped on black gym mats. After half an hour of sleep, Mike roused us with a gentle "Okay, it's best we get on with it now." As on every Tuesday, we held a team meeting before going on the water for our second session.

"We need to discuss selection for Lucerne," he said. Everyone sat up an inch taller. The first major competition of the year was a World Cup event in Lucerne, Switzerland. "I know I've said it before, but it bears repeating: the cream rises to the top over the months of winter training, and because we have a small group going for the eight, we cannot afford to interrupt training in order to seat race every seat. We want to avoid that, and I think you know as well as I do that it's not necessary."

He turned his attention to Rob Gibson, confusing him with Doug Csima. At some point in the years after Rob and Doug had joined the national team, he'd mixed up who was who and seemed to have given up trying to sort them out. I suppose they had some similarities. They were both known as power athletes, were within an inch in height, rowed the pair together often, and had dark complexions (Doug from his Hungarian background, and Rob from tanning booths, it was suspected). Mike mixed up their names half the time, and this time he was talking about Rob: "Doug is critical to the eight. He is a power athlete, and the eight, as you know, is a power event. Rob — I'm sorry, I've done it again — *Doug* is indispensable for the same reason. We know he pulls over 1,200 watts in a three-stroke max test. We need that kind of power off the line. The first five hundred metres is critical, and the statistics tell the story; the crew who leads at the five hundred most often goes on to win the race."

Mike looked past Rob to the athlete sitting behind him on an erg seat with his back to the handle, Gabe. He took a moment to recollect Gabe's vital information, then continued: "Gabe was out of the boat in 2010, but has returned stronger than ever and deserves to be in the boat. He is a skillful oarsman, as he's demonstrated in singles, pairs, and fours. We need Gabe's skill in bow seat."

To his left, on one of the couches, Mike acknowledged Andrew with a cursory glance. "Andrew is a leader, a strong oar with excellent technique. The eight needs him."

Will Crothers sat stone-faced in front of Mike, with his arms wrapped around one knee. "Will has shown a hunger to win stronger than anyone with his daily performance in the single and pair this year. He is an example for us all. We need that hunger in the boat, and especially in stroke seat."

As Mike spoke, I prepared myself for the disappointment of being left out of this string of accolades and what it would mean for my chances in the eight. Then this: "Jerry, of course, is new to us this year and has come on very strongly in a short time — a testament to his athleticism. We need Jerry in the boat. We would be lost without him." At this, a surge of dopamine crawled up my spine and into the back of my skull. I didn't move, didn't blink, but inside me embers glowed so bright I wondered if others could see beams of light shooting out my pores.

Mike continued, "Kevin is a leader; the team benefits from his experience. Derek is a talented strokeman, able to get the most of the rowers behind him, as demonstrated in the four and in the eight."

At this point, he paused again before addressing the difficult matter: "We know Conlin McCabe and Anthony Jacob will join the team after finishing their studies at the University of Washington. Conlin's 2k time of 5:44 is remarkable for a college athlete. We know the eight is a power event. We will need his power in the boat, no question about it. That leaves the matter of discussing selection for the final seat on port between Kevin and Derek."

Mike was a breeder of insecurity. One of his sayings was "If you can race 2 kilometres in 5:50, then what's to stop you from doing it in 5:49.9? And if you can do it in 5:49.9, then what's to stop you from doing it in 5:49.8?" Ad infinitum. Marginal gains could be had only by desperate, consistent effort, and there was nothing quite like a dose of uncertainty to keep the fires under our asses burning. Despite having a small group, all Mike needed was one solid threat on both port and starboard to keep the pressure on.

And just like that, Mike had finally revealed who he saw in the eight going into racing season: Will Crothers, Rob Gibson, Doug Csima, me, Conlin McCabe, Andrew Byrnes, Derek O'Farrell *or* Kevin Light, and Gabe Bergen. It was the kind of unofficial crew announcement made purposefully ambiguous to allow for future changes if necessary.

After the meeting, Rob slapped me on the shoulder. “Congrats, man! ‘We’d be lost without Jerry’? Pretty strong vote of confidence, if you ask me.”

I grinned. “Thanks, Rob.”

37

Although things were going to plan, a bog-like stolidity was taking over my mindset the same way the West Coast dampness seeped into our bones. I was losing all motivation and had begun hating Mike. His coaching methods injected doubt deep, deep down in a rower's psyche. He offered very little in the way of direct praise. His use of logic and reason was spotty. Everything that came out of his mouth had the tone of a foregone conclusion, and there was no changing his mind through conversation. Only one's performance in training and competition could influence him. And any performance that might influence his perspective netted less influence as time wore on. One season was a drop in his bucket of experience that went back four decades. When it came to rowing, Mike had made up his mind.

I could have quit at any time, but Mike somehow knew my nature. He recognized, perhaps better than I did, my willingness to endure the suffering. It was my choice to do every workout at maximum intensity, but he knew that some athletes don't frame it as a choice. Some athletes are slaves to their commitment. Mike was a master at creating an environment where each rower doubted themselves, where each of us routinely fell short, running as the ground fell away beneath us. It was just a matter of time, I was sure, before we all went down with major injuries.

I started criticizing Mike in the change room after training, saying it was ridiculous how hard he pushed us. We should be training smarter, I said. More technical rows, more recovery. The guys looked at me wearily. Mike was the path to the podium, and I was the uninitiated, learning lessons they'd already learned in past years.

For the first time in my life, I started keeping a journal:

> April 16, 2011 — Spracklen's Program:
>
> I have concerns about this man's logic, or lack thereof. He says we don't have the best athletes, so our training program has to make up for it. That follows if we have a better program, but Mike thinks very narrowly that more is always better. Guys are getting injured every week. Everyone is operating constantly at 75–80 percent. We are doing more than the Beijing guys did in the year leading up to the Olympics.
>
> The environment is poison; it's created by Mike to make athletes push through injury and common sense. There are times to train hard, but Mike seems to be the only coach in the world who thinks we should be at max output during every workout. He says we train at low rates during the winter to emphasize quality. The reality is we're just trying to beat each other out there by putting our blades deep and hauling as hard as possible — not necessarily that effective at race rates. Mike says we reduce the volume near the end of the week because our bodies are fatigued (even though I'm totally fucked by Tuesday most weeks), but the rates go up and just because I'm doing well among guys who are similarly exhausted doesn't give me confidence in my speed against international competition.
>
> I don't mind hard work. I've done everything asked of me so far, but I still have serious doubts about Mike's coaching and about the overall program. The only way morale is kept up in the locker room is by making jokes about Mike's sanity. I recognize I am still only 3.5 months into the program, so I am ranting here rather than confronting Mike at this point. I don't think I can continue for a second season if our results don't improve at Worlds this year. I do recognize the need to stick with things for a

> time and so I remain committed despite all these doubts and reservations. It's better to do one thing, to make a clear decision, than to flop around and constantly try new approaches. I made the decision to join Mike's group, so I am going to stick with it and follow Mike's coaching and go as hard as I can every day. I hope I will be rewarded for my faith (and for ignoring my intuition).

Conlin and Anthony joined the team in the second week of June. I shook hands with Conlin for the first time on the dock before a Monday morning row. He was only twenty years old, the youngest in our group, but also the biggest at 6'8" and 245 pounds. Anthony was 6'5" like me, but considerably lighter at 200 pounds. I was cautious meeting him, trying to get a measure of the risk. Immediately, I noticed his hips were so narrow I could almost clasp my hands around his waist and touch fingers to thumbs. I saw this as his advantage. I have child-bearing hips — big, heavy bones creeping over the gunwales, needlessly large and slowing me down on the water.

Conlin and Anthony's return brought tension to the locker room. No one was above thinking their seat in the boat was in jeopardy.

After they had been with us for a week, Mike called a meeting to discuss the implications once more. We sat in front of him on ergs and stretch mats in silence. He pulled out a piece of paper with his proposal on it. "We need to decide on the format for seat racing Derek and Kevin."

Originally, Mike had intended to seat race Conlin alongside Kevin and Derek to determine who would be in the eight, but Kevin and Derek both conceded that Conlin was essential to the eight's success. It didn't make sense to interrupt training more than was necessary. It was a sportsmanlike move to forego their right to a seat race for the betterment of the crew, but it wasn't all about magnanimity. Derek and Kevin knew Mike wanted Conlin in the boat. Like the justice system, seat racing is an imperfect process. Mike could have repeated the races, disqualified certain results due to conditions, or simply continued seat racing until the desired result was achieved. The rest of us in the boat wanted Conlin in it, too. Despite doubting ourselves and each other all the time, there was a consensus that

Conlin was a critical piece of the combination that would get us on the podium in London. This simplified the matter. Instead of a three-way race for two seats, it would be a contest between Derek and Kevin.

"Each athlete will be timed over two pieces: a 1,250-metre piece in one direction, and a 750-metre piece in the opposite direction," Mike said.

As an athlete, you want to be able to train in the fairest environment, with transparency in the selection process and unbiased coaching decisions. But that never happens in real life. Mike had been criticized for lacking transparency in his selection process. The hiring of Ken Shields to investigate his coaching had rattled his confidence. Mike was a visionary. He didn't know how to incorporate democratic process into his coaching. As soon as he was told "You must win *and* be fair with all the athletes," he was lost. As much as Mike's gruelling program was stretching my capacity to endure, I empathized with him. We could spend a month seat racing every possible combination only to go on and get crushed internationally, or we could trust Mike as our leader — warts and all — and focus on getting the best out of the crew Mike had decided on.

We were all putting our lives on hold for a shot at Olympic glory; of course athletes on the outside looking in would have demanded a seat race if it meant a second chance at a seat in the boat. But for those of us already selected, damn the bastards who tried to get in on appeal. We valued Mike's experience and ability to select crews. We didn't want a decision by committee. We wanted Mike to lead.

Conlin was roommates with Derek in a house just over the Cordova escarpment, five minutes from the lake. They were friends, and Conlin's big heart and sense of honour had him torn over the situation. He knew The Score (as Mike was apt to say), but he wanted to earn his seat in the boat just as Kevin and Derek were going to have to. Even an athlete of Conlin's calibre — with his superior physiology and strength — was not immune to the self-doubt imbued by Mike's training environment. A seat race may have been redundant, but it would have been an opportunity to affirm to himself as much as to the rest of us that he belonged in the eight.

It was the same for me with Anthony's presence. I felt stuck in fight preparation mode for a fight that kept getting delayed. I wanted to seat race him to prove my worth to myself and the others. Things could fall apart at any moment in my journey, and the only way forward was to attack, attack, attack. Mike wouldn't let on to the fact that he'd already decided Anthony wouldn't factor into his Olympic men's eight lineup.

Derek and Kevin stretched in the boat bay as the rest of us milled about, waiting for Brian's command to take the eight down to the water. Kevin looked focused; Derek looked worried. Both made eye contact with each of us, looks that said, *Give me all you've got.* I felt loyal to Kevin from our time together in the pair. I liked Derek, too. He was the first veteran rower on the national team to introduce himself and shake hands with me. The resident Mike Spracklen impersonator, he'd perfected a satirical British drawl and got us all laughing with lines like "I am not a serpent; I do not have eyes in the side of my head," and other odd Spracklen quotes collected over the years and passed on from previous generations of rowers. The laughter was necessary for our collective mental health, but none of those qualities mattered now. Friendship had to be put aside in pursuit of the fastest boat for the upcoming World Cup.

The water was dead calm, and the morning sun in the east warmed half our bodies. Kevin got into two seat in front of Gabe, and we shoved off. The usual banter on the way to Point One — busting Brian's balls and hurling affectionate insults at each other — was replaced with quiet focus. It was easy to put ourselves in Kevin's and Derek's shoes; this day would not only determine who competed in the eight at the World Cup, but also make it very difficult for the loser to work his way back into the eight in time for the Olympics.

We coasted by the red buoy at Point One and turned our 18-metre-long boat, ports holding water and starboards taking circular strokes, with arms only until we pointed at Point Two.

"Let's fucking go, boys!" Will shouted from stroke seat.

"Attention … row!" Brian set us off, and we wrenched our oars against oarlocks.

Our boat rose in the water as we accelerated. The sensation was like when my grandpa had hit the throttle in his Sea Ray, pulling us out of the water on water skis.

Two hundred metres in, we strode into rhythm, using the fraction of extra time between strokes to press harder off our footboards and put more power into our oars. I began the sequence of death and rebirth. Every stroke underwent a critical assessment in a tenth of a second: Had I backed off? Was my effort slipping? *Pull harder!*

It was 8:00 a.m., and the sun was now perched above the treeline and shining down on an angle that caused the light to reflect off the water and into my sunglasses, distorting my view with bouncing shadows. I wanted to shake my head until they flew off, but I couldn't risk catching a crab. The eight travels so fast that there's no time to wipe sweat from your eyes, adjust a loose shoe strap, or remove foggy sunglasses. Taking a hand off your oar at forty strokes per minute would be grounds for a violent ejection.

"Two hundred and fifty to go. Keep powering it!" Brian's voice buzzed over the four speakers placed throughout the boat. I let my eyes relax, straining my peripheral vision to look for Paul Hawksworth, our assistant coach, tethered to the 1,250-metre buoy. The final stages of any race pace effort can be expressed as a mathematical proof: one's perceived duration of time slows at an inverse relation to the remaining distance.

"Yeah!" Kevin's familiar call reached me in five seat. One word that meant, *Come on, boys! Give me everything you've got.*

"Down!" Finally, Paul called the finish and we slumped forward. A few screams of exasperation echoed across the water as the lactic acid reabsorbed into our bloodstreams. I writhed like a freshly hooked worm for several seconds longer than my teammates. My physiology was still morphing into what was needed to endure that level of exertion.

Mike didn't like how I expressed pain. One time after a gruelling workout, I stood inside the boat bay with him and tried to explain why my face became so contorted when I approached my physical limits. I said I was pushing myself hard for the sake of boat speed, and that my dramatic facial convulsions at the end of a hard piece were an unavoidable by-product of constantly stretching my pain tolerance. He responded with this gem: "Jerry, if someone were to take a knife and stab me in the heart, I would simply close my eyes, fall backwards, and die." Apparently, even death-inducing pain was no reason to show discomfort. I laughed. Mike didn't.

We spun at Point Two and paddled into the channel that attached Elk Lake to Beaver Lake to the south. As we caught our breath before the 750-metre piece began in the opposite direction, I flipped my sunglasses up into my hair and used the long-sleeved shirt I'd removed after the warm-up to wipe the sweat off my wooden oar handle.

The 750-metre piece should have felt shorter than it did, but the mathematical proof never fails, and the last 250 felt like 500 metres.

The crew felt punchy with Kevin in the boat. He'd emptied himself into the two pieces, and now it was Derek's turn. Mike nestled his pontoon in between our oars, Kevin climbed out of the boat, and Derek climbed in. We didn't row back to the dock because it would have taken too long and required another race warm-up, and by then the mid-morning wind might pick up, ruining the time comparison.

As Brian called attention, it occurred to me that I never felt quite ready for the work ahead. It was always a plunge into the abyss. No matter how many times we trained at race pace, I wasn't quite sure how I'd get through it.

"Ready … row!"

Derek was a finesse rower and an excellent strokeman. When stroking a four, he created a smooth rhythm that made it easy to apply power, with a feeling of extra time between strokes. Neither Kevin nor Derek were power athletes, but they were excellent oarsmen and part of their value was their ability to bring out the best in the other men in the boat. But Derek was seat racing for two seat in the back of the boat — Mike had decided that Will was the right guy to stroke us to London — so with six of us in front of him and only Gabe behind in bow, Derek had much less influence on the rhythm. Instead, he'd have to work with the rhythm Will and Rob established in stroke and seven seat.

As the boat heaved along, my only thought was to make sure my effort was consistent for both rowers. My mouth was full of sticky saliva. I sucked air hard into my lungs and spat onto myself to clear my airway of morning gunk. We charged toward the 1,250-metre buoy. At the 750-metre mark, a sudden gusting headwind slammed into our backs and slowed us momentarily. Brian told us to bump up the rate one beat and push through. As quickly as the wind hit us it was gone, and we lurched forward like my grandpa's Sea Ray after a water skier had let go of the rope.

Paul called us down. Rob dry-heaved in seven seat, I dropped my head in five, and Gabe let out a "Fuck me!" from bow. When Gabe started cursing,

I felt some consolation knowing we were all burning up the same, though we all had our suspicions about how Conlin experienced pain. When we measured our lactic acid after high-intensity pieces, Conlin would show a reading one-quarter the average of the rest of us, earning him the nickname

Conlin McCabe doing a three-stroke max watt test on the ergometer with Mike and Brian looking on.

Two-Point-O. (For Conlin, a typical reading was 2.0 millimoles per litre, an uncommonly low measurement of lactate in the blood after such intense exertion. For the same effort, Gabe tested as high as 16.0 millimoles per litre.)

I worried about the headwind that had hit us. If Derek lost, he'd have a case to demand a redo. Brian had boosted the rate to compensate, but did it? Deep down, I selfishly wanted to avoid another trial. The eight raced only a few times per year at race pace for distances greater than 1,000 metres, and I was happy to punish myself as little as possible. It was incredibly hard to commit to race pace in a non-race scenario like a seat race. Mike once said in a meeting that a crew is capable of a true all-out 2,000-metre race in the eight only two or three times per year. He said the psychological and physical toll of racing was too intense; if we attempted more, we would risk dulling the sword and backing off subconsciously.

I thought about this as we prepared for the final 750-metre piece. As much as I was coming to despise Mike, I knew he was right. Every day we ruined ourselves in training, but a 2,000-metre race effort was another level yet.

Rob and Andrew fired us up as we rolled to the catch.

"Let's go! It's the fucking Germans beside us."

They visualized lining up against the Germans at the World Championships, like they had in 2009. I visualized surviving the first ten strokes of the piece.

"Attention … row!" That pause between when Brian said "attention" and "row" became increasingly familiar — two seconds sliced into a trillion increments of time, all counted in a flash of panic.

We charged off the line, a locomotive compressing and chugging up to pace. It was the fourth piece. There was no sag. My body always gave me full power for the first ten strokes, no matter how late in the workout. It was strokes twenty to thirty that foretold how the piece would go, and this time my body co-operated.

We hammered it, we finished, sucked air and exhaled fumes of carbon dioxide. It was by all accounts as fair a seat race as you could get on Elk Lake.

Afterwards, Derek was standing by his car in the lower lot where we usually milled about at the end of the day. He was getting the guys' impressions about how it went. Brian, Mike, and Paul were in the upstairs office calculating the times. "I dunno, man, hard to say," I said. I wanted to give him something: "You're the best stroke I've rowed with, but Will's in the boat either way and Mike wants him at stroke, so that leaves it to two seat."

"Yeah, well, I feel pretty positive about how it went. I left it all on the water," he said. I thought about the surge of headwind, I thought about how punchy the boat had felt with Kevin.

Late that Tuesday afternoon, we got the email from Mike. Less than four tenths of a second gave Derek the win. We knew it would be close — one rower out of eight will have a narrower margin of difference in seat racing than in a four or pair matrix — but this was virtually a tie. Now the gust of headwind that I'd thought would give Derek recourse in a narrow loss acted as a tiebreaker in his favour; he had won despite less favourable conditions.

Athletes are attuned to The Score. You know when momentum has shifted away from you, when the belief in your goal becomes a private necessity. Some years you soldier on with only personal belief and conviction to keep your resolve strong. With the right combination of work, perseverance, focus, and timing, the season may again change so that others around you recognize what you've known all along: you are an athlete on the right side of The Score, an athlete whose merit lodges in the minds of his coaches and teammates without your having to say a single word.

With the loss, Kevin was on the wrong side of The Score. He took it well enough. He was so loyal to Mike that he decided to continue training with our group despite being out of the boat. He'd been training under Mike for over ten years and looked up to him like a second father. Where I saw a deeply flawed man, Kevin saw an oracle of wisdom and a rowing genius. Kevin's loyalty is perhaps best epitomized by something he said after a Monday afternoon 10-kilometre row on the erg: "The hardest person to beat is yourself, because whatever you do — you also just did."

… And if you can do it in 5:49.8, then what's to stop you from doing it in 5:49.7? And if you …

38

It was June 2011. I had been sweep rowing for only a few months and sculling for a little over two years, and now I was about to board a plane heading to World Cup III in Lucerne to compete against the best in the world. It was going to be my first competition in the eight.

I'd thought I'd be able to get some experience racing in the eight at the Elk Lake Spring Regatta back in March. Will Dean had been sick the night before and notified Mike that he might not be able to race. Mike had emailed me and told me I was in for Will. The next day, I'd shown up to the boathouse nervous and excited only to find that Will had recovered and I was back on the outside looking in. Will Crothers told me the news that morning in the boat bay, but Mike hadn't bothered saying two words to me. *He'll fucking see*, I'd told myself. Now, three months later, I was on my way to Italy because I had earned it, but certainly not in spite of Mike. He'd seen a place for me in the boat all along, even as I'd imagined myself the underdog.

Amy had been content to sleep on the couch in the months since I'd ended our final lapse. I'd snuffed out any notions of reconciliation and transformed myself into a deductive reasoning machine. Life was a series of if/then statements, and my primary goal was to survive Mike's training program long enough to have a shot at the Olympics. I just wanted to give myself a chance. I was afraid if I softened with Amy it would also cripple my resolve to continue rowing. I'd found my way into the eight because of my edge — every workout was a dogfight — and I was terrified of losing that edge.

For her part, Amy was ready to move on with big plans of her own. She planned to fly back to Ontario a few weeks before the team left for Italy to help take over a trailer park resort that her mom had agreed to invest in up near

Bancroft. It was a dream opportunity for her to do what she'd always wanted. I'd need help while she was getting the business ready and Ethan was still in school, so I asked my younger sister, Julia, to move in with me fresh off finishing her linguistics degree at Brock University. She skipped her graduation and flew out so that I wouldn't miss a beat in training. Amy stayed for a few days after Julia's arrival to be there for Ethan's birthday. The four of us crammed into 575 square feet, with Amy sleeping on the couch and Julia on a mattress I'd flopped down in one corner of the condo. When Amy left, she loaned Julia her car to transport Ethan to and from school across town. I offered Julia free food and my sincere gratitude for becoming part of my immediate support team. She took over from Amy, making our lunches every day — one sandwich for Ethan, three for me — and I cooked us all a hearty dinner at night.

My sister and Ethan dropped me off at the airport in 5:00 a.m. darkness on the morning of the team's departure to Italy. I hugged Julia, lifted Ethan off his feet, and pushed my lips against his cheek until my nose flattened. I wanted to bring him with me. The longer you hug your kid, the more you miss the feeling of their little limbs wrapped around you when they let go. One last wave, and they sputtered off in the ol' Corolla.

I stood in line to check in with my teammates. We were decked out in the new swag Rowing Canada had given us — sweatsuits, duffel bags, matching Team Canada shirts, and bright red jackets. We all stood a head taller than everyone else, and I pretended not to notice the many gazes cast our way.

"Basketball?" a man asked.

A blast of hot, humid air hit us as we walked off the plane and across the tarmac to the terminal in Milan. We passed through customs, all of us with the same reason for visiting, all of us scrutinized as though it was an elaborate scheme — what was this rowing World Cup?

We piled into a van for the drive north to Erba. Our arms and legs fused together with sweat in the humidity. Andrew drove, and we told him how he could do it better. Eventually we all passed out, our biological clocks still on Victoria time. When I woke up, I peeled my calf off Rob's. He smiled. "You were out for two hours, buddy."

The team had been going to the same hotel for years — the Hotel Leonardo da Vinci — owned and operated by a master chef named Maurizio alongside his fading trophy wife and their two daughters, Erika and Sylvia, both in their twenties.

At dinner, Maurizio, Erika, Sylvia, and two additional staff manned a buffet of the finest spread of food I'd ever seen catered for a bunch of athletes — athletes who would have been happy to eat any slop you put in front of them. There were trays of veal parmigiana, authentic Italian cavatelli pasta, an array of fine olive oils and balsamic vinegars in which to dip fresh bread, and great wheels of cheese stacked up high: Pecorino Romano, Gorgonzola, caprino stagionato.

I sat down at a big round table with athletes from both the small boat group and the eight. It was easy to put our differences aside off the water as we ate and joked and laughed. Maurizio walked from table to table inspecting our reactions to the food, drawing out emphatic nods of approval. He either didn't speak a lick of English or refused to speak it. He smiled mostly with his tired racoon eyes and employed a sign language of his own invention to communicate with us. When we didn't understand, he looked at us like we were idiots. When we did understand, he reared his head back with mouth agape in silent laughter.

That evening we had a meeting to go over the program for the next two weeks leading up to our first race in Lucerne. Mike said it was important to allow the body recovery time — roughly one day for each hour of time difference — while we adapted to the new time zone. I looked at the printout in my hands. The first six days in Erba were a gift. Mike had us doing only a short technical paddle in the morning and one moderately hard session in the afternoon. A windfall! I felt light, like the day I'd walked out of the courthouse with my dad, in purple prison garb and too-big Velcro clown shoes: free after preparing for the worst.

I whispered to Andrew, "Is this for real?"

"Yeah, just wait. This week you're going to see why Mike is the best rowing coach in the world," he said.

The next morning, Doug Csima said the same thing while we got ready for our morning paddle: "Mike is at his best in Erba. He takes his crews and fine-tunes them, you'll see."

I started wondering whether I hadn't given Mike the respect he deserved. So far, I had taken him for a megalomaniac with old-world tactics who could lead you to an Olympic medal if you survived his training long enough. All this talk of Mike working his magic in Erba led me to reconsider. I tended to size up people quickly and thought it was a good quality — my ability to get a read on someone in a short time — but I'd been wrong before, so maybe I'd missed something. Heck, I got a little excited on the van ride to the lake, like I was about to get access to some fraternity of secret rowing wisdom.

"Time for a Spracklen fine-tuning session," I said with a smile, wedged between Rob and Conlin in the middle row.

"Oh yes; yes, indeed," Derek sang out from the back of the van in his hilarious Spracklen impersonation: a perfectly executed combination of British colloquialisms and that British tendency to imbue each word with a dripping passivity, like its very utterance borders on grievance.

"You seeee, Jarry," he continued, "tension is the real killa. You carry tension in your shouldas. Loosen your shouldas. Do it now. Be relaxed. Wiggle your fingas. Yes, when you grip the oar you want loose fingas. Use your Saturday Night Finga." Derek wiggled his index and middle fingers licentiously.

At this, we broke into laughter. The Saturday Night Finger was a real Mike idiom. I'd thought the guys had been joking about it until Mike said it with a coy smile one Shawnigan day while coaching us in the eight. Spelling out exactly what the metaphor stands for is beyond the scope of this book (think somewhere between first base and a home run). Mike was not above dropping in the odd sexual ditty, and it may have been his only saving grace during winter training. Derek, having been coached by Mike for six years, had an encyclopedic arsenal of his sayings. The comic relief was a drug; I couldn't get enough.

The van bumped along. Derek continued: "Now, take a few strokes — ten to fifteen. You want a good, firm pressure to get an effect. No, no, no, let it run. You must use a loose finga — your *Saturday Night* finga. Try again, ten strokes. Yes, I can see straight away the difference. Your boat was singing along because you had no *tension*."

By the time we pulled into the driveway to the lake, my eyes were watery. I could have pissed myself laughing. I think it was the stress.

Sure enough, thirty minutes later we were stopped in the middle of the lake. Mike cut the engine and began: "You must not carry tension in your shouldas …"

This was supposed to be when Mike worked his coaching magic, but it was everything I could do not to burst out laughing, picturing Derek's goofy face. To make matters worse, Derek started whispering down the boat from two seat what Mike was going to say right before he said it. I'd expected the outing to be eight rowers sitting in awe of a rowing legend's insights, but there I was suppressing the giggles.

Jokes aside, Mike *was* giving us good coaching, even if he did sound like a broken record to Derek and the other guys who'd heard it all before. He talked through the nuances of the stroke from catch to finish. We rowed for a minute with legs only, holding our forward body angle at the catch, feeling the connection from our blades in the water to the footboard. He churned out analogies and metaphors to get his point across. It was his favourite part, like a poem he got to recite each year.

He said things like:

"Shoulders loose like you're hanging from a pull-up bar."

"Wheels always moving; never stop on the slide. It's one continuous motion. Imagine spinning a bike wheel by the spokes with your finga. If you go too slow, you'll lose your finga" — he whipped his finger through the air like a conductor signalling a climaxing horn section — "and in the same manner, if your catch is too slow, you'll check the boat."

"One cut through the water like a knife through what, Conlin?"

"Warm butter, Mike."

"That's right, like a knife through warm butter."

He had us row briefly, repetitively, focusing on one element of the stroke each time, assessing how the boat felt after each brief row. He told us to remove our outside hand and row with bent inside arms, then loosen and straighten them. "Feel the difference?"

Why did he wait until a week before the World Cup to spend time on this? I wondered.

Mike asked us to describe how each new focus felt. Together, we were trying to find how fast felt. When Brian made his race calls, we needed to know how the boat should feel, how we should react together. Maybe this *was* the right time to dial it in. Had we talked about it during the winter slog, the words may have become meaningless.

By day four, we were into race pace pieces: 4 × 1,000 metres. Will had replaced Derek as stroke, as planned all along, and the boat feel immediately deteriorated. Each 1,000-metre piece felt like rowing in sand, like each one of us was rowing the whole boat ourselves instead of the lifting sensation of eight men rowing together. And it wasn't just me this time; everyone felt the rowing was shit. Mike had put Will in stroke fully confident that he was the guy to stroke us in London the following year, but our 1,000-metre times were well off Olympic standard. Doug Vandor and Cam Sylvester in the lightweight men's double were our pace boat, given a set lead off the start to account for the differences in boat speed between us. They were whipping us every run of the lake.

Each of us had an idea of why the boat did or didn't go well. You compared the biometrics of your own stroke with your teammates' and put together theories as to what the problem was. Will's stroke was front-end loaded. With his oak tree–like trunk, he could apply near perfectly consistent power from catch to finish. My stroke put more emphasis on the finish, like the unfurling of a whip. I was exhausted trying to keep up with Will at race pace. I couldn't get the time, couldn't step on the front end of the stroke like he could.

Mike was worried enough about the situation that he decided, the next day, to swap Derek and Will between stroke and two seat — a seat position race.

With Derek back in stroke, the boat sang. It was like taking the brakes off. It was possible the boat was going faster with Will at stroke — fast doesn't always *feel* fast — but the psychology of the crew needed to be propped up. We knew Derek was an excellent stroke. Whenever we did side-by-side rows in coxless fours, Derek's boat seemed to win no matter which three guys he had behind him. After the swap, the feedback was unanimous: we wanted Derek at stroke.

There is a prestige to being the strokeman. It says much about your rowing ability and your character. If it bothered Will to be moved back to two seat, he didn't show it. He was a team player, frustrated with how things had been going but happy to be anywhere in the boat as long as we went fast.

There was so much focus on the World Cup that I'd almost forgotten to look around once in a while. Near the end of camp, the scenery entered my field of view. Every day before we shoved off there were a few fat Italian men fishing from shore, resting beer bottles on their bulging bellies and baking red in the sun. Sometimes an older woman would lie topless, sunbathing a little farther down from the fishermen, her breasts escaping down either side of her chest. It was telling of my barren sex life that I looked twice. The mountains to our port side cradled pockets of concrete houses with barrel clay–tiled roofs spilling out from near their bases right down to the water's edge. When we turned, the mountains gave way to soaring cliff faces that twisted and turned, nature's paths begging to be explored. The natural beauty surrounded us like a great coliseum, but we were gladiators imprisoned in our rowing shell, unable to explore at its beckoning. At the top of the lake, paragliders launched off a nearby peak and soared on thermals with spindly little legs dangling. I couldn't imagine a starker dichotomy between our activity and theirs.

Snapshots. That's all you get. Looking around while rolling your unisuit down to the waist before the work begins; looking around while routine is interrupted by someone's loose footboard; while waiting for Doug to take yet another piss, pointing his member over the gunwale of the boat, urine dribbling all over his lap; looking around when someone's back blows up in the middle of the piece (concerned but grateful for the break); looking around while we wait for Cam and Doug to take their lead, those little bastards, always out of fucking reach.

You harvest these moments when you can, because it's what you've worked for. But when you're there doing the thing you've imagined, you're too overcome by the pressure, the giving of your body and mind to the goal. The dream never fits the reality; whatever you'd imagined is not what it's like. Most of the journey happens inside of you: determination, perseverance, overcoming failure. But I also wanted to enjoy the journey — the food, the women, the land. It's why I took walks in the evening, hoping to run across that Italian waitress I'd met during our half day off in Como.

Team photo before leaving Erba for competition. *Left to right*: Doug Csima, me, Annie Spracklen, Mike Spracklen, Gabe Bergen, Lindsay Jennerich, Will Crothers, Malcolm Howard, Patricia Obee, Andrew Byrnes (*rear*), Brian Price, Steve Van Knotsenburg, Rob Gibson, Doug Vandor, Morgan Jarvis, Kenny Woo, Kevin Light, Conlin McCabe. Members of the lightweight women's double trained with us that year.

Maybe I'd run into her on some cobbled backstreet in Erba and we'd do the act in an alley, or something else equally romantic.

That kind of thinking is a recipe for frustration. Better to stay home and watch the Hollywood adaptation of *The Boys in the Boat*, because no sooner do you grasp the beauty of your journey than it vanishes, replaced with the shifting shoulder blades of another sweaty back rearing towards you. I wanted to taste the experience, but when we left Italy on the last day of camp, I left still hungry.

39

The morning we left Erba, we piled our big Rowing Canada–issued duffle bags on the cobblestone driveway in front of the hotel. I sat in a wicker chair beside some Italian pensioners who were having a smoke. I breathed out of the side of my mouth, away from the smoke, and chewed my lower lip while thinking about the race. A World Cup event — what the hell would that be like? Was it like a Canadian university football game? I couldn't stop thinking about it, especially when I sat still for longer than thirty seconds. Stillness is mental quicksand. The routine of training was my saving grace: wake up; go eat breakfast; go back to room; mix two bottles of electrolytes; take dried unisuits, compression shirts, and socks off balcony railing; take piss; slather sunscreen on face and body (the smell of it means pain is coming); pile into van; bring water bottles and oars down to dock; bring eight down; train; relief at another workout over; put boat away, then oars; sit in ice tubs under tree beside boathouse; pile into van; tell Andrew how to drive; eat lunch at hotel; sleep, or while away the time until the next session.

When that routine ended, my thoughts centred on the World Cup like a coin circling a Spiral Wishing Well. Obsessive, compulsive, the boa constrictor around my chest tightening. The only thing worse than the pain of a 2k was waiting for a 2k. I wanted to race that instant, to get it over with. My mind released adrenaline that threatened to drain my energy prematurely. The solution was getting up, walking, moving, going somewhere, anywhere. But we were going onto a bus that would take five hours to reach Lucerne, and there would be no escape from my obsessive thoughts. *This is the cost of becoming world-class. Suck it up, pussy.*

Our hotel in Lucerne, the Grand Hotel Europe, was a majestic brick of a building with a beautiful garden out front and room balconies enclosed in wrought iron railings. If our retirement years were to look anything like the European pensioners we were following around, we were getting a good preview. Everywhere we went there was a mixture of athletes in tank tops and shorts and white-haired pensioners in khakis with cardigans draped around their shoulders, newspaper and cup of tea within arm's reach.

Doug and I shared a room again. I tossed and turned all night.

The next morning we took the city bus through the city to the Rotsee — a 2-kilometre slip of water carved into the countryside. You'd swear it was man-made, but it's actually natural and has been the host of rowing World Cups for decades.

We met our team coordinator, Michelle, at the trailer and unloaded the two sections of the eight. Gabe kept the mood light by playing the foreman: "Aw-ight fellas, swing that bitch down this way. Fuck, watch the carbon. Jesus, Brian." He hopped around shouting orders, cracking us up as he went and occasionally spreading his arms wide with open palms, saying, "Not fucking bad, boys." I held the bow, and Brian ordered me up a touch, down a touch, left a touch, until the bow and stern sections were flush and Gabe and Andrew could fasten them together with ten bolts. Next, we took our aluminum riggers and backstays from the bottom of the trailer and prepared our individual seats in the boat. I had to ask Brian which holes to bolt into.

"You having trouble finding the hole again, buddy?"

The lawn in front of the boathouse was covered with a fleet of rowing shells set upside down on racks. We'd come down at 7:30 a.m. to avoid the congestion. Still, rowers were streaming in steadily now: Aussies with green-and-gold unisuits, Italians in blue, Dutch in bright orange and blue, Kiwis in black. I saw Mahé Drysdale — the Kiwi reigning world champion in the single sculls — walk by with his shell balanced on his head and his oars in his left hand. His chest was as deep as it was wide, holding cavernous lungs and a heart that could jump-start a car.

Once on the water, we zipped back and forth on the course a few times, only passing by the Slovenian men's double and the German women's eight. Cowbells rang along shore as the animals grazed the grassy slopes rising from the banks. The water was a dark green, reflecting the foliage of the trees clustered along the banks, their branches stretching high over the water. The beauty was lost on me. I kept thinking about the set of the boat. The separation at the catch seemed worse. Who the hell was leaning to port? *Can we get the damn boat off port side?*

Mike had me in five seat, smack-dab in the middle of the engine room — seats three, four, five, and six, named after the fact that coaches often put their most powerful rowers in these seats. What did he expect from me? I had power, but not as much as Rob and Conlin had. Probably he put me there because the boat was most stable in the middle and he knew I was still learning. But my pride chose a different narrative: *He put you there to lead the engine room. You're a beast.*

The night before the first race, I wanted to toss off my blanket and get it over with that instant. Night racing on the Rotsee under the stars, racing blind under the moon, the shores invisible, with only cowbells giving us sonar. It would be carnage in those skinny lanes. I fell asleep.

The next morning I shit three times. Once when I woke up, once after our early morning paddle, and once again forty minutes before the race. Some people throw up when they get really nervous; I evacuate my bowels.

We finished breakfast in the half-silence of pre-competition focus — the amplified sound of cutlery clinking on plates, looking around gravely, bobbing heads in agreement when we caught each other's eye, forcing food down the gullet even though the nerves ruined my appetite.

On the bus, we sat quietly. Doug's eyes darted around, calculative, probably processing our arrival time based on current traffic. Will sat across from me in his Patagonia sun shirt. I wondered if his confidence was rattled from being swapped out of stroke seat. Gabe sat on the bus wheel well, a bushman dislocated in this city of expensive watches and fashion-forward office workers. Andrew never changed much. Same demeanour as always. If I didn't know him, would he look like he knew anything important was about to happen? Probably not. Derek looked unusually grave, his easy sense of humour stuck away somewhere for now. Brian scanned our faces, looking for clues as to how ready we were. Did he need to say anything, give us information, or just be quiet?

We arrived at the course an hour before launch. The sky was grey, like most winter days on Elk Lake. Mike had gone down earlier to check over the boat. We huddled briefly by our boat and planned the minutes until we'd be back and ready to take the boat to the dock.

Rob, Will, and I went to the communal men's change room to put on our World Cup unisuits. They were black with a blood-red CANADA up the sides. I felt a surge of pride as I let the shoulder loops snap against my skin. I was never overly patriotic, but among all these foreign athletes I was fiercely Canadian. As a kid, you want to beat everyone in your class, school, town, and then you want to be the best in your province, then your country. But when you compete against other countries, you realize that you're the product of your friends and foes growing up, and you badly want the sum of your experiences to trump those of your competition.

I did my pre-warm-up on the erg under one of those big-top white tents, fixing my eyes on the clock hung against the canvas wall at the front of the room. The erg tent was open to all teams, and beside me sat the biggest guy from the Dutch eight. He looked like the Russian boxer from *Rocky IV*. His arms and shoulders were sinewy pythons entwined with muscles slowly shifting under his skin with each stroke. He was well proportioned, with a skull as symmetrical as a mannequin. I figured he must have been grown in a petri dish by Dutch scientists. My first instinct was to pull hard strokes to let him know that, while not quite as muscle-bound, I had some power hidden in my butt and legs. I held off, knowing it would be stupid to let the presence of a competitor affect my warm-up routine.

We met back at the boat at the same time, nobody missing. Mike pulled out a weathered race schedule. Paper sounded nice in his hands; he tended to gently massage it with his fingertips while he spoke, giving off soft scrapes and crackles. We had five minutes to kill and spent it stretching beside the boat. We'd taken it off the racks shortly after arrival for Brian's thirty-six-point inspection and then replaced it on the top rung, above the German women's eight.

"Hands on," Brian said.

No more dress rehearsals; this was it. We grabbed the gunwales.

"Ready, up."

The white Hudson hull popped up high above our heads. There was so much nervous energy in us that if we'd let go, the boat may have gone ten feet in the air. It was one of the rare situations in my life when something felt out of reach, with 6'8" Conlin behind me, locking out his elbows.

"Down to shoulders."

We split, four to either side. The weightlessness disappeared as the boat came down hard on my left shoulder. The lawn sloped down toward the water, so our starboard side gunnel dug into our traps. We marched in lockstep 50 metres to the dock, past the Brits, past the Aussies, eyes ahead, jaws set. The Germans shoved off just as we stepped on.

"Down to waist. Ready, go!"

Brian's voice was businesslike. He'd been here many times. This was his domain. I latched onto the certainty in his voice to boost my confidence.

As soon as we shoved off the dock, I felt a rush of insecurity quiver inside. That kid who had been too shocked to hit back showed up. All my life I'd had a recurring dream of fighting schoolyard bullies and being ineffective; I'd throw a punch, but there'd be no power behind it, like trying to punch someone under heavy water. I wished I could defend myself in my sleep, but I couldn't, and I didn't know what it meant, but I knew I was determined to overcome, to force myself into uncomfortable situations. It's why I got in fights as a kid, and it's why I was in that rowing boat for my first race in the eight against the best in the world.

We rowed into the warm-up loop ahead of the Americans and behind the Poles. Brian's voice grew more intense with each piece: "No one trains as hard as we do. Next twenty, don't save anything. In two … one … right here." The warm-up course was short. We had room for only two hard twenty-stroke pieces before needing to turn around. The Polish crew used short, arms-only strokes to turn their boat, taking a long time. Finally, Brian had had enough. "Fuck these guys, we're going ahead. Starboards, back it; ports, give me some power." As we blatantly cut off the Poles, they looked at us with surprise more than anger. It takes a long time to turn an eight. Brian was symbolically giving them the finger for fifteen seconds straight. He was the defending Olympic champion coxswain, and this was his first international race since winning the gold in Beijing. He was sending a clear message about who was in control.

Time flew by, and suddenly, too soon, we were backing the boat into the starting gates. *Jesus Christ, how did I find myself here?* A World Rowing official lay chest down on a narrow dock that hovered over our stern. He grabbed it, we stopped backing, and Brian called adjustments to Gabe and Will in bow and two seat. Doug turned his head and whispered back to me, from six seat, "It's going to go fast. Let's do this, brotha." He sounded like he had at our first Sacramento camp. There we were, the two of us, in the engine room. The others — Gabe, Will, Andrew, and Conlin behind me, Doug, Rob, and Derek in front of me — primed, ready. The next stroke would be the start of the race. Everything I'd learned about rowing unfurled into individual components in my mind, like the exploded view of an engine schematic. How much pressure in my grip? How far apart do my knees go? Is my handle wet enough, too wet? Bury the blade or let it float?

The starting announcer's voice rang out over the PA: "Two minutes to start." My heart pounded in my eardrums. A throng of people gathered on shore to watch the start of the race. Most of them had come to go for a swim at the public beach that was less than 50 metres from our boat (the rowing fans gathered along the last 500 metres of the course). It was just their luck that they'd happened upon a World Cup race while floating on inflatable lounge chairs, sipping beer.

Our heat was a four-boat race. Germany — undefeated since 2009 — was in the other heat. It was impossible to predict how another year of training and different lineups would affect results. Only the winner of each heat would advance directly to the final. The remaining crews would have to race in the repechage race and come first or second to join the two winners of the heats in the final, three days later. (The repechage race allows all crews who did not win their heats a second chance at qualifying for the final, which ensures the most competitive boats race in the final.)

The starting official began listing the countries from lane one to four: "Netherlands, Canada, Great Britain, Ukraine." It was our cue to roll our seats up three quarters of the way to the front of the slides. I wasted no time in squaring and submerging my blade. I was too early. By the time the announcer called Ukraine in the last lane, I'd lost all tactile sense of how my oar was positioned in the water. I desperately wanted to tap my handle down and lift my blade out of the water to flick it from feather to square and feel the familiar clunk of the oar collar seating into place against the oarlock. But it was too late.

"Attention!"

The starting horn blared. My body stiffened, my legs pressed, my shoulders strained in their sockets. One stroke — still level with the other boats. Two strokes — still level. This was different than all the race starts we'd practised. There was no sensation of building speed with the Dutch and British eights blasting alongside. It was like running the wrong way on an escalator, or swimming up current. I wanted to lurch ahead of the other crews, like I was used to doing in my single. *Screw it, I'm laying down some bombs and getting us out of here*, I thought. But there is no escaping the averaging effect of being one eighth of a crew; you either do everything together or you fall apart. During the first 500 metres, I sunk my oar deep, dredging the bottom of the lake, weightlifting the boat. I was building an energy deficit that I would soon pay for.

At the 750-metre marker, the Dutch had already begun to pull away and I began paying the price for overexerting myself. Our stroke rate sagged down to thirty-five from our target of thirty-eight. My upper body started collapsing at the finish. At one of our last meetings in Erba, I had told Mike we needed the spacing between strokes that Derek could give us. I'd said boat feel was more important than the rate. "Jerry, boat speed is determined by power, length of stroke through the water, and rate of striking. We cannot allow the rate to slip," he'd responded.

At the 1,000-metre mark, Brian's voice grew desperate. He shouted at us, "Come on, boys! We need to stop them *now*! Give me legs!" When that didn't work, he dropped his tone, speaking under his breath with an appeal to reverse the losing fate we were sealing with each stroke: "Our bow is on the Dutch seven seat. I need you to put me on their six seat. It's not enough. I need more."

The race was over for me with 1,000 metres to go. My whole body felt like my recurring dream of being unable to punch my adversaries. Instead of loose arms and shoulders linking to powerful legs and core, I had been taking the weight at the catch with bent arms, and now they sagged with lactic acid like two waterlogged pool noodles. My mind went fuzzy from the exertion. I became a passenger riding along, dead weight forced onto my teammates. I could have wept in shame. All I could think was, *When will this awful experience end?* Then guilt for wanting out, and a rise of the usual morbid psychology: *Don't you dare lose without hurting yourself as much as possible, you pussy.* The Dutch were being pressed by the British. We were a length back and out of it. The Ukrainians struggled behind us in lane four. My form disintegrated completely in the last 250 metres. I looked as new to rowing as, well, I was. There was no hiding it. Even in their extreme fatigue my teammates held their form, while I heaved and collapsed between them like some drunk sailor rowing to save a drowning comrade in the middle of the ocean.

Two short blasts of an air horn sounded, indicating a close finish between the Dutch and the British. The crowds gathered along the bank cheered. The sound travelled to me as if through a dense wall. My head felt fat. I was suffocating. At last the air horn blasted again — six seconds after the Dutch and Brits — and I slumped forward in anguish.

40

That evening after dinner, Mike sat waiting for the rest of us to take our seats. He always stayed in an executive suite so that he could use his room for private meetings. We sat on ottomans, on couches, or on the floor. It was after dinner, and six hours had passed since the race.

"I want to talk in more depth about how the race went today," Mike said.

We'd had a brief chat after the race to get our first impressions on how things went while it was fresh in our minds. Now it was time for a more thorough deconstruction.

"How do you think it went?" he asked.

"Mike, it felt like there was some separation. It felt heavy," said Rob.

"Yeah, it didn't feel crisp," Will added.

At this point, Mike looked at us one by one to get our feedback, like roll call.

Gabe: "Sloppy, heavy."

Doug: "Start was decent, faded fast."

Andrew: [Something too long for me to remember.]

Derek: "We were dropping bombs instead of keeping the rhythm ticking along."

Me: "Yeah, it felt like we never established a good rhythm."

Conlin: "Could have pulled together better."

"Do you know what your stroke rate was?" Mike asked.

Silence.

"Thirty-six strokes per minute, at times sagging down to thirty-four," he said, letting out a guttural sigh. "I had the Dutch at thirty-eight and a half. You cannot win a race under-rating the other crews by four strokes per minute."

Mike looked at us, dumbfounded.

"Tomorrow in the rep, you *must* maintain thirty-nine strokes per minute," he said.

Jesus Christ. My heart sank.

"We've been over this and over this and over this. At one minute into the race, you need to push. Yes, you're feeling grotty, but so is everyone else, which is precisely why we attack at that moment. You can't afford to let the rate slip," said Mike.

I felt a wave of despair ascend from my guts and up the back of my neck. I couldn't take it anymore.

"Mike, what good is it boosting the rate higher if we can't row together at thirty-five? Shouldn't we focus on getting the rhythm together first?" I asked.

He smirked, dropping his head and then looking up at me as if peeking out from under a blanket — that oh-you-poor-idiot-who-doesn't-know-any-better look.

"You can talk about the rhythm all you like. You can go out there tomorrow and row at thirty strokes per minute and *feel* great. But you'll *lose*." He hung on to the words "feel" and "lose" with a dripping sarcasm. "Boat speed is determined by three factors: Length of stroke … "

Yeah, yeah, I'd heard it before.

I'd never rowed 2,000 metres as hard as I could at thirty-nine strokes per minute. When we'd left Victoria, most of our race pace pieces had peaked around thirty-six strokes per minute. That night, instead of dreaming of limp punches, I dreamt of losing grip on my oar handle, catching a massive crab, and being ejected from the boat.

"Okay, boys, you know what we have to fucking do." The tone in Brian's voice was different in the warm-up before our second race — he was calling us out. No more excuses about rhythm. No more whining about boat feel. Sure, I thought, the boat might chew up my uncertain oar like a wood chipper, but at least there was no doubt about what we were going to *try* to do. I gave in to the moment. How I was supposed to race 2,000 metres again, less than twenty-four hours after one of the worst physical experiences of my life, was beyond me. I could still feel the concrete in my legs from the previous race.

This is going to be a disaster.

"Set the tone, boys. Don't give them a fucking inch."

Jesus Christ, Brian, just let me survive this.

Why did I feel like I was being taken to my execution? It was just a race. Every goddamn quote about facing adversity I'd ever heard flashed before me. I wished I was good enough to row the single so that when I crumbled it would be all on my shoulders. The eight demands your best. You can't crumble with eight other guys depending on you, can't wind it down and say, "Today's not my day." The fundamental thing moving the boat is the understanding that seven other rowers are suffering just as much as you are. Until they stop, you don't stop. You can't believe they continue, but they do. It's thousands of hours of training side by side, wondering who's going to break, just to become teammates in a long, skinny boat, wondering how the hell you're still going 750 metres into the race.

So there I found myself, submitting to the moment. No, *submitting* is the wrong word. I wanted to laugh out loud like a crazy fool, "I'm fucked, I know it, and I'm still going to try as hard as I can!" Courage is the cousin of stupidity. I felt more stupid than courageous.

It was a six-boat race this time around. The Americans had finished third in our heat, and they were the crew to beat. The British, who had come second to the Dutch, were in the other heat. As soon as the race had been seeded the night before, I'd fabricated reasons to hate the Americans. What had I seen in them the previous day? Not much, really. Frankly, they seemed like decent guys representing their country. Maybe their three seat had held my gaze a little too long. *Yes, he'd written me off.* When it came time to question my reason for existence 750 metres into the race, I didn't want to be telling myself, *Aw, heck Jer, those Americans are a class act, really earning it out here.* Instead, I wanted to tell myself, *Every stroke I take will put a knife one millimetre deeper into the hearts of every man in that boat. Time to make them hurt.*

On the start line, it was déjà vu. I could swear the same fat guy was floating on the same black inner tube over by the beach, beer in hand. Bikini-clad girls teased my focus. The sound of cowbells jangled on the grassy hill on our starboard side. The water was dark and dimpled.

Rate, rate, rate. That's all I told myself. Blade depth, catching without missing water, level hands out of the finish? Forget about it. I purged all that. I'd give Mike his rate, but like hell it would be good clean rowing.

My teammates were experienced; they could handle it. Each of them had raced at thirty-eight or higher in past international races. Andrew had been at forty strokes per minute in his gold medal final in Beijing. What was he thinking? How did our crew compare to Beijing in that moment? I wanted to plug into his memories and download his experience so that I could form an expectation for how the race should go.

The starting official began the eulogy: "United States of America, Canada, Poland … " The Poles started slapping their thighs, shouting and turning and clasping forearms. Jesus Christ, they were animals. I gave my quads a little wiggle, just in case I was missing something.

"Attention!"

Eternity.

ENHHH! The horn. The first two strokes are long and strong, the next three extend slide length, build for five, then drive into pace in two. The start was better than I'd expected. The boat was cutting along the surface instead of bobbing up and down. At 750 metres, I wasn't wondering how I would survive. We were in control, pushing out on the Americans into first place. I felt a tingling sense of glee mingle with the lactic acid. Somehow the pain becomes worth it when you can see the backs of all the other crews in your peripheral vision. At 1,250 the Americans made a push, but we responded, neutralized it. "We've been at thirty-eight and a half the whole way, boys. Keep it here," Brian said. With 250 metres to go, I knew we would win. Rowing with a big lead is like playing poker with your opponent's cards face up on the table. You see their push, you call their bluff. When their move ends, you start inching away again and you can see the pain you're inflicting. It masks your own pain; you're in control. The only thing worse than extreme pain is not knowing when it's going to end. As we sprinted to the finish, we had a three-quarter-length lead on the Americans — an almost insurmountable lead in a men's eight event — with Australia, New Zealand, and Russia in pursuit.

We crossed the finish line to win the race. I lost my head and bellowed a victory roar. The roar of relief. *Relief.* It washed over me as fast as the lactic acid dissipated. We'd won. We'd *won*! Yes, it was only the repechage, so coming first or second meant the same thing — a berth in the final, the race that counted — but this was as emotional a victory as any I'd experienced.

We nodded respectfully to our competitors, turned the boat, and rowed along the shore back to the dock.

"Way to execute on the race plan, boys," Brian said. "Jerry, how does it feel to win an international race?"

"Fuck, yeah!" I kept saying, over and over in a crescendo, relief and endorphins flooding my system. I was like a mixed martial arts fighter who manages to land a lucky punch and then proceeds to circle the octagon, miming the championship belt around his waist, as if he'd known he would win all along — the kind of guy you can't wait to see get knocked out the next time he steps into the ring.

As we continued up the shore, I heard a shout from shore: "Daddy!" Ethan was standing in front of my dad, waving and bouncing up and down. I was shocked. "Hey, buddy!" I yelled. "Go, Canada!" Finally, Brian had to calm me down. "Jerry, keep your head in the boat. Tomorrow's the race that counts." He leaned over the gunwales on starboard and shot me a smile. I regained my composure.

My parents had taken Ethan with them on vacation to Holland, and though I knew they were going to try to make it to Lucerne to catch some of the racing, I hadn't expected to see them until the next day, hence the emotional outburst. It was like seeing my next of kin at the hospital moments after narrowly surviving a car wreck.

We met later that afternoon for lunch. I hadn't seen Ethan in three weeks, and when he saw me coming he sprinted and jumped into my arms at warp speed. I laughed and smooshed my face into his cheek. But as soon as we sat down, my mind was already on the next race. My parents had made a detour in their vacation and brought my beaming, loving son for a visit, and all I could think about was how soon I could shed them and get back to the hotel. "Daddyyy ..." Ethan was smiling, hanging off my shoulder. I was not in the mood for physical contact. It provoked me. I was in fight mode, and the slightest touch triggered a violent inclination inside me.

"Sit on your seat, Ethan," I said.

His face fell. I felt like an asshole. I hated being away from him ever since Amy and I had broken up. Any time I saw him after being away for more than a week, there'd be an unusual dynamic to our relationship. Ethan would be polite for the first few minutes, treating me like I was more of an uncle, or, God forbid, some unengaged weekend dad. *It's me, Ethan*, I wanted to say. *I'm the same dad I've always been since you were born!*

It made me sick to think of my fatherhood role diminishing over time. I wondered what was going through his little six-year-old mind. I imagined the billions of synapses forming in his brain as I looked at him. Was I doing everything I could to give him the best start in life? Was my pursuit of rowing costing his proper development?

Horsing around with Ethan after the first heat of the 2011 World Cup at the Rotsee rowing course in Lucerne, Switzerland.

During the meeting later that evening, Mike did a poor job concealing how obviously pleased he was with himself.

"You've seen now that at the same power and length of stroke, a higher rate of striking will give you more boat speed," he said. "Tomorrow, you've got to get your nose in front by the five hundred and hold through the middle one thousand. The last five hundred is up to you. Who wants it more?"

We moved on to assessing how we stacked up against the other crews in the final. It looked like we were ranked fourth, as Germany and the Dutch had won the heats and the British had almost tied the Dutch. The Americans had also beaten us in the heat, but we'd beat them in the repechage. I thought if we rowed like we had in the repechage, we had a shot at the podium in the final, and maybe even a shot at the undefeated Germans.

That night before bedtime, I ran over everything with Doug. He lay in bed with his sleep mask on. "I don't know, man. Last year, we led everyone by a length and still couldn't hold on in the last five hundred," he said, referring to the 2010 New Zealand World Championships. He pulled his mask off, stretched his arms, and cradled his head. "Mike says it's up to you in the last five hundred. Maybe he's right, but my legs were spaghetti by the fifteen hundred. There was nothing left to give."

"We should relax a bit off the line, not waste so much energy," I said.

"Maybe. Mike's right, though, statistics show the leader at the five hundred almost always goes on to win the race. Though we might be changing that stat now," Doug said, laughing.

Ours was a mind-numbing strategy. Go out harder than everyone else, then hold on for dear life, using sheer force of will to hang on to the lead in the last 500.

"Our best race in New Zealand was the B final. We finally gave up the fly-and-die strategy and rowed the whole way at thirty strokes per minute. The Chinese were at forty, and we still won easily," Doug said.

"Is Mike such a megalomaniac that he can't see that we need to change things up?"

“He knows more than you or I will ever understand about this sport and how to get an eight on the podium,” Doug said. “You think he’s crazy, but every now and then you experience some of his genius and it catches you off guard. But if we come DFL tomorrow, I am fucking done with this sport. I’ll retire,” he concluded, sliding his sleep mask back in place.

He was joking, I think.

Three races in three days. This was a new level of assault on my body. I wondered if I’d ever get through a race without wanting to rest every ten seconds as if I was still playing football. My teammates were tough, mentally and physically trained, psychologically more prepared, used to racing back-to-back-to-back, but still … I couldn’t help wondering how far behind I was physiologically, and how much longer until my body and brain got used to the trauma of racing. Maybe I wasn’t meant to be an offensive lineman or an elite rower — just somewhere in between, excelling in recreational sports after a day at the office.

The trip to the racecourse took on some normalcy the third time around. The sound of the air brakes on the bus stopping in front of our hotel; the murmur of Swiss-German locals reminding me of something my mom had said (that Swiss-German was hillbilly German, equivalent to a deep southern accent in English); the squishy patter of runners on the sidewalk; the first woody knocks of carbon while picking our oars out of a pile; the sound of spandex sliding against skin; and finally the splat of the boat hull displacing water.

The sky was grey and leaking light drizzle in headwind conditions. It was our first race against the Germans that year. During the warm-up we were in front of them in the holding pattern. They didn’t look as physically intimidating as the Aussies or the Dutch, but they rowed as if all the fulcrum points on their bodies were connected by steel rods. A far cry from Mike’s critique of our starboard blade work during a film session earlier that summer: “It’s like a *spider*,” he’d said, rolling his fingers in front of his face. A spider with one particularly errant leg in five seat.

The starting announcer began his deadpan routine: “Two minutes.” His voice hidden in a tower somewhere, faceless, echoing across the water.

It was the voice of an old family friend. I injected nostalgia into hearing that voice. *Yes, old pal, thank you very much for the warning again.*

"United States of America, Poland, Germany ..." He began roll call early. The two-minute warning was never actually a full two minutes. Lying bastard.

The oar felt hot in my hands; my blisters had awakened from the back-to-back racing.

"Attention!"

Eternity.

Doug's back was rising in the middle of a breath when the horn went. He took the weight, his lats tensing and spreading wide. Strokes one, two (*a little rough*), three, four, five (*down on port*), five to ten (*coming together now*), gear shift on thirteen (*still some separation*). We were off to a rocky start, and the Germans already had their nose in front.

It's hard to keep the faith when things don't go well off the start, working so hard but losing inches in a sea of bodies. There's always the hope that other crews have gone out too hard and will pay in the final 500 metres, but you don't believe it when you're rowing poorly. The overwhelming urge is to put things right yourself; a crew turning into eight individuals separately determined not to be the reason why the boat is going slow.

Instead of focusing on Brian's race calls, I laid down five bombs to put it right. Then Conlin took his turn, then Rob his. But we didn't do it at the same time. We paced ourselves off the British in lane six. We were in lane five. The Americans, in lane one, were pushing the leaders in lane three, Germany. We hadn't kept any secrets; the rate was high, the effort was there, but the rhythm was shit and we found ourselves in third place through the first 500 metres.

All these early warning signs didn't help my psychology heading into the midway point of the race. I started to feel the two previous races in my body, like sand coating my muscles. I couldn't stay loose. The rain came down hard now, stinging the backs of our necks and making our oar handles gummy.

At 1,500 metres, I was in agony like I had been in the heat. Déjà vu. Brian's voice grew more desperate. We were paying the price for our inefficient efforts, slipping back with each stroke now. (As this was happening,

I was thinking my particular pain was a special kind of hell that is reserved for idiots who go where they don't belong, but that was my ego. We were all burning up just as badly.)

My neck could no longer control the oversized bowling ball of a head attached to it. It gave way, sending my noggin in all directions like a bobble-head on a car dash. If Mike had been concerned about my pain face, what would he have said to this? The pain was written all over my body like a sixteen-foot highway advertisement: *I'm Fucked and We All Know It.*

The finish horn sounded four times in rapid succession. Germany first, then the Dutch, Great Britain, U.S.A. Three seconds later we crossed the line in fifth place, with the Polish coming sixth a second after us. I tried and failed, like usual, to avoid twisting from the pain of the lactic acid swishing around inside me. Kristof Wilke, stroke for the German eight, undid his shoes and let his legs dangle in the water. Their crew was hunched over in pain too, but theirs had produced a victory.

During the debrief with Mike, he was surprisingly empathetic. "Hi, Jerry. Hi, Will. Hello, Conlin," and on like that, greeting us softly with consolation as we came off the water. Had I known then what adjustments he would be making to our training program when we returned to Elk Lake, I may have felt a little less sorry for myself in the moment and sorrier for what was coming.

Fifth place was unacceptable. It was an improvement from Worlds in 2010, but we trained as hard as we did to win. And if not to win, at least to be on the podium. Maybe this experience would be as good as it got. The future looked like an Olympic qualification might be our greatest success as a crew. I left Switzerland with one thought about rowing: *Thank you, that'll be all.*

41

In two months we'd be back to Europe for the World Championships in Bled, Slovenia. In two months, Mike was determined to find more speed. "The standard rises every single year, and so we must increase the training program to keep up," Mike said upon our return to Canada. *How is it possible to increase our training volume?* We were already on the brink of major injury every single day. Our medical support team operated like they were in a wartime medical tent, patching up wounded athletes as best they could (releasing SI joints, intercostal muscle strains, ribs on the verge of snapping, cartilage orbiting kneecaps like space junk, raking our muscle strains and tendonitis with deep tissue massages) and sending them back into battle, grudgingly. No, adding to the program couldn't be the answer. We needed to row better — like Germany. If anything, that would require dialing it back a notch.

I began loathing Mike. Every time he talked about the program in his matter-of-fact manner, as if everything he said was common sense, I wanted to lash out: *Mike, you're fucking crazy.* His reasoning was full of holes. The human body evolved over thousands of years. How the hell were we supposed to adapt in two months to the increased training load? We'd barely survived the training heading into the World Cup. There were no more notches on the dial. He was adding notches. He was cheating reason.

Mike believed we'd get stronger by striving through these brutal workouts, knowing we'd fail but seeing how close we could come. It was a prescription from coach to athlete to overcome the dulling effect between mind and body.

"The body lies," Mike would say.

He always spoke of The Body as if it were this separate entity that needed to be beaten into submission by the mind. What enlightenment. All along we had been tricked by our bodies, and Mike had come along to bring us out of the cave: *No, there really is more! I know you think you're trying, but the body bloody lies! It will forsake you at any moment. On guard, men!*

Now it was around this time that I started playing ping pong between my principles and reality. On the one hand, I had made a choice to stick with Mike until the Olympics. On the other, it was proving much more difficult than I'd imagined. I was steadfast in my conviction — Mike was our path to the podium — and at the same time, absolutely convinced that he was sabotaging us.

"It's *your* medal," he'd say. "I'm only here to show you what it takes. It's over to you how bad you want it."

He was just the messenger, just a conduit for the truth. If we didn't like what needed to be done, we must not have wanted to win as badly as we'd thought. Between the morning row and the second session on Saturday (500-metre sprints times a million), most of us fell within a range of mild depression to severe anxiety depending on what lies our bodies were telling us: *Your rib is about to crack, your disc is herniating, your rib* is *cracked. Has it broken through the skin? No? Soldier on.*

Andrew was Mike's lieutenant in the locker room. "It may not make sense to you now," he'd say, "but it'll make sense when you're on the podium." He would know. It was his second quad with Mike, having won gold with him in 2008. Still, I'd think, *Fuck, Andrew, give me some rationale based on reason and not some religious cult everything-will-work-out-if-you-just-believe nonsense.*

Perhaps the most difficult part of dealing with the increased training load that summer was knowing how marginal our gains would be. The crew was set. The only way to make up the gap between us and the podium, never mind the Germans, was to row better or increase our aerobic fitness. And when it took a whole year of training to shave a second or two off our time, it was hard to imagine it possible to turn things around in two months.

I'd like to tell you we rose to the occasion, that we showed up at the boathouse every morning that summer with competitive fire flashing in our eyes, eight men marching abreast, like line infantry. The truth is, we trudged bleakly one by one from the upper parking lot to the warmly lit change room, uninspired. The Olympic dream was this innocent little boy inside of us, God bless him, who'd been buried alive in a casket, his heart barely beating on. But that's the journey — giving everything you've got for a tiny sliver of possibility, knowing your best may not be enough in the end, but needing, *needing*, to know you held nothing back.

In rowing, I'd thought I would escape the emotional turmoil that had plagued me after Amy and I broke up, as I worried about Ethan's future. I'd thought rowing would be this binary product of inputs and outputs — what did emotion have to do with it? Everything, it turned out. What I couldn't do with Amy, I did with rowing in two short years — I married it. I went all in. Held nothing back. I committed to Mike, to the pursuit, and to my teammates, who were doing the same. When Mike pushed me through the barriers of reason and logic, I could no longer keep things emotionally neat and tidy. I had to trust him even when I thought he was full of shit. I had to trust in the fact that my decision to commit was more important than what I thought about that decision in any future state. I made a promise to my former self, and like hell would I break it. An inner battle between reality and my chosen principles waged on:

> *There must be a better path to the Olympic podium.*
>
> *What the hell do you know? Mike's been there before. Go with experience.*
>
> *But he's old, he's going crazy, losing touch with reality. Your body will break before you see an Olympic race.*
>
> *He knows exactly what he's doing. You just need to keep your shit together for one more year.*
>
> *We need more recovery, more technique work.*
>
> *Excuses, excuses. You know what needs to be done. Suck it up, pussy.*

Just as future prospects seemed grim, there was a surprise announcement. Mike called a meeting one Saturday morning after our first row. We spread ourselves across a row of ergs in the simmering heat of the boathouse loft with our unisuits rolled down to the waist. Mike sat with his back facing the big bay windows. Beside Mike sat Malcolm Howard.

As soon as we saw him, we knew what was happening. Malcolm had been training in the single scull with Allison Dobb as his coach since the beginning of the 2010 season. Malcolm was following in the footsteps of Derek Porter, who had successfully made the transition from the men's eight to men's single after winning gold in the eight at the 1992 Olympics and then going on to become world champion and Olympic silver medallist in the single.

The single sculls is an event reserved for the most genetically gifted among rowers. Malcolm fit in with this group. A towering mass of slow-twitch muscle fibres, he possessed the elite single sculler's trademark chest cavity — deep as it was wide — housing two lungs like great fire bellows ready to suck unfair amounts of oxygen into his bloodstream.

He didn't just look the part. Malcolm finished as high as fourth place at a World Cup in 2010. It would be his best result, as he went on that year to a disappointing sixteenth place finish at the World Championships in New Zealand. He was a steam locomotive, nearly unstoppable when up to full speed, but he gave away too much of a lead off the start. Unfortunately, Malcolm was quite mentally stable, which would have disadvantaged him amongst his competitors in the single. I can't imagine a more mentally gruelling event than the single sculls. It's an event best reserved for people who had insufferable childhoods and possessed the kind of bad memories needed to fuel the necessary self-loathing. (This statement could be applied to competitive rowing in general, but the single sculls is a particularly desolate boat class).

"Malcolm has indicated to me his desire to return to the eight," said Mike. "We all know the calibre of athlete he is, and the boat would no doubt be stronger with him."

No one moved. A few of us nodded silently, acknowledging the news while simultaneously calculating what effect this might have on our own place in the boat.

The announcement was the kind of boost we needed. We'd struggled maintaining our middle course pace, and now we had a specialist on board. There weren't many rowers in the world capable of sustaining the exhausting middle 1,000-metre pace Malcolm could hold. No question, this was good news, but it meant Derek would lose his seat just one month after beating Kevin. Sure, he could try to demand another seat race, but the remaining portside rowers — Will, Conlin, and Doug — were all stronger on the erg. A strokeman's skills do not usurp power in a Mike Spracklen eight. Conlin was off the water with a rib stress fracture at the time, but he would be back in the boat as soon as he was healthy. Will was Derek's closest rival in erg performance, but Will was regularly beating the rest of us in singles and, with Gabe as his partner, in pairs training. And despite the switch that had put Derek back in the stroke seat in Lucerne, Mike was determined that Will was the guy who would stroke the crew at the Olympics. Lucerne was a hiccup. Mike's vision hadn't changed.

Under these circumstances, Derek met with Peter Cookson and Mike later that week and decided to switch from the eight to the four in Terry Paul's small boat group. He sent us all an email saying there was no point in holding back our regular training with another seat race, knowing full well that Conlin would return in time for the World Championships.

Malcolm took over five seat, moving me back to three seat. Andrew switched from three seat on starboard to six seat on port. He was one of a minority of rowers who can row well on both sides of the boat. Finally, Will resumed helm of stroke seat.

Bowman Gabe Bergen guiding us back to the dock through heavy fog on Elk Lake.

Gabe christened the new boating order by giving us each spirit animal nicknames as follows:

Bow seat: Gabe Bergen — Diviner of Animal Spirits
Two seat: Doug Csima — Racoon
Three seat: Jeremiah Brown — Emu
Four seat: Conlin McCabe — Hippo
Five seat: Malcolm Howard — Great Dane
Six seat: Andrew Byrnes — Ostrich
Seven seat: Rob Gibson — Mustang
Stroke seat: Will Crothers — Red-Tailed Hawk
Coxswain: Brian Price — Weasel

Those weeks before we returned to Europe had me at my most prolonged insecure state since joining the national team. Ethan had flown back with my parents after the World Cup to be with Amy for the rest of the summer, leaving only Julia and me in the condo. Despite Julia's presence, I was mostly isolated with my thoughts. I'd gone from an outsider who should have been grateful just to make the team to a member of a team desperate to be the best in the world. I didn't want to train as hard as we were without knowing we had a realistic shot at the podium. With Malcolm back in the boat, we'd been given a big boost in horsepower and psychology. But what if it wasn't enough? Success was the only thing that could validate the extremes Mike put us through, and the thought of it eluding us cast a pall over me.

Mike pushed us hard, his popemobile following us up and down the lake. During rainy workouts, I occasionally lifted my gaze from my line of wake toward the black wiper clearing Mike's windshield. Obscured behind the foggy glass, not much changed in his appearance. Shoulders pulled back, microphone held near his face, ready to deliver instruction. Sometimes his eyes seemed to glaze over, and I felt as though we were being swept up in his deep and unknowable motivation. I imagined his love for the sport was overshadowed by a seething, dark, and angry determination. In a way, I knew part of what drove Mike came from the same well that I drew from. That inner voice that says, *I know what it takes, and I'll do what it takes, and I'll show every bastard who ever doubted me for a second.*

Training days went ahead, with most of us shaking our heads in disbelief at the start of the day and walking to our cars beaten up by the end of it. Frozen in my mind: an image of Rob walking slowly to his car in flip-flops, staring at the dirt five feet in front of him, thumb wedged under the strap of his gym bag. It's the body language of a man held captive by the pursuit. A kind of sadness in knowing you've given yourself to the journey, that you'll endure everything your enigmatic coach throws your way. It was like we were complicit in some crime against our own psyche. The allure of the Olympics was too powerful, too meaningful, to allow us to resist whatever soul-crushing training awaited us.

I remember one Saturday in August that year when all possible factors that could destroy a rower's will affected me all at once. The sun had beat down on us with a pulsating throb all week. I'd lost precious pounds to dehydration, and what energy I had left had gone into the morning check mark workout: that brutal, impossible climb to forty-two strokes per minute in two-beat-per-minute increments over the course of four lengths of the lake. Now we were in the middle of the last workout of the week. As Mike coaxed us on — "The body wants not to push this hard, but you must will it onward, you *can* do even more" — the intercostal muscle weaving around my rib cage felt as though it'd been sliced open and two joints in my lower spine screamed at me to stop. My hands burned hot wrapped around my oar. I inspected my left hand and winced at the searing sting of newly revealed flesh lacing my palm and fingers, shining a silvery pink like a salmon fillet. I now recognized my oar hanging among many from the rafters by the maroon patches of dried blood saturated in its grains. The roughed-up wood of my oar handle had long ago turned into a slippery matte finish, smothered soft by a mixture of blood, blister serum, and sweat.

"Think of the Germans, boys," Malcolm said. "No fucking way they're putting themselves through this!"

His words hung in the air, supported by our silence. His rally cry was not about effort. We all knew we'd throw what we had left into the next piece, and then again into the one after that. Whenever Malcolm spoke up, it was about sharpening up our mental acuity to ensure we

Canadian men's eight being worked hard.

met the mental and physical resistance with force. It was necessary to lean in to the pain to get the effect Mike intended. Just bearing it wasn't good enough. It's the kind of effort that is hidden in everyone but usually reserved for flight-from-death scenarios. Part of how we trained under Mike was creating an artery to that source of energy, and the only way I knew how to summon it was with a great deal of anger. So much rage needs an anchor, and I hooked mine into Mike. I wanted my ribs to break and burst through my skin so that I could scream, "See! Do you believe me now, you fucking bastard?"

42

Another flight to Europe, and another notch on the belt tightening around my chest. We faced the first real threat to our dreams. The World Championships in Bled, Slovenia, were also the Olympic qualifying event. If we ended up in the B final like the crew had in New Zealand, we'd face the possibility of not qualifying for the Olympics and being forced to race the relegation regatta months later.

The routine in Erba was the same: the first three days of rowing was a cinch. It was still surprising coming from Mike, even the second time around. After the World Cup, he'd increased the intensity and volume of our training into the zone where ribs crack and tendons fray. Yet, he was sticking to his method of allowing time for our bodies to adjust to the new time zone before pushing us hard. Pathetically, I found myself feeling more charitable toward Mike. *Aw shucks, he's not such a bad guy.*

Given a break from the grind, it's hard for eight men not to descend into shouting jokes from bow to stern, with even Malcolm setting up some long-winded jabs at Brian amid the harpoons being launched from Gabe in bow. "Christ, Brian, one job for your little bitch-ass up there, and you can't even steer," he yelled through suppressed laughter. Brian returned insults with stamina. Every coxswain should have thick skin, but Brian wouldn't just take sit there and take it. He had a chip on his adolescent-sized shoulder. For every insult he received, he hurled back three of his own.

"Gabe, get your windmilling oar down to the water at the catch, you skying motherfucker."

"Maybe if Byrnesy put more than half his blade in the water, he'd actually lock on."

"Jerry, maybe you'd keep up with Will if you didn't stick half your loom in the water."

And on it went.

On the second-last day of camp, I found myself unable to keep my frustration contained any longer. Mike was going to ruin us. He'd written "stretch rate" into the program the night before, and upon arriving at the boathouse the conditions looked awful. Lake Erba had become roiled up by wind, and our riggers slapped through the crests of waves as we plodded through our pressure pyramid warm-up toward the top of the lake. We were back into training at full intensity, and it felt like being woken up five minutes after falling into a deep sleep. My veins pulsed, bubbling, removing cobwebs and opening up passages that had started to collapse with the ease of the first days of camp. My legs felt fat, like they were storing all the cheese I'd eaten at dinner the night before. A gusting headwind grabbed our blades and pulled them up or down like a child's flat hand stuck out the car window on the highway. As my system sputtered to life like an old diesel tractor after sitting idle for months, Brian launched us into the first hard piece of the camp.

"You must maintain rate. Higher, higher. Don't let it slip, Brian!" Mike's launch pressed upon our starboard side as we struggled to find form. The wind swallowed the output from his megaphone so that all we could hear were the muffled words "rate … higher …"

"Come on, boys! We're at thirty-five. Get it up to thirty-eight. In two … that's one … two … ready, go!" Brian's voice crackled through the PA speakers, nipping at us, cajoling us, but his eight horses were faltering, calling upon reserves that had already been depleted.

"Thirty-six and a half here, boys. It's not enough! Will's going to give us another half beat in two."

I fixed my eyes on Conlin's massive back whipping toward me on each stroke, trying to stay with him, Doug doing the same behind me in two seat. Finally the last piece ended. The relief of survival crept over me as my breaths morphed from sucking wheezes to two-stage gulps of sweet oxygen. Then the voice of the devil resurfaced, fully audible now with the wind behind him.

"Brian, set your course into the wind. We will practise stretching the rate into a headwind. Yes, we will get value out of the headwind," said Mike.

A surge of anxiety hit me. I'd barely been able to keep a grip on my oar during the last piece. Mike was pushing me over a cliff. Brian called out instructions.

"Jesus fucking Christ," I mumbled under my breath, as we moved forward to the catch.

"Just shorten up your slide length, and keep your hands moving," Doug offered from behind me. I hung on to his voice like a lifeline during such times. I never knew how I'd get through Mike's relentless approach, but I thanked Jesus just as much as I cursed him that I was rowing with seven guys who'd been through it all before.

"In two. Ready, up!" Brian unleashed the mayhem.

Two tons of flesh started hurtling itself back and forward, faster and faster. The wheels under our seats zipped along at an increasing pitch.

"Fifty-two … up, up!" Brian asked for another gear. My arms stiffened.

"Fifty-four … fifty-six …" We were reaching the limit of what was possible. Our body movements resembled controlled seizures, jerking violently back and forth.

Then it was over.

"Brian, what did you get up to?" asked Mike.

"Fifty-six."

"Fifty-six? I know you guys can do better than that. That was a warm-up. Let's really stretch it up this time. See if you can hit rate sixty."

I clenched my teeth, furious now at what I saw as needless risk.

Halfway through the second stretch rate, my forearms cramped and my grip locked onto the oar. "Fifty-eight, boys. Ready, up!" Brian shouted. My legs froze at half slide. I stopped moving on my seat, lost grip in my left hand, got it back, fought to stay in time. Rob was leaving us all behind in seven seat. His thick shoulders blasted backwards with more power and speed than the rest of us, daring us to keep up. *Fuck, Gibson.*

"Down!" Brian ended the ordeal.

I was red hot with anger. Someone was hurting me, and I wanted to hit back. I blew up.

"What the fuck are we doing?" I shouted at Brian, the word *fuck* launched like a poison-tipped spear. I wanted to do damage.

"What's the problem, Jerry?" Brian said coolly.

"There is absolutely no fucking point to this exercise!" I snapped back.

Mike had heard me and was nearing us now. He pulled his launch over to starboard side and tapped the outboard engine into reverse to level up with me in three seat.

"What's the issue, Jerry?" he asked.

"Mike, we're just rowing like absolute shit to hit some ridiculous rate. I'm not even using my legs anymore. It's fucking senseless. Fuck!" I yelled.

"I'll explain to you one more time why we do this, Jerry. You're new to the eight this year, so perhaps you haven't had the benefit of hearing this yet," Mike said in a calm voice laced with threatening undertones.

"We stretch rate so that race pace becomes *easier.* It is not about the quality of rowing. We push up to rate sixty so that when we row our race pace at thirty-nine, we find it *easier*. We find we have more time. It is no different to how we stretch the length of our stroke during winter while training at low rates, or how we stretch power with power strokes at the end of the week when the body is fatigued."

I stared straight ahead as he spoke.

Rob looked down the boat at me with a grin. "You okay, Jer? Just keep the hands moving, brother."

"Keep it loose," said Malcolm.

The key to extremely high stroke rates is to stay as loose as possible to prevent seizing up. As we rowed into the final twenty-stroke piece, I quit fighting and gave in. It wouldn't be perfect, but I'd get through it somehow.

On Brian's call, we drove the rate up higher and higher. I kept my jaw unhinged and relaxed. Fifty-five … fifty-six … I flicked my oar around with the lightness of a badminton player's touch, feeling the wood grains dancing lightly against the hide of blistered skin on the insides of my fingers. The oar circled back and forth in the oarlock, feather to square, feather to square.

"1:13, 1:11!" Brian screamed out our pace per 500 metres. Excited by the sheer power, it drove us even higher.

Fifty-eight … sixty … Approaching 28 kilometres per hour, fast enough to pull a water skier, a speed matched by only a few crews in the world, if any.

"Down!"

The boat coasted quietly through the choppy water, oars suspended at ninety-degree angles to the boat, pausing, then splatting onto the surface. No one was injured. My oar had not severed the bottom of Conlin's spine, as I'd feared.

Then, in the same calm voice, Mike said, "Now, how did that feel, Jerry?"

"That one was actually pretty good!" I said, smiling.

Maybe Mike, one of the most decorated coaches in the history of the sport, knew what he was talking about. I hated when he was right.

"Fuck yeah, boys!" Gibson called out.

43

2011 World Championships. Bled, Slovenia.

"You've got to attack the first five hundred metres, you know that now," said Mike. "The Netherlands will want to challenge in the third five hundred. You need be prepared for it."

When Mike went over final strategy and race plan on the eve before race day, he spoke in poetic phrases that soared, dipped, and fell in resolution.

"Push through the forty-five-second mark, find your length and power through the middle hundred strokes, then it's over to how badly you want it in the last five hundred," he said, as if reciting from an old manual.

Malcolm punctuated the end of Mike's paragraphs with testimony: "Guys, you know what we have to do out there. It's going to feel like shit, but if we commit to every one of those strokes in the middle one thousand metres, we're going to be in a good position," he said.

Next, Andrew struck up: "Listen to Brian, and do the calls together. Let's push those finishes."

Doug and I rolled our eyes. When Andrew spoke, it didn't have the same authority as Malcolm. Despite the fact that he was an Olympic champion, Andrew had a lackadaisical air about him. It was part of his easygoing character, and it drew our ire.

The meeting neared its conclusion. Brian took us through the race plan call by call: "First stroke, long and powerful, don't cut it short; next two, sit up and drive legs; strokes three to five, drive legs; six to ten, full slide length, start to bring in the body swing. On stroke thirteen, we drive it and lengthen."

He spoke as if giving instructions for a wartime siege, pausing between race calls to allow us to visualize the race unfolding. My mind's eye gave me only a blur of limbs, like an infant trying to make sense of a world it did not yet know.

"Last ten strokes, all power; empty the tank."

As Brian wrapped up the race plan, Gibson breathed audibly through his nose, Will's rigid jaw tensed, Andrew appeared mildly affected, Malcolm looked around the table at us, nodding, Gabe stared down at his interlaced fingers, Doug chewed on his lower lip, Conlin gazed straight ahead with raised brows, and I sat forward on my elbows, resting my chin on my hands and exchanging glances with each of them. Under the dim light of the room, it appeared a group of men were in the late stages of a high-stakes poker game. Mike played with the piece of paper in his hands and watched us with a sweet smile on his face. He looked paternal.

The next morning, we gathered in the hotel lobby at 7:00 a.m. to travel down to the lake for our pre-race row. The morning warmth of the sun bathed us as we rowed up to the start of the racecourse. I could feel the potential in the twitching of my legs and arms, and felt an urge to release the power into my blade. Brian spoke in a low voice, turning us onto one of the two warm-up lanes closest to the north shore. The Dutch eight had waited with their boat on their shoulders while we'd shoved off, and now they rowed across the bottom of the start area perpendicular to us, revealing portside blade work that left much to be desired. I harvested the observation, letting it fuel my mental aggression. *We will destroy them.*

Olympic qualification — the uncertainty of how it would go this time, the brutal voices in my head demanding resilience in the face of fear — dominated my thoughts by the time we hit the water again for the heat. Everything came too soon. Brian called the first hard twenty strokes before I had come to terms with the pain awaiting us. The five-stroke practice start, the ten-stroke start, then the over-rate fifteen — boom, boom, boom, hitting me like a boxer on the ropes, still reeling as the next punch lands. It was all in my mind, of course. My body behaved like a sled dog answering the call. A well-trained body resists a feeble mind, resents that it should be limited by one.

"Two minutes," rang out the voice from behind tinted glass in a structure that stretched out from shore and rose two stories above the water — central command in the aircraft control tower.

At last the boats were announced lane by lane. No words passed our lips; we instinctively rolled our seats into the starting position, the sound of rubber wheels underneath us gliding against the smooth wells of the tracks, the soft knock of oarlocks rotating and falling into position with the blade on the square, submerged. I sat breathing deeply with my left hand resting on my oar handle. It felt like a dried-up husk of corn; I'd scuffed it up impatiently with forty-grit sandpaper an hour earlier.

"Attention!"

The horn.

Will's round shoulders jerked and paused in slow motion once his blade locked onto the water. Was I behind already, or was Gibson in seven seat already ahead? Five more strokes. A rocket blasting off. Everyone holding their breath until the ship cleared the station. The feel was good: connected, strong, efficient. After only twenty strokes we began to inch ahead of the Dutch, and by the 500-metre mark we had three seats. Within the blur of effort I was faintly aware that the Dutch were racing their trademark race: ease into it, and then challenge late. Even as we moved away from them I grew irritated, knowing they weren't showing all they had. Surely, our gains would be short-lived and we'd be forced to give away some of our lead when it hurt most in the third 500 metres.

But this time was different. In the middle of the boat, an insatiable blade churned the water again and again. It wasn't the longest stroke, or the most powerful, but Malcolm's blade was unyielding. The effect was a solidity coming from five seat that encouraged the rest of us. It's much more motivating to add to a good thing than to fill in a deficiency.

Through the third 500, we took another half seat on the Dutch, stretching out to a half-length lead. By the time we entered the final stretch, our collective anticipation of victory spurned us on to the final sprint sequence: boost rate for three strokes, hold for four, repeat four times, then ten final strokes, submerging oneself in paralyzing lactic acid.

It was our second win in my short time with the crew — another heat — and it may as well have been the final for the vindication I felt at having suffered for a *reason.* The sky was cloudy, and wind whipped across my flushed cheeks. I coughed up stringy saliva from my throat and sucked oxygen into my windpipe, every breath like sandpaper. "Nice job, boys," surfaced here and there after some normalcy of breathing returned. A slap on the shoulder from Doug in two seat felt as affectionate and welcome as any physical contact I'd ever experienced. One more battle in the quest toward Olympic glory had gone our way.

44

Winning our heat gave us two days off before our semifinal race. The time off had allowed me time to visit my Aunt Beate's family, on my mom's side, who were returning to Germany from vacation and had stopped by for a quick visit. We sat on a patio beside the laneway that led up to the hotels where most of the rowers stayed. A steady stream of them passed behind us as we chatted. The last I had seen them all — Beate, my uncle Bearnd, and my cousins Timon, Janis, and Leonard — was when they had visited Canada in 2007. They found it surreal that, since then, I had started learning a new sport and randomly appeared on their vacation route home, participating in a World Championship event. My bald uncle Bearnd stared at me, processing the story as I told it.

"So you just decided this?" he said, unbelievingly.

From the moment I greeted them, they hadn't taken their eyes off me. They were in awe of the circumstances.

Bearnd continued: "You said, 'I'm going to become an Olympic rower,' and now two years later here you are in Bled, racing against the best in the world with the opportunity to qualify for the Olympics?"

This summary turned the hardest thing I would ever do in my life into some kind of bar story, something stripped of all the context and left with the thinnest possible plot line.

"Uh, yeah, I guess that's the gist of it," I said as the waiter came with our food.

My uncle Bearnd craned his neck towards me, like he couldn't make sense of me. "*Unglaublich*!" he said, reeling backwards.

We spent forty-five minutes chatting while my cousins took turns arm-wrestling me one at a time and then all together. I was an elite athlete in their eyes: strong, determined, unrelenting. I was their superhero older cousin. But little did they know how fragile my mental state was, or how I had mentally left the conversation several times to examine rowers out of my peripheral vision, trying to find weaknesses, trying to find something to exploit. I asked a few questions to change the subject away from rowing, but as my aunt and uncle relayed their family updates, my thoughts kept darting away to the semifinal ahead.

I was glad to finally say goodbye; my mental state was not conducive to being around family or friends. Their presence would be one more thing I couldn't control, their hope and encouragement more expectation I didn't need. Isolation was what I craved. I didn't want to resurface to a normal state of existence because it would take too long to get back to the callous mental state required to extract peak performance from my body. It was better to stay where I was mentally, as if in a cold, damp cave, rather than coming out and warming up against the good in life. I wanted to surface only for a fight to the death. I feared the carefree kid in me, the curious wanderer, the goofball looking for laughs. What got me to an Olympic qualifier was not the side of me that friends and family would recognize. It was an unhealthy determination to assert my will over my own feeble inclinations. It was an inner war that quietly waged on.

After two days of rest, the British took the place of the Dutch in our cross-hairs. We were in lane four for the semifinal, and they were in lane three on our port side. Beside the Brits were China and the Czech Republic, and rounding out the field to our starboard side floated Australia and France.

The scouting report from Mike told us that the French, Chinese, and Czechs would not pose a threat, but the Brits would be looking to stamp out any ambition of ours early on in the race. The Aussies also could not be discounted, having pushed the world-beating German crew right through the last quarter of their heat. This was the race that we couldn't screw up; a top-two finish meant a place in the final and automatic qualification for the Olympics.

As the last crews backed into their starting gates, my heart began thumping against my ribs. Time stretched itself out like usual.

"Czech Republic, China, Great Britain, Canada ..."

Quiet all scattered thoughts and turn yourself over to the trained response. Don't overthink.

"Attention!"

Someone in the crowd on shore shouted something — like the one fan who yells "Get in the hole!" after every tee shot by a PGA Tour golfer. I was so focused, the voice was garbled as if hearing it underwater.

Then the horn.

All reserves of adrenaline activated inside my body, bouncing around inside like electrons, everywhere and all at once. Summoning all physical and mental potential, sparks on the ends of every hair on my head.

An assembly line of water churners jolted against oars, taking up the slack, suspended for a moment, overcoming the inertia of putting a 1,800-pound vessel into motion.

We surged ahead with the Brits and Aussies, the three of us moving away from the rest of the field quickly. By the 500-metre mark, we were neck and neck. Our positions stayed the same for the second 500, but then things began to shift. Slowly, like tectonic plates separating, we moved ahead of the Aussies and the Brits crept ahead of us. In the critical third 500, the Brits asserted themselves and moved confidently into the lead. The Aussies were content to protect their third and Olympic-qualifying position against the rest of the field. I suppose we were content to also qualify in second behind the Brits.

As soon as we crossed the finish line, the veil of pain lifted and guilt washed over me. Win or lose, there was more to give — there always is. Mike was right: if you can row 2,000 metres in a given time, what the hell stopped you from rowing it a hundredth of a second faster?

"That's a step in the right direction," Andrew said, swinging his head around Conlin and Malcolm from six seat. "Olympics bound, boys." He sounded like he might offer us a tour of Lake Bled next. Heck, why not throw in a few 250-metre pieces on the way back to the dock for added benefit?

The pain in my body still gripped me, and I hated Andrew for his composure. I despised his ability to maintain form through the end of a 2,000-metre race and how quickly he found his voice afterward. *How did he recover so damn fast? Was he holding something back?* It's the oldest question that sits in the back of every rower's mind in any boat other than the single scull: Will my teammate do everything possible to hurt himself for our collective mission? *Would eight Jeremiahs have beaten eight Andrews today?*

For months, I thought Andrew was only giving 95 percent, but when I finally rowed the pair with him in training, I learned the truth. He was pulling fucking hard. The difference between us was how we manifested the will and energy required by the task. Andrew — the Olympic champion — derived his energy from a stolid inner focus that skipped past my antennae and went straight into his oar. I raged, cursed, rowed ugly, and fed off anger, which I sent through my oar, our boat, the water, the sky, inevitably collecting at Mike's launch. Maybe I could have learned from Andrew, but one year from the Olympics is no time to try to change your nature.

With second place in the semifinal, we had qualified the boat for the Olympics, yet our seats in the boat were far from secured. From outside the boat, and certainly within the Canadian national team, it appeared Mike had his eight guys. But we knew how easily our seat could be lost to a rival or an injury — a sentiment reinforced by Mike's race breakdown that evening back in the red-carpeted hotel meeting room.

"You backed off, didn't you?" he said, trembling with anger.

His thin lips barely moved as he spoke. Occasionally, he dropped his gaze bottom-right, as if deflecting the scolding of an old schoolmaster. I wondered what had happened in Mike's upbringing that accounted for certain mannerisms.

"You thought to yourselves, 'Well, we've got the qualifying spot, so that's enough,' didn't you?" he said.

Silence.

"Well, we're here to win, aren't we? You tell me: Are we here simply for a trip to the Olympics? For a nice vacation?"

He wrinkled the training program in his hands until the paper was soft as a blanket.

Finally, Rob spoke up: "No, Mike. I think we know what we're here to do."

"Then why aren't you doing it?" Mike snapped back. "Why did you let the British crew off the hook in the last two hundred and fifty metres instead of pushing them bloody hard until the end of the race?"

Rob stared back at him, speechless.

"You know, psychology is important. Do you think they're scared of us now?" Mike asked, pausing, then shaking his head in the negative. "No, they're more confident now because they know they can break your will."

A flash of anger — my will was the beginning and end of me.

"Right, then. Tomorrow you have a chance to correct it. You *can* beat the Brits and you *can* beat the Germans, but only if you row *bloody hard*!" he said, nodding in agreement with himself.

"Brian, the race plan, please."

More fans gathered around the bank for the final. Cyclists on the lakeside path straddled their bikes, waiting for the start. I glanced behind me — a mistake. The lane buoys stretched beyond sight, eventually swallowed up by mountains far off in the distance.

The warm-up had been good. Rob looked back at us from seven seat. "Let's fucking do this, boys," he said. I wished everyone would be quiet — Rob, the fans, the other crews, wished Richard Schmidt in the German crew, that bastard, would stop the three deep breaths and loud exhales he always produced as the crews were announced. Most of all, I wished the wind would stop. It had been building all morning and meant we were in for a bumpy ride. If it were up to me, all races would be indoors on flat water.

The thought of the coming pain made me angry and impatient. Why couldn't we all just jump out of our boats, swim ashore, and have fist fights until we knocked each other senseless?

Malcolm said something. I missed it. Then we were off.

The Germans went for it in the first 500, backstopped by the confidence that comes with having been undefeated for nearly two years. This was the last race of the season, and rumour had it their sponsor, Wilo Group, was paying strokeman Kristof Wilke and his teammates $75,000 for a win. The British had their sponsor, Siemens, plastered more prevalently across their chests than the Union Jack. On our chests? A humble maple leaf. But make no mistake, we were equals. Every man from all three of our countries had the opportunity to train full-time; it didn't matter whether it was on the equivalent of $65,000 U.S. per year (the British, thanks to their lottery funding) or on $16,000 U.S. per year (us, thanks to the people of Canada through government subsidy). In my opinion, so long as you could cover your basic cost of living, the field was equal.

As we crossed the 1,000-metre mark, a cross-headwind slammed into us, darkening the water with tight, curling ripples. I felt the wind creating lift under my blade, like an airplane wing. It always feels as though the wind is picking on your crew only, and two seats ahead of me in five I watched Malcolm glance over to his right, then left, making sure we hadn't lost three seats in one gust of wind. We hadn't, but the Germans were powering away from us and their bow had disappeared from my peripheral vision. One lane over the British were down two seats to us, but, to our vexation, the Aussies were leading us by a seat on our port side. Their grunts and shouts were audible over the churning of blades and barking of coxswains.

With 500 metres to go, the gusts of wind started slamming into us more frequently and with the worst kind of inconsistency — swooping down on us from port, then starboard, then head on, like an army of invisible phantoms. I was still learning to row, goddamn it. I didn't need this additional level of difficulty.

In the final 250 metres, the outcome was determined when one of the Aussies, as if my prayers had been heard, caught a huge crab. I couldn't see it. I was drilling two holes into Doug's back with a death stare, lost in my own private battle of not losing to myself, not letting down my teammates.

"Boys, we are moving on the Aussies right now. And we're closing on the Brits. Give me another seat!" Brian ordered, his white knuckles tightly gripping the gunwales.

The Aussies took another bad stroke, sending a plume of spray into the air. Then Malcolm almost lost his oar off the top of a wave, taking the next catch on an angle, and causing his blade to be sucked downward by the force of our speed. He fought it off, shortening his next stroke to get back in sequence. Five strokes later, Gabe's blade did the same thing. I couldn't feel my arms anymore. My brain was shrouded with lactic acid, and I had only enough mindfulness to keep pushing into the void.

The horn sounded once, then rapidly three more times. Germany, Great Britain, Canada, Australia. A few moments later, Poland, and finally the Netherlands. We'd taken the bronze. I was still trying to regain my vision when Andrew slapped me on the back and pulled at my unisuit in celebration. "Back on the podium!" he cheered. *Jesus, Andrew, how can you speak right now?*

As far as we had come as a team, as far as I had developed as an individual within our team, I drew no satisfaction from third place. I sensed that the British had been within range, and I burned thinking of Mike's words after the semifinal: *Do you think they're scared of you now? No, they're more confident now because they know they can break your will.*

PART FOUR: THE FINISH

You'll tell yourself, "I'm feeling grotty, I can't continue, I want to stop," but you can continue. The body lies. You know this feeling is coming, so prepare mentally for it. Don't listen to the body. Push through, and you'll find you can, if you're determined.

— Mike Spracklen, on pushing through the pain
45 seconds into a 2,000-metre rowing race

45

Amy worked quietly at spreading raspberry jam onto a slice of whole wheat bread. She and Ethan had made the trip back to Victoria in September 2011 for the start of Ethan's grade one school year. She looked down at her work preparing my lunch for the next day: two triple-decker peanut butter and jam sandwiches, a bagel with mayo and Black Forest ham, two protein bars, and two hard-boiled eggs. The three weeks off after Worlds had flown by, and the next day was our first back on the water.

Ethan had gone to sleep after only three warnings of punishment were he to get up again. Now I lay on our worn brown leather couch, not really reading a book. Amy worked deliberately under the kitchen pot lights, and I watched her over the top of my book.

Two and a half years had passed since we'd broken up, and she still made my lunches for me. We didn't talk much. Only the sound of jar lids tightening, knives chopping, and grocery bags rustling filled the silence. I feared at any moment she would decide enough was enough and declare that she was moving back to Ontario to be closer to the friends and family she missed so dearly. At the same time, the faint possibility that we would get back together hung in the air between us every day. It would have been easy to fall back into familiar territory. We'd been close for eight years; we had a wonderful son. She was beautiful, and I found myself leaving the condo with Ethan on Sundays to avoid the temptation that came with my testosterone level's recovering on our one day off. Things were in a delicate balance.

We resumed training, and on our fourth day back we were at Shawnigan Lake in two coxless fours. Although it was October of 2011, we were firmly in 2012. We operated on an August 2 year-end — the day of the Olympic final. But two hurdles remained before we could place singular focus on the Olympics: the National Rowing Championships in November, and the Lucerne World Cup II in May. Only a month away, the Nationals presented a vulnerability to attack from Terry Paul's small boat program — something not lost on Mike.

"We must perform well at Nationals. You know the score: if we don't perform well, we'll open ourselves to attack from the other rowers who will then want to be considered for the eight," said Mike.

"Peter Cookson has been working hard for us, and I think we can consider him an ally, but" — his voice dropping — "you know Phil Monckton has it in for me."

Phil Monckton was the vice-president of high performance at Rowing Canada, a powerful, broad-shouldered man. I'd felt small in his iron-clasp grip when we'd met briefly and shook hands in early 2011. He'd won a bronze medal in the 1984 Los Angeles Olympics and come fifth at the 1976 Montreal Olympics, both times in the quadruple sculls event. Years later, Brian Price told me Phil was pushing to keep me in sculling in early 2011 — something that would have made sense to most at the time, myself included — but Mike had fought back to give me the opportunity to become a sweep rower. As much as I resented Mike at the time, I had unknowingly been the beneficiary of his direct sponsorship.

The 2011 Nationals were held in Welland, Ontario, a short drive from Niagara Falls. When we arrived, snow flurries flew in every direction except down, tossed about by an icy wind. The rental car's thermometer read -2°C on our way to the hotel. The sight of my own breath made me realize I'd forgotten my pogies (rowing mitts with holes in the sides to slide your oar through).

After settling into our hotel, Andrew and I drove to the course to do a short 6-kilometre paddle. My oar was white with frost from the cross-country trip in the trailer, and after twenty strokes my hands turned a similar white.

I cursed into the back of Andrew's head from bow — something he was used to by now. "Don't worry about it," he said. "We'll get warm by the time we get to the start."

We glided down the canal, which was still being used by massive freight ships to bypass Niagara Falls and traverse the 99-metre vertical difference between the northern and southern terminus. The sight of Scott and Dave passing us in the opposite direction was a surprise as we entered the starting area. They had seemed a world away these past months. Two crews going in opposite directions get a good look at each other on account of facing backwards, and I watched Scott and Dave long and critically. They, along with the other small boat crews, had disappeared from our lives in early 2011, after the team was split in two. Terry Paul and Mike staggered their workouts so that neither training group was on either Elk Lake or Shawnigan Lake at the same time. When there was unavoidable overlap, the two groups would start their runs at opposite ends of the lake to avoid crossing paths. Mike saw them as the revolutionaries trying to overthrow his imperial claims to the lake and the way Canadian heavyweight men trained.

A couple of months after Derek O'Farrell had exited our program, I asked him how things were going. "Jer, it's a fucking dream come true. I don't hate my life every waking second for once. I actually enjoy training again," he'd said. Before the switch, his facial expression had perpetually resembled a child about to get a needle. The tense pulled-back lips and sunken cheeks had been replaced with a glowing smile. Their program was, well, liveable.

Do you want to be comfortable, or do you want to win? This is the question we hoped remained pertinent as we did Mike's bidding and drove ourselves into the ground every single day. If there was, in fact, a more tolerable path to an Olympic medal when it was all said and done, I would be consumed with something many orders of magnitude greater than what can be conveyed by the word "resentment."

At the moment, I resented my poor circulation to fingers and toes. That night my Saturday Night Finger swelled up to the point where I could bend it only halfway toward my palm. I dismissed it as another of many niggles, like the stubborn L3 and L4 joints our chiro regularly popped back into place in my back. We all knew our bodies were destined to be bags of problems, and mostly we got on with it, hoping one of our niggles didn't grow into a serious injury.

By the day of the finals, we had done the job — all of our pairs from the eight had made it through. All except Malcolm and Conlin, who were sidelined due to a dubious rib in Malcolm's expansive chest. They pulled out after the first heat as a precautionary measure, neither of them needing to prove themselves. Their physiological superiority lifted them out of the general burden of proof put on the rest us. Conlin took no solace in this fact. When Andrew and I boated for the final in gusting winds, Conlin stood in the boat bay, nodding at us and pacing around, dying to compete but without a partner. "Kick some ass, boys," he said.

The previous night, Doug and I had gleefully taken shots at Malcolm while sharing a ride to a restaurant for dinner: "The guy gets a little niggle, and he pulls out. Easy decision when you know you're going to get beat," said Doug. "What a prima donna," I'd said, laughing and wiggling my swollen Saturday Night Finger in front of my face. "Look at this fucking finger! Someone call the doctor!"

Doug had mastered the art of befriending you in the moment and then cutting off your legs when you weren't around. He was an averaging agent on our team; if you were having a good week, he'd go through his general ledger of missed workouts — sometimes stretching two months back — and administer "freshness" demerit points that, in his mind, overturned a string of workout wins that one might have been enjoying. If you were in a funk, struggling to keep up with the group in training, Doug would more often than not be the one to give you a boost at the end of the day: "It's just where your body is in the cycle. You'll turn the corner soon," he might say.

Little did I know, my swollen fingers would become a severe injury during the coming months and put my Olympic bid at risk. I would be a prime target for Doug's undermining takedowns. As sensitive as I was to the opinions of my brothers in the boat, I always perceived Doug's jabs in particular as attempts to put my character into question. Doug Csima: the Machiavelli of the Canadian men's eight.

It was wishful thinking that any of us might topple Scott and Dave in the pair event. We trained in a power event, the eight. The pair required more precision and finesse. In the eight we needed to meld together to heap power onto stroke after stroke. Boat feel was important, yet a fine oarsman like Scott Frandsen would make no substitute for a bucking bronco like Rob Gibson when it came to our event.

We entered the gates for the final with a blowing tailwind acting like a wind tunnel and grey clouds so low I could reach my oar straight up and penetrate them. On the horn, we shot ahead of everyone by a length in less than thirty strokes. We needed it to be a 500-metre race — then it would have been ours for the taking. After the first quarter, Scott and Dave started reeling us in with crisp, clean strokes. Their oars cleared the rough water, making it look effortless, while Andrew and I slapped the crests of waves moving in the same direction as us. We were at the mercy of the windswept current. It took three strokes to move through one swell, and ten more to move a few feet beyond it. The cold air scraped my windpipe. My race calls became hoarse and unintelligible.

"Harghhh!" [Hard!]

"Uh-hch!" [Again!]

"Ledgsh!" [Legs!]

Far over in lane one, Gabe and Will knocked us into third place. I became furious with how quickly my mindset fell, content to maintain third place. As a Spracklen soldier, I had capitulated in the worst possible way. Mike had trained us to be our own worst critics, and there I sat behind Andrew, wheeling back and forth on my carbon seat, with my fat ass poking through the holes, stuck between exhaustion and self-loathing for having let myself off the hook. *Goddamn it, the race is still on!* Even my masochism wasn't severe enough for my liking.

Once I cut myself down mentally, I moved on to Andrew. He'd stopped shouting encouragement after 1,000 metres. Were we in this together? Mike's oft-given warning echoed in my head: *Everyone reaches a point where they will stop trying.* I tried to learn what that point looked like for each of my teammates. What was their tell? It's in the body language; you see an inch lost on the shoulder drive at the finish, or a slight lag at the pickup of weight at the catch. Or perhaps it was all illusion at the hand of fatigue.

Scott and Dave won. They beat us all by so many boat lengths of open water that I can't recall the exact margin, only that we got beat badly. Perhaps a saving grace, Will and Gabe came second by a more respectable margin — not so far back that Scott and Dave's wake had disappeared before they dropped their blades in at the same spot, as was the case for me and Andrew. For Scott and Dave, it must have been sweet victory indeed, and a metaphorical punch to Mike Spracklen's gut.

The subplot of mutual detest between Mike and Scott and Dave, both of whom had rowed for Mike far longer than my time with Mike would amount to by the end of the London Games, was far beyond my reality. Combined, the two senior athletes had been rowing longer than I'd been alive. I was simply a visitor in their world, dropping in for a quick fuck-it-all-and-go-for-it. The truth is, I agreed with them. Mike did seem like a megalomaniac in the rowing world, and I admired them, based on disputable facts depending on who you spoke to, for standing up to Mike. On the other hand, I wouldn't base my opinion of Mike on heresy that floated around the boathouse. I was in the middle of a gamble, and I intended to see it through. I would continue to bet on Mike.

46

Christmas passed, and several more fingers on each hand joined my Saturday Night Finger in a permanent swell. I could barely keep a grip on my oar. When I finally gave in and showed Mike my problem, he said, "Yes, that's odd. I've seen the condition in many rowers before — rower's finger, we call it — but what's unusual is how long it's lasted like this."

His diagnosis brought no comfort. I started skipping the Monday afternoon 10-kilometre ergometer workout. Guilt and shame. To ride the Wattbike at the back of the room while your teammates slug it out on the erg is to rot in hell. I was accumulating so many freshness demerit points that even if we won the Olympics, Doug might have grounds to question the medal around my neck. Now my journey forward looked impossible because of … fingers.

Rest in Mike's environment meant weighing the potential consequences of losing your teammates' and coach's trust against the need to get healthy. "I take flak from Ken Shields for pushing the athletes too hard," Mike had said during one meeting, "but I create a training program that I believe gives you the opportunity to win, and it's up to you to manage your injuries appropriately. If you're sick, rest. If you're injured, take the time to heal." In other words, weighing the risk of further injury versus falling behind the group in performance was up to each individual. We understood that only the most severe injuries warranted a break from training. Some balk at this old-school approach, but sometimes you *do* need to tell yourself to suck it up. Other times, you must listen to your body's complaints and take the time to heal. An inability to do so, and suffering a major injury as a result, is a form of quitting.

So I found myself sitting on a big rolling ship headed to Vancouver on a Wednesday in late December. Amy was busy doing extra shifts at the Lululemon job she had begun that year to help out with the holiday rush, so I convinced Ethan it would be fun to come along. I told him we'd get to ride a big ship across the Strait of Georgia to visit Daddy's doctor, who was also the Vancouver Canucks' team doctor.

Ethan, now five years old, sat beside me reading *The Lord of the Rings* — a book I couldn't get through in high school. His eyes flicked across the page, devouring paragraphs in hungry chunks. Occasionally, he moved his lock of blond bangs to the side, picked his nose, or pulled his legs up underneath him, all while staying locked to his position on the page. Books were his portal to another world, and watching him read gave me an urge to rest my big wounded paw on his head and say, "Good boy. I love you."

Dr. Wilkinson's office was located in the University of British Columbia laboratory building, beside a red dirt track. We arrived early, so I sprinted off down the 100-metre straight, yelling back, "Whadaya got, boy?" Ethan whooped with joy and took off after me. He hung in for 500 metres before slowing to a walk with his hands on his hips, overcome by his all-or-nothing child pacing. I kept running, putting in six laps at a brisk pace, ignoring Ethan's complaints of boredom until Dr. Wilkinson's sleek Audi pulled into the parking lot.

Inside, Dr. Wilkinson went over the procedure with me in his soft South African accent. The building was quiet and mostly empty on Saturdays. The sound of his rummaging through cupboards for necessary supplies put me in a trance, my heart still thudding from running. He had a soothing voice, a pitch and timbre refined over years of treating anxious patients. I learned what I was in for through what he told Ethan. Daddy was going to get a little poke from a needle to take some blood. Then the blood would be mixed up in a special mixing machine (centrifugation), and finally, Daddy would get a few more pokes in his fingers to put the healing blood (platelet-rich plasma) back into the sore spots. Ethan, my acting guardian, stood beside me with half his face buried into my shoulder. He was in awe of Dr. Wilkinson, the Vancouver Canucks' team doctor who referred to the NHL superstar Sedin twins as Danny and Hank.

I forced a smile for Ethan's sake as Dr. Wilkinson inserted the plasma deep into my Saturday Night Finger, which now looked like it'd had one fun Saturday night too many. He'd left out a few details in his story to Ethan: first, that he would insert the needle multiple times in each finger, down to the bone and deep into my palm; and second, that the freezing had no effect when the needle sliced through tendons. "This may sting a bit," he said with a genuinely troubled look, long after it had started to sting. It felt like my finger might pop from the pressure of the thick plasma filling the area. "Daddy's getting a little bee sting," he reassured Ethan. "Nothing too nasty." Ethan had had enough of seeing me impaled and decided to go back to the *Sports Illustrated* magazine he'd started reading in the waiting area.

Winter wore on unremarkably but for the slowly building sense that time was hurdling us towards the final judgment: the Olympics. Only our weekly meetings punctuated the monotony of training. There, Mike would talk over the program and ask us for our input, though he never changed anything that went against his fundamental coaching philosophy. Any well-disguised objections by the crew were met with glazed responses, as though Mike were simply the messenger of irrefutable truth relayed to him from a higher power. He was the oracle, the sensei, the rowing mystic at the mercy of his gift.

Watching film of us training was like getting teeth pulled. Mike once tried to make an example of two eights that were training side by side. The boats were being filmed from the launch on an angle from behind on starboard side. Mike had said, "Watch how the eight on the left surges through the other eight when they respond to my 'hold the finish' call." Sure enough, the one boat appeared to surge ahead, but the surge was due to the launch, with the cameraman speeding up and closing the angle, not a superhuman hold-the-finish call.

Nothing sent Mike scooching up on the edge of his chair more than slow-motion video. I could almost see his tail wag as he pointed out our technical flaws with his laser pointer. The sharp red dot wavered in his hands and made your heart flutter if it danced too close to your frozen image on the screen. Sometimes Mike would start critiquing one of us in slow-motion footage while we were turning the boat around for the next piece, or after he had called us down in the workout and we were hunched over in exhaustion: "See, *see,* look at the erratic path of your hands!"

"Mike, we're turning the boat around for the next piece there."

"Well, you should maintain good form at all times."

Other times, while watching slow-motion playback, Mike would compare our body positions with our blade entry. His point was that the blade should be inserted at the catch before the body starts moving forward, or you're missing water. The principle is fine, but I think he forgot he was watching it in slow motion after fifteen minutes, because it was like he expected the slow motion athlete to act in real time. You can spend years honing your technique but you will always use some slide length while your blade is entering the water, or else you'll check the run of the boat.

Mike was what analog is to digital; art is just the stuff science hasn't caught up with, and just as some gap will always exist between what we can and can't know empirically, there will always be leaders like Mike to bridge the gap. Sports scientists can point to all the ingredients that make up a gold medal athlete, but they still can't deliver one. Mike could deliver one, but looking back I'm not sure if the reasons he thought he was successful were truly what was behind his success. I always thought, behind the twitching face delivering the sermons on technique, it was Mike's honing of his intuition over decades that brought him success.

Sometimes when the training was particularly tough, we would curse at each other. It was rare for someone to curse directly at Mike on or off the water, but it happened occasionally. One time, Mike came into the dressing room after Monday morning training holding a letter from a concerned lakeside jogger who was complaining about the profanity bellowing across the lake.

"Jerry," Mike started, "why aren't you able to control yourself? Are you an *asshole*? Is that what it is?" He thrust the letter towards me. My mind was still scrambled from the pain of the open-rate workout that had just ended. I jumped off the bench and took two stomping lumberjack steps toward him. "You're goddamned right I'm an asshole, and so are you!" I shouted. Mike gulped and stepped back, his face turning a shade of yellow similar to the change room walls. I continued: "I'm putting every-fucking-thing I've got into your workouts, so don't come at me with this fucking bullshit."

"Very well, Jerry," Mike said, smiling sheepishly, suddenly realizing he had entered the cage of a provoked animal. "I'll see you at eleven o'clock for the next row." He turned and hurried out to the safety of his Acura TL, where I imagine he locked his doors and took a few deep breaths.

I looked at my teammates. Gabe was lying in the corner with his head resting against the concrete block wall. "Gotta hand it to you, Jerry. Not too many people can pull that off with Mike," he said, laughing. "He shit his pants." Malcolm had a huge grin on his face. "Man, that whole time I was thinking, 'Jerry is going to punch Mike in the face, and Mike is going to die.'"

The truth is, Mike liked it when guys started to crack and lose their tempers. It was a sign that his program was working.

During one week of self-immolating intensity, Mike actually added cursing into the program.

"If you want to curse, then we will get it out of your system by allotting time for cursing at the start of the workout," he said.

So, with the steam rising off our backs after the next Monday morning warm-up, Mike had Brian announce over the PA on his launch, "Thirty seconds of cursing … ready, go!"

Getting advice from Mike Spracklen during a tough week of training.

At this, a year's worth of resentment and anger vulcanized inside of me. Most of the guys screamed "*FUUUCK!*" straight up into the air, like a pack of howling wolves, but I pointed directly at Mike with a glare you could walk on and hurled the nastiest expletives I could muster at the source of my frustration. I don't think Mike expected such a direct attack. Cursing was subsequently taken out of the program, and no doubt Mike received letters from a few more concerned citizens who'd been jogging along the lakeside trail that morning.

Those were dark times. I was in such a black hole physically and mentally. I felt trapped between the present and greener pastures that lay beyond the Olympics: the place where trips to Italy meant soaring off cliffs under the inflated wing of a paraglider, not rowing like a Greek slave under the scorching sun.

At the end of the day, I would often drive home guilt-ridden about how I had treated my teammates, particularly Brian, who took a lot of abuse from all of us. I realize now that I wanted to be allowed to fail. Mike was an enigma to all of us, and he didn't allow us to take our foot off the gas for one instant. Under Mike, you could never say you didn't work hard enough if, in the end, you didn't achieve your Olympic dreams. You could say that you should have done things differently, or maybe you succumbed to injury or suffered other setbacks at inopportune times. But you could never say you didn't work hard enough. When the going got tough, when I felt paralyzed because the oxygen couldn't reach my bloodstream fast enough to supply my burning muscles, I wanted to be let off the hook. Mike simply wouldn't allow it. Instead, he fostered an environment in which you had to prove to yourself and your teammates every day that you belonged in the boat. I can look back now and see how that kind of environment pulled the best athletes out of us, but in the moment it just felt like hell.

47

In our last Sacramento camp before World Cup II, Mike switched me and Rob in the eight. I went to seven seat, and he went to three seat. Brian later told me that Mike had planned it all along going into 2012.

Seven seat, at first, felt like being transported back into the single three years earlier, with pontoon training wheels fixed to my bow. Rowing with six rowers behind and only one in front takes more confidence than rowing in three seat, where you can see the rhythm as much as feel it. I had memorized every unique biomechanic motion of the men in front of me, of our starboard blades sweeping through the air and how they entered the water; Rob's blade stabbing it like a murderer, Malcolm's gulping it like a sperm whale; how Doug, in front of me, started shooting the slide as he got tired about the same time I'd start opening too early with my back. All subtle shadings in a sketch of near synchronicity that I relied on to find my own place in the equation.

"All right, Jer, just like in the pair, bro," said Will before the first pyramid workout, now directly in front of me. I felt disconnected from the rest of the boat as we geared up to speed. My strokes were rushed, the water heavy like concrete mix. Mike had coached us to imagine picking up the weight of the boat off the man in front of you; a slight anticipation allows eight blades to enter the water at the same time. "If you don't do it, you'll make it awfully heavy for stroke and seven," Mike would say. Now I understood.

By the time the afternoon wind lapped up the surface of the snaking Lake Natoma in Rancho Cordova, Brian had taken us up to thirty strokes per minute and I was exhausted from over-anticipating the catch and not allowing the guys to get in a hair before me. To use one of Mike's favourite metaphors, if four people each grip one corner of a heavy slab and lift at slightly different times, the slab won't budge, but if everyone lifts at the same time, it will rise effortlessly. Mike was full of rudimentary physics metaphors that made me feel like a frustrated third-grader. *What about the vector of the applied force? What about the differences in application of force on the way up?* If the humans in his metaphors weren't robots with hydraulic pistons for arms and legs, that was their fault.

The next day, with a shiver of sadness while turning the boat onto the course for the first piece, I gave up thinking so hard and let myself slip into my subconscious. The boat taught me what to do. It was a breathing beast, surging and gliding underneath me, back and forth like the pendulum on my old piano teacher's analog metronome. Unlike metronomic time, however, our rhythm was a groove — human, ebbing and flowing, with constant miniscule corrections. Find it, keep it; lose it, seek it. Micro-adjustments, each stroke getting closer to truth and justice, starboard and port becoming one oar. When done well, the feeling is like adding power to a bicycle that's flying down a steep hill — a generous feeling, like the boat can only go faster.

The next day, we hit race pace. The day after, we stretched the rate to fifty strokes per minute and I survived in my new seven seat — no giant crab ejecting me out of the boat, no oar impaling Will's freckled back. Even the constant unsolicited coaching from Andrew, who had moved from four seat to behind me in six, abated. When Rob let out a "Fuck yeah, Jer!" from his new place in three seat, I knew Mike had made the right move.

Winter carried into spring in a way that found me startled by the thought of the biggest test still being in front of us, not behind us, with the mountain of work we'd bored our way through. "Medals are won in the summer but earned in the winter," I had once heard Kyle Hamilton, the stroke of the 2008 gold medal eight, say. If it were down to sheer force of will spread out over the previous six months of cold and grey and petulance, then I figured we had all earned a gold medal, and this business of having to go and win it seemed an unfair last step.

The explosion of spring roused my fight-or-flight circuitry, like millions of monarchs awakening from their chrysalides and taking flight in my gut. Perhaps every athlete taking on the world loves and is addicted to the sense of foreboding that builds on approach to the Big Contest.

Every time I would lie on our sports therapist's massage table to get my back cracked, or to relieve strains in my intercostal muscles, I found myself slipping into the same dreamy contemplation of my position. Thoughts swam freely for a while before spiralling into a vortex, with the pointy end concentrated on Mike Spracklen. Resentment had been building over the past seventeen months against the man I had determined was my best shot at an Olympic medal. I wondered if I would survive him.

48

World Rowing Cup II, May 2012. While walking over the cold marble floors of the hotel lobby in Lucerne, mid-rear in the pack of my rowing brethren — all of us decked out in red, white, and black unisuits that pressed our genitals against our bodies like freeze wrap — it appeared, by the angle of the rain, that the world had been turned on its side.

We stepped through the sliding glass doors. I swung my backpack over my shoulder only to have it hit me in the face, courtesy of the wind gusting from the north. Mother Nature was blowing hard that day — all exhale and bottomless lungs.

A few days earlier, we'd finished in Erba with a race simulation 2-kilometre time trial in the eight. Mike didn't prescribe them too often, in acknowledgement of the pain we were expected to endure to produce an accurate measurement of our speed. It had taken the same Big Race mental energy to keep my nerve while stepping off the Hotel da Vinci's wide-tiled terrace that morning and piling in the van with my eight quietly breathing teammates. Five minutes, thirty seconds was the time we produced. According to Malcolm, the water density was different in Lake Erba than in the waters cradling the hulls of crews winning World Cup and World Championship races in the low 5:20s. Apparently 5:30 was a good enough time on the stickier waters of Lake Erba in May.

We caught the 10:05 a.m. express from the hotel. The wind pushed the bus toward one side as if permanently lowered for wheelchair access. I watched the road, its wet black asphalt intersections painted with so many green, red, yellow, and white road markings, twisting and turning and dashing in organized chaos.

Alternating downpours of sideways rain and hail sent financiers and watchmakers (and whoever else had reason to work in downtown Lucerne) scrambling for cover with folded newspapers and trench coats pulled over their heads to fend off the marble-sized ice pellets. I wondered if it would start to hail down on us during our race and blind us. I needed to watch Will's back to help me anticipate slight changes in the rhythm. Every race came with an unexpected challenge. Today it would be rowing with eyes closed.

As we neared our stop, the thunderhead clouds broke enough for some sun to cut through in isolated golden staffs, but the wind raged on.

Two British heavyweight male rowers who'd made the trip with us got off first and walked ahead. They were dressed in elaborate Team GB warm-up suits, with lion's head logos wrapping around their upper bodies. The lion had a red-and-blue-striped mane, and it stuck out its red tongue at us. *I'll rip that tongue out of your mouth*, I thought.

The British were staying at the same hotel as we were. Crossing their paths in the grand foyer on the way to our separate breakfast rooms set my jaw rigid. I hated them, hated their respectful air (seemed condescending), their pleasantries (as if we weren't going to war in mere days or hours), their de facto sense of entitlement (as if the Germans' dominance was all very much a nuisance only they could put right). I made sure when I met their glances I had ferocity in my eyes. Let them suffer any consternation I could evoke.

When we got to the long flight of stairs that took us from the street above down to the Rotsee racecourse, the drone of the race announcer's voice came into focus. His pitch was elevated with excitement. The British four had just set a new world record in their heat. I knew the British four were the best in their boat class (strongly challenged at times by the Aussies), and I ascribed their record to the depth of talent in their boat. Our eight was making progress. We had another season of training under our belts and were eager to see how our speed would stack up against the rest of the field before the Olympics.

Brian managed the strong, straight tailwind during the warm-up like an annoyed old captain who'd seen similar conditions before, commanding starboard to hold and ports to pick at the water between turns. The tailwind gave him less time to work with travelling downwind and much more time than usual going into the wind. The rowing felt like sledding — walking uphill, and then sliding back down with the wind at our backs.

These were world record conditions. The best time in the eight was held by the Americans, who had broken the record of the defending 2003 world champion Canadian crew (also coached by Mike) in the opening heat of the 2004 Athens Olympics eight years prior.

Rowing with the wind is most effective with a relaxed upper body and a very quick catch. Rowing against it requires added attention to tapping down at the finish in order to get good blade height to clear the waves. A firmer grip to control the oar on the recovery is also required (the wind was so strong that day that I had to use my wrists as well as my fingers just to feather the blade). Though you still need enough relaxation to absorb the shock from hitting the odd wave with your oar.

Brian encouraged us going into the wind: "Nothing stops us. Fight through it!" Our final twenty-five-stroke start, with the wind at our backs, was blistering fast. We were on form and ready to go.

The British were on our right, eyes ahead, the murmur of their coxswain audible between our own coxswain's instructions. "Remember, clean finishes in these conditions," Brian said. The Polish began shouting their customary battle cries, but I was too busy being pleased with the feeling of consistent pressure against the face of my blade to notice. The water pushed against our blades, threatening to rip us from the grip of the boat holder who was struggling to keep us in the gate. My husked up wooden oar handle pressed into my fingers — just enough pressure for the elevated grains to crush and grip against the padded hide of my fingers. We hadn't even started, and I already had a lock on the water. A gift.

What happened next was magical. The wind had blown all the clouds away, and the sun lit up the waves with dazzling light, bouncing off the water into my eyes, against the boat, against Will's red spandex.

The starting official began calling us out, and as I rolled my seat forward with Will, the pressure of the river running against my blade keeping my body taut, like a rat trap ready to pop.

"Attention!"

Every muscle, tendon, and joint was a loaded spring.

The horn.

The first stroke was a home run swing. The boat shot out of the gates. The next stroke was another home run, and the next, and the next. Metaphorical major league baseball records were falling by the second, and the rowing world record, the thought not daring to cross our minds, was within reach inside ten strokes.

I have a theory that the rest of us finally fit into Rob's power curve that day. The water was moving so fast, we could finally keep up with him through the drive. Every single stroke felt like flashes of brilliance we'd experienced in training but were never able to sustain. *Shoomp, shoomp, shoomp*. The boat was as stable as a train barrelling down its tracks. With each new puddle of water sent from our blades, we moved on the British. They and the rest of the field struggled with the conditions while we took flight. I worried we would derail at any moment — a sneaking suspicion that stayed nibbling at the root of my confidence even as it grew. We were thieves stealing perfection. Surely we would be discovered and the watery beast beneath us would send us hard onto port, furious with our gall to attempt perfection on its roiled back.

"Yeah, boys!" Conlin yelled from four seat.

With 500 metres to go, we had open water on the Brits. They threw themselves at their oars with aggressive strokes, as if they were in an airtight room, using up precious oxygen and slamming their bodies against the wall in desperation. Every now and then one of them struck a wave, sending a spray of white into the wind. Seeing an opponent struggle normally filled me with opportunistic hunger (often triggering the *Mortal Kombat* throaty-voiced "Finish him!" command in my head), but this time I was nearly tranquil. The pain was somehow tolerable for once. It didn't seize and rush through my body unpredictably. It travelled slowly up my quads at a pace that I knew would leave my head — my consciousness — above the worst of the lactate, when usually I was already three leagues beneath it.

"Boys, you're putting on a heater today. Keep on rolling!" said Brian.

Shoomp, shoomp, shoomp. It was too easy.

"All day!" Rob yelled out in the final 200 metres.

"Just keep it right here, boys," Brian said calmly.

There was no need to sprint. We crossed the line comfortably to win the heat. Only then, after rowing it out for a few strokes, did Brian break the news.

"That's a world best time: 5:19.35!"

"Holy shit, Brian," Doug boomed gleefully. "We didn't even sprint. We should have sprinted, should have padded the record!"

"Guys, remember it's just the heat," Malcom said, "but that's pretty awesome."

When we reached the dock, I felt eyes watching us, as warriors might be watched returning from a battle of impossible odds. Exhilarating. Three years earlier, in May of 2009, I was still floundering on the surface of Elk Lake in my single like an injured Canada goose unable to take off. Now I was one of a privileged group of nine men who, together, had travelled across 2,000 metres of water faster than any other man-powered vessel in the history of humanity. (This particular description took some time to arrive at, and is the one I used to remind Ethan of my demigodliness, up until the Germans broke our record five years later.)

Later that afternoon, I sat on the carpeted floor of Mike's ritzy hotel room. Long white curtains covered the walkout to a balcony wrapped in black wrought iron railings. The wind had died down and now gently swept the curtains inward at their base, where Will sat cradling his knees, his red Oakleys propped above his forehead.

While we waited for Mike, Brian said he'd received a congratulatory email from Kyle Hamilton, who, in addition to leading his crew to gold in Beijing, had rowed two seat in the 2004 Athens eight that had lost to the Americans in their heat (a race that also saw the Americans break the world record). That race had rattled the Canadian crew, who were the two-time defending world champions and who had gone on to a crushing fifth place finish in the Olympic final.

"We heard from Kyle, did we?" Mike said, smiling as he entered the room.

Mike was extremely proud of Kyle, a rower who had gone from a stretch to make the boat in 2004, to team captain in 2008, rowing stroke seat. When I'd watched Kyle lead a relentless attack during the Olympic final in 2008, I had been struck by how unflinching his face was underneath his hat, sunglasses, and thick goatee. Only a slight parting of his lips to breathe and the occasional teeth-baring snarl revealed that he was not, in fact, a machine.

"Yes, Kyle was a great leader and oarsman." Mike sighed, looking past us into memory.

We all looked at each other, smirking. One of Derek O'Farrell's best skits was embellishing Mike's frequent usage of Kyle as a role model for the rest of us:

> **FADE IN: MEN'S LOCKER ROOM – DAY**
> MIKE is giving a speech to his crew moments before their Olympic final race.
> **RISING ACTION:** KYLE HAMILTON calls MIKE.
> **MIKE:** "Oh, hellloooooo, Kyle … What's that? No, no, no, I'm not busy a'tall."
> MIKE holds his hand over the receiver and mimes the words "*It's Kyle!*" to the blank, blinking faces of his crew, then gets up and leaves the room, chatting away like a teenage girl.

We began the meeting by giving Mike our perspective on the race, one by one.

"I don't know how to describe it," Rob said. "It felt effortless."

"Yeah, it was dialed in."

"The finishes were crisp. Catches were biting spot-on."

"Smooth and effortless. It made you want to apply more and more power."

And so on.

What do you say after a world record performance? The way forward was simple: *Okay, now go do it again in the final.*

In closing, Mike warned us not to get too excited. He cast a sideways glance my way. "The last thing we need is for one of you guys to go out to the bar tonight and get drunk, or do something to put the crew's performance in jeopardy." I wondered if some of my guilty teammates had manipulated Mike's memory, making him think it was me who had thrown a beer bottle and shattered a hotel window after a 2009 World Cup; that it was me who had damaged business signage in Bled in 2011 after failing to hurdle them in a drunken sprint, returning to the hotel with half a wooden sign in hand. Malcolm shot me a look from across the room like a sibling gleeful that I was unfairly under suspicion by father. I felt caught between laughter and offence.

Two well-behaved days later, we sat in the gates, ready for the final to begin. To our port in lane three, Kristof Wilke, the German stroke, slapped his thighs and exhaled forced breaths that sounded like a cat coughing up a hairball. The rest of his crew glared straight ahead. Anger showed on their faces. With our world record performance, two seconds faster than their winning time in the second heat, we had undoubtedly injected a dose of fear into the Germans. I recognized the fear in their body language. It was the kind of fear that I woke up with most days in the pit of my stomach; the kind of fear that slowly rises up your sternum as the race gets closer; the kind of fear that must be doused with anger and displaced by violent physical output.

We had lost some of that fear. We talked about taking nothing for granted, about forgetting the world record all together, but a sense of superiority had seeped in all the same. And so we were in for a rude awakening.

The water was flat, with gentle ripples. Mike once said that ripples were better than a glass-smooth surface. It allowed some air underneath the hull and reduced the surface tension as the boat cut through the water.

To the Germans' port, the Brits twitched, fiddled, arched their backs and stuck out their chest to make room for deep breaths; all little movements that revealed the nervous energy bubbling inside them. Beyond the Brits were the Dutch, and beyond them sunbathers lay on beach towels above the giant *S-A-M* of the blue Samsung sponsor banners lining the first hundred metres of the course.

The first stroke was not good, nor was the tenth or twentieth or hundredth. Gone were the smooth train tracks beneath us, and in their place tension and weight. Our oars caught like a pile of loose change hitting pavement instead of one unified stroke. I still don't know if the reason was due to complacency or too much determination not to be complacent.

By 1,000 metres we were in third place behind the Germans, followed by the Brits. Now we were angry, but too late and in the wrong way. Our eight bodies separated and came back together on carbon seats like Slinkys, rushing then catching up. The Brits, through sheer indignation with us perhaps, had moved firmly into second position and nearly drawn level with the Germans through 1,500 metres. We tried harder, but continued losing inches. Brian's race calls took on a bleating tone as we ran out of course. "Come on, boys, we can't wait. I need power with legs down. Ready, *now*!"

To no avail. The world record heat was a distant vague dream, elusive and teasing. To make matters worse, we still had to burn ourselves down to the wick to hold off the Dutch for the bronze. The lactate phantom clung to the base of my skull, stretching its tentacles around every muscle in my body and making my face hot with blood rush. The crowds cheered early as Germany and then Great Britain crossed the line a few moments before us. We held on for the bronze. Unconsciousness would be better than the pain — if only I could go hard enough to black out entirely.

Our hotel rooms were quiet holding cells as we packed for the trip home. There would be no drunken celebrations involving broken hotel windows, or boarding the bus to the airport with half a business sign in hand. Only thoughts of missed opportunity and what lay ahead for us at the Olympics two months away.

49

I missed Ethan terribly, but appreciated the solitude that I needed to focus on training. Julia came to live with me again, spending most of her time out of the condo socializing with her friends. In the evenings after a day of pulse-blasting, intestine-churning training, I'd sit at my kitchen island half awake in a training fog, feeling the warm tingling blood ooze through my limbs to begin repairs, silence ringing in my ears.

I felt lonely, but relieved for the break from fatherly duties — extreme, penetrating guilt accompanying that relief. Being away from Ethan would be fine had we managed to keep the nuclear family structure together, the model burnt into me all my life by my dad as the only way to prevent having a dysfunctional family — not able to understand that dysfunction is found in all family structures. At some point Amy would move on, get married, have more kids. The thought of another man in my son's life filled me with nausea and sent wild worst-case scenarios running through my head on infinite repeat.

Ethan and Amy had travelled back to Ontario after his birthday in May, where Amy had home-schooled him for the remainder of the school year while running her camping and trailer park resort up north on Lake St. Peter. Amy and I were both hard on ourselves, both determined to make Ethan know that we still cared about each other and loved our bright six-year-old more than ever. It's their parents' time that kids need most, and I was giving nearly all of mine to rowing.

The Olympics, the apogee of this journey, now started entering my mind regularly again — the first time since I'd forced myself to shelve the dream in the first months of full-time training. It had been necessary to expel the big picture in order to stay focused on the daily incremental steps that would get me there. Now, the peak jutted back into my mind's eye, looming large, almost within reach. It was like looking down a long dark tunnel with the faintest light flickering at the end, the cold wet walls ready to collapse at any time. I wanted time to collapse in on itself and put me on the Olympic start line right then and there.

June 2012: The ocean air drifting over from Cordova Bay, carrying the scent of salt water. The sun high over Elk Lake, alighting sparkles upon the water and drying out our soggy bones. I knew I would make it now. Barring an act of God, I would go to the Olympics. What a dangerous thought. Soon, the right to call oneself an Olympian. An *Olympian.* Incredible. Dangerous.

Dangerous, because to embrace the goal three weeks before we left for our pre-Olympic training camp in Italy was to court complacency. Going to the Olympics created a dichotomy of never thinking I was good enough and simultaneously believing that I was. Knowing not to quit all those days in Mike's furnace because maybe — however slim the possibility — I would make it. Maybe there *was* a champion in me. That was worth fighting to the death for.

Tension rose in each of us. On June 28, the Canadian Olympic Committee held a press event to announce our selection to the Olympic team. We shuffled around on gravel outside the east boat bay, clad in black Team Canada jackets with the Canadian Olympic Team logo over our hearts. While the photographer tried to get us all in the frame, I stood briefly in the front row. "For once in my life, I'm not hiding in the back for the picture," I joked, before shuffling to the back.

The next day, nearing the end of another tough singles workout, Rob and I started having at each other on the water. At first, I thought we were cursing each other over one of the usual spats: waking down the guy behind you, rating high on a controlled stroke rate piece, or taking off from the start of the piece a split second early. "Fuck you, Jerry, you motherfucker," said Rob. "There's no 'I' in 'team,' asshole!" For every F-bomb Rob hurled my way, I responded with two of my own. We were like chest-puffing sixth graders lacking the vocabulary to put together proper insults, stringing together sentences with the word *fuck* as subject and predicate.

Rob and I had never had an altercation that lasted beyond the workout in which it began. The same went for all of us in the eight. Ninety-nine percent of the time, what happened on the water stayed on the water. Soon after docking, the rage from just minutes earlier would dissipate and usually end up in a laugh by the time we hit the showers. This time, Rob was having nothing to do with me.

I asked Doug what the hell was going on when we got back to the dressing room. "It was your comment about being in front for the team pic yesterday," Doug said.

Tension was higher than ever with the Olympics so close, and Rob had taken my stupid joke to heart.

Fuck him, I thought. I left the boathouse and drove home to ice my hands, eat, nap, and get ready for the third session of the day.

The negative energy was still in the air at the end of the final workout, and Rob and I still weren't talking. My mind had cooled off, finally ready to consider the situation during the drive home that night. I realized I'd been too dismissive of my comment even if I did think it was harmless. Earlier in the season, we'd have moved past it without needing to talk about it. But it was too close to the Olympics to allow needless conflict to continue if it could be solved with an apology.

I diverted my course home and headed to Rob's house, a rented upper floor wedged into the Cordova Bay hillside, with a view of the Georgia Strait. "Mr. Jerry Brown," Rob said with a smile, as he moved some garbage away to open the front door. Maybe he wasn't as pissed off as I'd thought. "Look, I'm sorry about the comment the other day," I said. "I came here to put it behind us."

"Consider it done," Rob said, stretching out his hand. I clasped it.

"We good?"

"Yeah, we're good, buddy."

He poured me a glass of water, and we spent the next twenty minutes talking in his kitchen while peering out over the rough ocean waters. We talked about the media interviews, the buildup, the attention of those outside the rowing world slowly catching up with us.

Far off in the distance, Mount Baker rose above a thin line of clouds. Beyond Mount Baker, 7,500 kilometres away, the waters of Dorney Lake lay calmly waiting for us.

50

The plane shot through the sky. I bent my neck down to look out the oval window at the blanket of clouds floating underneath us. When my neck got sore, I concentrated on time. Moments piled upon moments. The Games were close enough for me to finally sense time sifting away for good — perpetually about to race, about to take the stage, waiting to perform. It was as if there was a rough whisper coming from somewhere behind me, saying, *The Olympics are coming. Here come the Olympics. Don't fuck it up. The Olympics. Once in a lifetime. Never again. Never again. The fucking* Olympics.

I talked to myself: two voices — one mostly quiet, the other loud and relentless. On my face I was gone, silent, spaced out. But my mind raced with negative self-talk. The voice told me I wasn't good enough. It told me there was so much that could go wrong with nine men in a boat — equipment malfunctions, ribs breaking at the wrong time … ribs! One hundred and ninety-two ribs in our boat. No doubt one of them would snap in the Olympic final. And how about danger from other crews? In the 2008 men's eight heat, the Australian rudder broke and sent them veering into the Canadians' lane, nearly ramming into them. Brian had seen it coming and narrowly avoided disaster.

The plane began descending into Frankfurt. The clouds got closer and closer, then enveloped us. Out the window was all fog — the kind Mike might elect to row through despite the poor visibility. I played superstitious games I hadn't played since I was a kid: If we hit turbulence, we'd win a medal. If we bumped hard on landing, we'd finish dead fucking last. If we broke through the clouds in exactly ten seconds, we'd win the gold. My eardrums popped — an omen?

51

Frankfurt to Erba. Erba to the U.K. Italy came and went. Muscles flexing and releasing, sweaty backs, hungry strokes. Andrew trying to kidnap me in our hotel room so that I couldn't go for my evening walks. Me telling him it was part of my training, that I needed the walks to keep my sanity.

All in all, I'm not sure if we even touched down in Italy. In a blink we were back in the air, headed to London.

52

When we arrived in London it had just stopped raining after weeks of downpour. We piled into an airport shuttle van and drove from Heathrow International Airport to Eton Dorney over moist earth steaming in the hot sun. It was warm and sunny with clear skies when we stepped out of the van. There was a lazy, late-summer feeling in the air that seemed at odds with the most important competition of our athletic lives being a few days away.

A brief walk in the surrounding neighbourhood revealed row after row of empty streets lined with rusty-red brick houses, all with the same square dimensions and brown-tiled roofs, orderly and plain. We were staying in Slough, England, and it was just as bland as the name sounds.

That night the air conditioner in our room wasn't working, and the heat of the day sat flush in my cheeks. I lay in my bed wide awake, flipping my pillow to the cool side every ten minutes, getting hotter and more stressed out over losing sleep. I listened to the air conditioner blow my own fumes back at me while Andrew purred away. In the morning I demanded that we get a different room. The hotel attendant spoke like an automated phone system, telling me someone from maintenance could have a look at the air conditioner the following day. I leaned in close, sounding like the pretentious patron of a five-star hotel: "You will fix our air conditioner right now or give us a different room immediately. Where's your manager?"

They sent a maintenance guy up to tinker with the machine, but hours later it was still blowing hot air. I asked Heather, our athletic therapist, to switch rooms with us. She was unenthusiastic. "Try it again tonight. It should be cooler than last night. If it's still bad, we'll switch," she said.

I wanted to unleash the worst of me on her, to tell her she was only there because of how hard we, the athletes, had worked to get there. I wanted to tell her to pack her things and go back to Canada. All this toward someone who had looked after me from day one on the national team, and to whom I owed a debt of gratitude.

"Heather. I need your room tonight."

The pressure was getting to me already. That night the air conditioner in Heather's room let out intermittent belches of cold air — enough to lower my body temperature and let me fall asleep to the sound of the sputtering machine.

Breakfast was a British version of the selection we usually got abroad. The bacon was fossilized in grease, the eggs were yellow and of a creamed-corn consistency, and the toast was crunchy like croutons. The meal was saved by porridge with raisins and, my favourite, buttery croissants. I knew if I took a little of everything, my body would get what it needed.

In the afternoon, the nine of us took a van from the hotel down to the racecourse for a light-pressure paddle. Andrew weaved us around double-lane roundabouts on the disorienting left side of the road. The English elms, cedars, and hemlock trees lining the road had sucked up the moisture from weeks of rain, and now the leaves were fat and broad in the sun. The branches hung low with the weight of the foliage, and I stretched my arm out the window to slap a few leaves as we drove by.

Mike said this first row was to give us the chance to look around like wide-eyed children and absorb the grandeur of the Games. "Get it out of your system so we can be focused starting tomorrow," he said.

We parked and walked to the course entrance, which was heavily guarded by British army reservists decked out in full fatigues, from the berets on their heads to the camouflage pants stuffed into their black combat boots. The perimeter of the course was lined with fencing topped with barbed wire. Soldiers paced along like the fence like a scene in *The Great Escape*. From what I saw, the British were ensuring any martyring terrorist knew they were better off exploding themselves in some other crowded place.

After clearing security, we hopped on a bus that took us around the starting gates. Six blue and red banner flags blew in a cross-headwind on the north side of the course. The Olympic rings were everywhere: on the flags, on the blue banners along the banks, and on the grandstands. The bus drove along perpendicular to the start of the course, and I looked out the window to see the grey stretch of water disappearing into the distance. Lane markers dotted the water like an airport runway. The water was more exposed to the wind, a bit choppier than Lucerne. Here, the man-made course was carved into a flat, grassy plain, with time and space on either side for the wind to gather freely.

The bus dropped us off near the finish line for a short walk to the dining hall, our team tents, and the boathouse. We crossed paths with the British four: Peter Reed, Alex Gregory, Tom James, and Andrew Triggs Hodge. They stopped their conversation to turn and greet us as we walked by a stack of rowing shells. They were genuine and gracious. Next, Rob and Will broke away from us across the paved pavilion between the boathouse and docks to greet an American men's eight rower whom they'd trained with at the University of Washington. They clasped hands and shoulder hugged, saying, "How are you?" and "How is so-and-so?" and "Good trip over?" All I saw was two of my teammates fraternizing with the enemy. I wanted to run and dropkick the American rower onto his back and tell Rob and Will to snap out of it. I was still a visitor among journeymen rowers — men and women who had battled each other over the years and forged friendships. When it was all said and done, I would have less than two years of international rowing experience — hardly time to foster any relationships with the people who populated the race lanes beside me.

An athlete attending The Greatest Show on Earth has learned that heroism in sport is misunderstood by most spectators. The idea of heroism centres on rising up to meet a great challenge with courage, but every athlete on that pavilion, tinkering with their boats, or chatting about logistics, or slathering sunscreen on toned muscular limbs, knew that any heroic performance in the coming days would be a product of the daily preparation that had begun months and years before.

I made a point of staring intently at whoever met my gaze. All internal fear became masked by my anger, that emotion quick to fill the void that otherwise harboured insecurity. If they looked at me and saw that I wanted to damage them, maybe they'd shrug it off, but maybe, just maybe, it would put the slightest ripple in their day — one tiny impression on top of thousands of others, good and bad, tipping the scale. Maybe, with a thousand pounds per square inch of nervous energy crushing them in the moments before the Olympic final, they'd look across and remember the face that told them *One of us will die before this is over.*

53

The first couple of days went smoothly. We got to the course at 7:30 in the morning when the grass was still wet with dew, slipped our shining yellow Empacher war machine into Dorney Lake, and opened our bodies with some light work. We got our morning row in before the practice lanes turned into a highway traffic jam. In the afternoon we returned to do short race pace pieces, keeping the feeling of speed in our bodies before the first race, like Formula One drivers zigzagging to heat up their rubber during the formation lap.

One day before our heat I noticed something was off. The stress of the previous day with the air conditioner had evaporated, and the battle anger gently lifted out of me like the silky grey smoke of an extinguished candle.

I was so calm. Twenty-four hours before the biggest moment of my life, and no elevated resting heart rate, no sweaty palms, no butterflies — all symptoms of the adrenaline that should have been building in my body. My mind was blank.

In the afternoon I went for a walk to concentrate on the race and let the nerves in, trying to ignite the fire that should have been burning bright inside me by now. I saw people pull into their driveways after a day of work, carrying in groceries, children scurrying behind. I thought I might like to join them at their dinner tables and ask them about their day. The walk wasn't working.

In hindsight, I know now that I was experiencing a state of shock. The pressure to perform had totally overwhelmed me, my natural fight-or-flight instincts overridden. All the physiological symptoms of preparing for battle were absent. Instead of sweaty palms and a tight chest, I was apathetic, even a bit lethargic. I couldn't snap out of it. Mike had described this exact situation to us earlier in the year. "You want to feel nervous at the start. If you're not nervous, then you're not ready. But if you're too nervous, you'll feel sheepish and tired, and this will detract from your performance as well," he'd said.

I remember watching a nature documentary showing an Arctic wolf chasing a white bunny across the barren Arctic plains. There was nowhere for the bunny to hide, and the wolf closed in fast. But before the wolf caught up to the bunny, it suddenly stopped. The bunny could have kept trying to escape a little longer, until the wolf caught it, but it stopped as soon as it realized that death was inescapable. I had built up the Olympics so much in my head that I had become that little white bunny the day before our heat. It was as if my brain had shut off my physiological response to threats and left me emotionally paralyzed. Not nervous, not excited, just … nothing.

The morning of the race wasn't much different. We did our pre-row and went through our race simulation rowing at a firm three-quarter pressure, going over the race calls we decided on implementing for the race. Brian spoke in a quiet voice to prevent our race calls from echoing across the water and into the ears of other crews or coaches who may have been riding their bikes along the bank. I can't imagine anyone was trying to listen, but Brian's lowered voice matched the mood in the boat: bristling, focused, expectant.

"Push through the minute, power legs together, squeeze last six inches, no miss, one cut," he whispered.

We went back to the hotel to count down the minutes until it was time to return for the race. I went to my room and rubbed my thumbs against a piece of forty-grit sandpaper I dug up from the bottom of my bag, underneath the Team Canada rowing clothes and the water bottles.

Hello? Jeremiah? Are you there? Where have you gone?

The grandstands were full of people when we returned to the racecourse, and excitement was in the air. Black perforated plastic had been laid across the grass from the bus stop to the pedestrian bridge that overlaid the entrance to the warm-up course — a three-lane-wide strip of water separated from the racecourse by a ten-metre-wide grassy bank. I walked along the sloping path, carefully mapping out the flattest ground like a senior afraid of falling — this was no time to twist an ankle. Fifteen-metre-high temporary grandstands had been erected on either side of the course along the last 300 metres. The intermittent roar of the crowd made me feel like a gladiator waiting to be brought into the spectacle. We passed the last of many checkpoints, manned by smiling volunteers and police officers who were not smiling so much, and I felt a slight swell of pride in my belly. *I am an Olympian,* I thought. A fleeting thought.

We walked, red Team Canada backpacks slung over shoulders, to the white canvas team tents between the boathouse and boat storage area. Somewhere, everywhere, a female voice rang out from the PA system, announcing the schedule. The voice had that indistinguishable accent of a United Nations translator fluent in eight languages: "Racing in ten minutes, the women's quad."

I finally started to feel nervous again, a faint pang trying to hammer through my shell and wake up my insides.

The whiteness of the tent gave off a clinical feeling, like we were being quarantined at the site of an apocalyptic virus. Doug nibbled on the skin at the base of his fingernails; Gabe stared at the ground, sullen; Will was the first to hop on one of the stationary warm-up bikes in the tent; Conlin sat on a storage bin with the hood of his white Patagonia sun shirt drawn over his head (he'd ordered eight of the shirts, which made us look like Klan members walking around with hoods drawn in the sun); Gibson pushed up his lower lip and breathed audibly through his nose, something stallion-like about his exhales, as though forced out from under the weight on his chest; Andrew sprayed sunscreen on his arms and shoulders, careful not to get any on his palms; Malcolm surveyed each of us with nods of encouragement and a look that said, *This is it, boys. Here we go.*

An hour later, my teammates and I would be in for a rude awakening.

The final preparation before we went on the water was a pre-race activation by our team chiropractor, Mike Murray. We took turns lying face down on his massage table in a separate tent, getting our muscles karate-chopped from head to toe. Murray worked away like a Japanese drummer. He muttered quietly to himself when he worked — a habit born from decades of handling bodies on his table — probably finding that his grunts soothed his clients. Part magician, part psychologist, part chiropractor, Murray could make you feel new again.

"Flip over, Jerry," he said. I turned onto my back, and he continued chopping, hovering over my quads for some extra attention, his muttering fading away until nothing but the sound of hands slapping skin filled the tent. As I lay there, moving my body to Murray's hushed commands, I felt the way a knight must have felt putting on his armour before battle. I stood up and felt, without having spent any energy, like I had just been in a wrestling match. The blood spread through my body like a flood plain. I was primed and ready for battle.

There is no question of if — only when. When will you go through the suffering to come?

After the body activation, we met Mike in the back of the boat bay. We talked over the race plan in quiet voices because the Dutch men's eight was twenty feet away in the next bay. Bits of orange unisuit and legs and arms were visible through the open two-by-four wall and racks of rowing shells.

"You *are* capable of this," Mike said. "If you row your race as well as we all know you can, there's no one in the world who can stop you."

We'd drawn both the British and the Germans in our heat. The top three crews in the world all in the same heat — what the hell were the organizers thinking? Despite being ranked third, our goal was to win the gold medal, and so our heat amounted to a dress rehearsal for the final. Like the Canadian eight four years prior in Beijing, we would go out and win the heat and then do it again in the final. Two races, gold medal, thank you and good night. Or, so we thought.

Mike gathered our lanyards and shook our hands. He gave us each a little nod and look that said, *You will now sacrifice yourself for the cause. Godspeed.*

"Ready, up," Brian ordered. "Take it away."

We marched to the dock in rigid lockstep with Mike trailing us, eight Olympic lanyards hanging off his forearm like a butler holding a linen tea towel. The boat felt heavy and dug into my shoulder. I felt the stares of rowers and coaches scattered about the pavilion, pausing momentarily to take us in. The men's eight and men's single sculls are often referred to as the blue ribbon events in rowing. These events are to rowing what the 100-metre race is to athletics.

Mike was still gathering our discarded rubber sandals after our first two strokes cleared us from the dock. The oar's wooden grains in my hands comforted me, the first push of the legs and pull on the arms satisfying, something familiar in a hostile environment.

We rowed away from the hustle and bustle of the dock and steady murmur of the crowds, toward the pedestrian bridge overhanging the entrance to the warm-up course. The bridge was lined with people looking down as we slipped underneath.

A cool breeze chilled us. A few people from our throng of family and friends shouted "Go Canada!" from up high, looking over the back wall of the grandstand. I saw Will's shoulder flinch when someone shouted his name. If anything, I would have told our supporters to shut up until the last 500 metres of the race — that's when we'd need them. Not now, not in the warm-up. I wanted us to be a boat full of snipers sneaking up on the enemy, taking them out without them even knowing we were there.

I had given my family strict instructions not to contact me in any way until after the last race was over. It was in keeping with my desire for isolation. I feared seeing my family might allow the softer side of me to show up. Consequently, my dad had purchased tickets for the final only and would be coming over from visiting our German relatives in a few days, along with my mom, Jenny, Julia, Amy, and Ethan.

The only family I knew in that moment were the eight brothers in my boat — yet even they seemed oddly distant from me.

Brian called the first hard twenty at twenty-two strokes per minute. We slammed into it with all the power we could summon. The boat felt hard through my hands, vibrating like hitting a baseball off the end of a bat. "Okay, boys," said Brian. "I asked you for a twenty-two, and you gave me a twenty-six and a half. I get that you're pumped for this, but let's hit this next piece at a twenty-four."

The next hard twenty strokes felt disconnected. We were masking our failure to find rhythm by heaping on gobs of power. We were like eight boys trying to shoot the same slingshot as hard as we could at the same time; instead of carefully pulling back the rubber band and finding the load together, we pulled blindly and the rhythm fell from our sling, the effort wasted.

"All right, guys, you're still high by four beats. Settle it down a bit here," Brian said, speaking to us like someone riding a nervous bronco, trying to soothe the beast attached to the reigns in his hands.

Nearing the end of the warm-up, we managed to come within two strokes per minute of our target stroke rate. My nerves had returned in the form of uncertainty: something was off, we all knew it, but your gut instincts are muted in the pressure of — for six of us — your first Olympic race. The Olympics is noise, fanfare, shiny glitz, bright colour, hype, and excitement. It seeks to undo you.

All around us the six other crews churned up the water with a loud *whoosh*, *whoosh*, *whoosh*, approaching and fading, approaching and fading. From over Will's shoulder I watched Brian look at his stroke coach monitor, up at Will, back at the monitor, across the glittering water, thinking, processing. I was working too hard to shake the indifference from the previous twenty-four hours, and Will was humming in stroke seat, the energy pushing up the stroke rate. We misunderstood a lack of focus for a sign we were about to do something special.

Covering the PA microphone with his hand, Brian spoke in a low voice with Will, conferring over the boat feel and high rates. "All right, guys, Will can feel the power down here. Rates are high, but it's a good sign. We're ready to beat the Germans," he said.

The Germans had looked flawless when we'd passed each other going in opposite directions. I could feel their rhythm just by watching them — their perfect entry at the catch, their bodies flexing with the load in synchronicity, their finish clean and sharp.

Having the world record put it in our heads that we should beat the Germans if we got it right like we had in the World Cup heat. But it also made us think that we had to summon something extra, some special Olympic version of ourselves.

Wrong.

There is no extra effort available to give, and the Olympics is not the time to try something different from what you've prepared. Yet, we tried to do both anyway.

We made final preparations in the starting gates with our oars held in one hand, a halo of shimmering sun where the blade touched the water. I sat rigid, looking down at my feet, thinking about the massive effort seconds away. *This, too, will pass; this, too, will — no! Be here! Stay present!*

A new voice echoed across the water from far away. It belonged to an upbeat Olympic official who was introducing our crews to the crowd 1,700 metres behind us, a sea of humanity invisibly tucked into the horizon. When this different voice introduced the British crew in lane one, a great roar rose up and rolled over our backs. Smaller cheers followed for us, the Germans, and the Dutch. There were only the four of us in our heat.

Then the familiar voice — that old sentry — invisible in the starting tower, comforting in his detachment.

"Great Britain ... Canada ... Germany ... the Netherlands ... Attention ..."

The horn went, the light behind Brian turned from red to green, and the underwater machine holding our bow shot forward into the water like a fish striking bait at the surface, flashing, disappearing.

We squeezed and yanked the first stroke as hard as we could. We pulled ourselves up to the catch for the next stroke. All hamstrings, no glide. *Zip, zip, zip*, the wheels on the slides sounded high-pitched underneath us. After fifteen strokes, the crews around us shifted gears into a strong forty strokes per minute, but we kept on sputtering in the midforties, unable to find any unity in our rowing.

By 500 metres, we had somehow managed to stay ahead of the Brits in lane one, but the Germans had taken a half-length lead. Over the next 500 metres, the British moved through us, then the Dutch. They all left us behind to try to figure out what had gone wrong in our boat. It must have appeared as though we had given up — an injury, maybe. We were in the epicentre of a disaster, the worst race experience since my foray into the sport three and half years earlier. *Jesus Christ, not now! Not this time!* We had nothing left in the tank. We were eight large men jabbing at the water with short, jerky strokes, watching our Olympics turn into a shocking embarrassment.

As we crossed the 1,500-metre mark, all three crews had an open water lead on us. The Germans were so far ahead that their wake entered our lane, throwing us further off balance, further out of sync. The roar from the crowd consumed us prematurely. The noise should have meant only 300 metres to go, but this time it meant 350.

Brian had long since stopped pleading with us. "Just row it out. We're not sprinting," he said with disgust. He couldn't believe the failure he was witnessing in front of him. I was never more mortified in my life. The pain raged inside me. Bad races always hurt the most. There is nothing worse than being burnt up and out of contention and still 750 metres from the finish. I wished someone would take my oar from me and beat me senseless with it.

When we crossed the finish line, the noise from the crowd had completely subsided. People were already leaving the grandstands to use the washroom before the next race. We finished twelve long seconds behind the Germans. We were like a college crew who'd been invited to row against Olympic crews just for the chance to say we'd been there. We were spectators.

"Fuck me," is all Brian could muster after the embarrassing beep of the finish horn reminded everyone that Canada had been in the race too. "Ports tap it, starboard hold. Let's get the fuck out of here."

There's simply no margin of error available when you're facing the best in the world. We lost the race within the first ten strokes. There was nothing Brian could say to try to salvage our bad start. He had tried everything he could think of to get us back on track, to no avail.

When we got off the water, Brian and I were picked by the Canadian media to explain what had happened. *Didn't they want Malcolm?* God damn the little pang of importance I felt at being picked to represent our team, my ego daring to show itself in this way after such a dismal race.

When I got to the media section of the grandstands, a woman wearing makeup as thick as cake icing greeted me. She pulled me down into the media pit overlooking the podium dock we seemed unlikely to ever set foot on. Her eyes darted from me to her notes to her phone. "Let's roll, Matt," she said to her cameraman. She'd probably been rushing around to get all her interviews done, probably wished I'd hurry up so that she could make her next assignment. Meanwhile, my world was collapsing by the second.

"Jeremiah Brown, from the coxed eight-man rowing event, joins us now. Jeremiah, not the start you guys wanted. Tell us what happened in the race and where you go from here."

She clearly knew nothing about rowing.

I answered her question with a clichéd statement, like every athlete ever interviewed: "Well, you know, we went out there today and made a few mistakes, but we know what we can do better and we'll come out with a better effort in the next race."

I turned to leave, but she asked me to stay to do the same interview in French and have me repeat the same response in English. Suddenly, I had the urge to push her into the water.

Mike decided to wait until we returned to the hotel to go over what had happened. On the bus ride back to the parking lot, I stared at the sheep carelessly grazing beside the course and wished I could trade places with one of them.

Back at the hotel, Mike called a meeting in one of the conference rooms. We all sat in silence in leather office chairs around a long polished wooden table, waiting for Mike, who sat at the head of the table, to rip into us. Unbeknownst to the rest of us, Brian and Malcolm had talked with him beforehand and had taken the brunt of Mike's anger.

"Okay," he said, letting his forearm drop on the table, the silver chain of his watch clunking loudly. "Let's discuss the race."

We went around the table, taking turns. Our responses were the complete antithesis of our world record race breakdown.

"We were disconnected from the start."

"The finishes were washing out, and we were rushing to get to the catch."

"It felt like we were getting rate with our slides instead of through the water, we —"

"That's it, isn't it," Mike interjected. "You started too high. What rate did you hit, Brian?"

"Fifty-three."

"You see, you were out of control," said Mike, "like a bunch of children chasing a ball down the street. Frantic and out of control." He looked at us, considering how in the hell such careful preparation could come to this. "We train length and power year-round, we build up the rates gradually, so that the rhythm becomes second nature at race pace, but you went out there and blasted off the line at fifty-three strokes per minute."

Mike looked at Will. "It's your responsibility to control the rate, Will. You're the stroke; you're the leader; you've got to get it right."

Will nodded in silent agreement.

"Let's leave it there for now," said Mike.

When we stood up to leave, condensation outlines of our arms and elbows remained on the polished table, slowly lifting back into the air of the warm room.

Before dinner I sat in my hotel room on the edge of my bed, considering the possible outcomes of our next race. If we repeated our performance in the heat, our Olympics would be over. Our families would be left with tickets to a race without us in it. If that happened, I figured I would disappear to Portugal or somewhere other than Canada, where the cost of living was low, and live out my remaining days in obscurity.

While I couldn't sit still in our hotel room, a preposterous thought crept into me: *Andrew already has an Olympic gold medal, so maybe the thought of failure doesn't matter as much to him and Malcolm and Brian? Maybe this is all gravy for them?* A paranoid and cowardly thought. I walked to the window. If I could just keep moving, I might be able to escape the racing thoughts encircling my head like a swarm of mayflies.

Out the window I could see Windsor Castle in the distance, its towers poking up above the treeline. I looked back at Andrew. He was reading a finance magazine, his outward demeanour as severe as mine would be if I couldn't remember something on my grocery list. "What's going through your head?" I asked. "How are you so calm right now?" He dropped the magazine to his chest with his finger wedged in to save his page. "I'm feeling the pressure just as much as you. There's no point in making it worse by dwelling on it," he said. We talked until there was nothing left to say, and then waited in silence.

At dinner the whole rowing team was quiet. The eight of us sat together, working our clinking forks and knives into our dinner. When the odd athlete or trainer at another table smiled or laughed softly, I seethed.

After dinner, Peter Cookson and Phil Moncton called us into the hallway for an impromptu meeting. It turned out they wanted to present us with the Olympic rings we had been fitted for a month earlier, when the team had been announced.

"Look, guys, we believe in you. We know you'll get the job done in the rep," said Peter, sounding choked. "Phil and I want to give you your rings as a token of our appreciation for all the work you've done to get to this point."

Jesus Christ, we haven't lost yet, I thought. What the hell were they thinking? The whole presentation came across as a consolation ceremony, as if we'd already been eliminated from the final. They called us up one at a time to shake hands and accept our rings. I took the ring and shoved it deep into my pocket. I didn't want their empathy. *How dare they risk compromising our mentality like this?* Good intentions, yes. Horrible timing, unacceptable.

On Sunday, July 29, 2012, I woke up briefly forgetting where I was — half a second of groggy-eyed confusion, and then the rush of recent events and nerves lighting up my body and mind like a neon bulb flickering to life. *Oh. Shit.*

That afternoon, after the day's scheduled races were over, we drove to the course in the van, quiet like soldiers being transported to the front lines. We had one day to fix things before the repechage. Mike borrowed a bicycle to ride along the path parallel to the course, one hand on the handlebar, one hand on a stopwatch hung around his neck. He spoke to Brian by walkie-talkie from shore. A cold front had moved in and made the rowing feel like Elk Lake in October. By the end of a full race warm-up, I was starting to lose my fingers and toes to the cold.

Mike had a hard session planned for us: three 500-metre pieces — the third stretching above race pace — and one final 750 into the biting wind. Most coaches would consider that amount of work the day before a major race to be too risky, but Mike knew the greater risk was our psychology. We needed to find the sustainable max effort that we could hold with rhythm and power for the entire race. Mike called this our red line. Most of all, we needed to remember what fast felt like.

The rowing was the most committed miserable thing we did that year. We blasted into the headwind at Brian's command, searching for the perfect equilibrium of power, stroke rate, and rhythm. Mike told Brian our split times weren't fast enough. Brian, in turn, told us. We turned the boat and tried again. The spray from Gabe's and Rob's oars stung my hands.

Every stroke fuelled by such anger — how could we have worked so hard only to let ourselves down when it counted most? Every stroke a thesis in perseverance, in resilience. Our Olympics was just beginning. But it felt like the end, it felt how moments feel before something doesn't go well.

This is not *the end for us.*

54

Back at the hotel, I spent the afternoon looking out our window thinking, thinking, finding myself in a cold mental pit of my own digging. For the first time in a few years I allowed myself to consider what fate had planned for me, for us. Until now, all such considerations had been rooted out by taking action over and over again. Worried my body might break? *Push through for another week.* Worried about selection? *Fuck it, just pull hard, nothing else matters.* Always leading to a greater goal on the horizon. I preferred that horizon to stay well out in front to give me room to overcome the failures along the way. Now the horizon was a towering cinder block wall close enough for me to feel my breath waft back in my face. No more chances to correct, to get back on track. Would we break through, or was this it? I tried to suppress the thought, like swallowing something dry stuck in my throat. *Suck it up, pussy.*

That evening we gathered in the conference room once again. The setting sun, like a punctured egg yolk, spilled orange light over the trees and grass outside, entering sideways through the window blinds and striping us in the last warm light of day.

Malcolm looked around with a grim face that telegraphed the weight we all felt.

"We'll start by going over the next race one at a time," Mike began. "I want each of you to say exactly how you envision it unfolding. Best if you all close your eyes and listen."

His pitch was already elevated. He held the program pinched between thumb and index finger like usual, kneading the paper so that its soft crinkle was the loudest sound in the room. It was Will's turn to go first.

"We take off, first two strokes are long and strong. Build rate from three to five, staying tall, driving legs. Five to ten, keep building, start to bring in the body swing. On thirteen, we drive into a strong forty-four with rhythm."

"Hold on, Will," said Mike. "I don't want our race plan said back to me. I want to know how you see the race unfolding. What are the other crews doing alongside? How are you going to respond?"

Will took a moment to think it through.

"Okay, the Brits try to get a canvas on us by the five hundred, but we hold off their initial push. We're in control, and as we push through seven-fifty we start to inch through the Germans. We don't give them anything in the third five hundred, and we hold them off with our sprint to win the race."

"Okay, then," Mike said, sounding unsatisfied. "What about you, Rob?"

Rob barked out the Coles Notes version of what Will had said, and then we continued around the table in similar fashion. When my turn came, I wanted to say I didn't know what would happen and ask what the hell this was all about, anyway.

"It's about focus," Mike said after we'd all given our predictions. "If you go into this next race without focus, you'll be sorry. You'll be very sorry." His voice had taken on a grave tone, and his bushy eyebrows twitched uncontrollably. What could he say? What could he do to get us back into the right headspace for the next race?

Not what followed.

"How will your family and friends feel if you don't come through tomorrow?" he asked.

We stared at him blankly, looked at each other. Silence. I watched Rob's eyes narrow a little, trying to understand why Mike would say something like that.

Mike's face was now shadowed with some mix of fear and anger and foreboding I hadn't seen before.

"If you lose tomorrow, there will be children crying in the stands," Mike said, looking my way. "At least one little boy will be."

My neck twitched and I glared back at him. *Did he just say that?* In that instant I wanted to lash out, to fling myself across the table and tackle him to the floor. I hated him in that moment, hated him more than at any point during the most miserable training of the last nineteen months.

Malcolm believed Mike had said it purposely. "Mike knew an angry Jerry was a fast Jerry. It was a calculated move," he'd tell me years later.

It was a miscalculated move. One that nearly caved me in. The spike of rage left as fast as it came, swallowed up by emotional fatigue. Mike was undoing everything I had worked on to keep my sanity. The hardest thing was suppressing thoughts of loved ones so that I could stay buttoned down in the pressure. By invoking my son, Mike only succeeded in losing my trust and making me want to find Ethan, gather him up in my arms — his skinny arms around my neck, his head nestled into my shoulder — and walk away from it all.

Mike had seen the red anger take over me time after time in side-by-side training, when the rows up and down Elk Lake were attacks on each other, when we wanted to crush each other as much as the Germans and Brits. People don't usually respond well to being hit when they're down, but I do. Under the moroseness, there is a circuit inside me that flickers to life. Mike saw that I was able to transform the part that felt sorry for myself into anger, and the anger into speed.

But this was different than those battles on Elk Lake in the single and in pairs. You can express your individuality in small boats, but the eight demands everyone's focus on the same things at the same time. If any individual rower went into battle rage and tried to be a hero in the eight, 2,000 pounds of teammates and carbon and aluminum would chew him up and spit him out so that he was nothing more than a dead piston on an 8-cylinder engine. If anything, we needed to dial ourselves back a touch so that we could execute our race plan. We tried too hard early on in the heat. The problem was not lack of effort, it was a lack of focus. Mike was appealing to our emotion when he should have been tempering it.

A year's worth of silence had passed in the space of a few seconds when Gabe finally spoke: "Look, there's no reason to panic. We know what we did wrong. We just gotta go out there and do it right this time. Execute the race plan. Race our race. That's all we have to do." It was the most Gabe had ever said in a pre-race meeting. He was the oldest one of us and had seen his share of mental collapses. Like hell he would sit idle and be part of another one.

"Wise words, Gabe," Mike said. "You're right. But doing it is another matter, isn't it?"

Another insufferable pause.

"You know my job is on the line here," Mike said, softly now, a plaintive look on his face. "Rowing Canada is looking for a reason to axe me. You know that."

Mike had a nervous habit of swallowing repeatedly as he spoke, and I watched as the loose skin under his chin constricted, like a lizard devouring an insect.

Earlier in the day, Doug Vandor and Morgan Jarvis in the men's lightweight double and Lindsay Jennerich and Patricia Obee in the women's lightweight double — both Canadian crews capable of medals — had underperformed in their races and looked to be out of medal contention. Mike now faced the prospect of all three of his crews crumbling at these Olympics, and for Mike the eight's failure would be the most crushing of all.

But we had a contract. Mike's job was to keep his bearings and prepare us as best he could. Our job was to put all of our strength, our focus, our souls behind those oars. Mike failed us that day. As far as I was concerned, from that point on we'd lost the man whose training program had given us a chance to win. It was up to the nine of us in the boat now.

I left the meeting with a sense of foreboding like a bag of rocks tied to my ankles, pulling me down into darkness, the belt so tight around my chest that I couldn't breathe. The only saving grace to the worst-case scenario ahead, I thought, would be Mike's firing.

If the thirty-one-year-old guy typing these words could speak to the twenty-six-year-old athlete living that experience, I might tell him that this is life: people you count on will fail you, and it is still your job to bail them out. *You wouldn't be there without Mike's belief in you. Now go and bail him out.*

55

In February 2009, just a few weeks into my rowing journey, I returned to Ancaster, Ontario, for my grandpa's funeral. A few weeks before, I had visited him on his deathbed with a few of my cousins and watched the man we'd looked up to all our lives turn into a corpse. I had sat by his bedside with The Beck, Chunk, and Cotton Ginny — my grandpa had a nickname for each of the grandkids. His body was foreign, with its haunting guttural breaths and bluish skin, the wave of silky white hair he always kept perfectly swept to the side now tousled and wilted like dead grass stuck to his forehead. Still we sat by his side, talking to him, hoping he'd come back to life, yearning for his big smile and jokes and praising of the Lord.

During one of our last conversations when he was still healthy, I remember saying to him how amazing it would be to compete at the Olympic Games. This, after the 2008 Olympics, when the thought of taking up rowing was still a private exploration. I was searching for his approval and didn't expect his response. "Hah! Those people work so gosh-darned hard, commit their whole lives to it, and for what? Most of them end up with nothing! I think they're all mad!" he'd said with a snort.

I smiled whenever I thought back on that brief conversation over the course of the next three years, as I worked gosh-darned hard to commit not a lifetime but a portion of my life so wholly to the pursuit. I smiled because I knew my grandpa would have been my biggest supporter, telling everyone at church about his grandson, The Mighty, who had transformed himself into a mighty Olympic rower.

But now it turned out maybe he was right. I *was* on the brink of madness.

Before the Games, we'd all agreed to go dark: no social media, no reading the news about us, no checking emails. We didn't want to risk being distracted by the hype around the Games.

In a moment of weakness, I broke down and opened an email from my dad:

> Regroup and work towards the standard you set in Lucerne, and we'll be there to watch you achieve it in the final on August 1. We're confident you and your teammates can finish what you set out to achieve.

I thought of how disappointed my son would be after watching the race. He was only six years old and thought my teammates and I were invincible. I responded:

> Ya, tough one. Tell Ethan not to give up on us too quick. We'll be better in the rep.

My dad was probably feeling just as twisted inside as I was, but his response gave me back some perspective on life:

> That's the spirit. He's got all the confidence in the world in his dad, The Mighty. Think of how proud Grandpa is looking down from above!

The email shone some light into an existence centred on rowing, an existence that had become stripped of anything else. My dad's childhood reference was enough to bring back good memories. It reminded me of the grandpa who'd loved me unconditionally and my son and dad who would still love me no matter what happened the next day. A brief moment of comfort in my weakest hour.

That evening before bed, while Andrew lay with his head propped up on a pillow reading about stock investment strategies — curious, given our $18,000 per year income — I walked to the window to watch Windsor Castle disappear into the dusk. The next day we would race Poland,

Ethan and my dad watching our first Olympic races from Germany.

Australia, Great Britain, the Netherlands, and Ukraine, with the top four crews moving on to the final.

Despite the stucco ceiling pushing down on me and the wallpapered walls closing in, I knew in my gut that we had worked harder than anyone. We deserved to be there. I knew it because Mike Spracklen had been chased from countries for working his athletes too hard. Maybe our race tactics would do us in, or our inability to focus when it counted most, but it wouldn't be for lack of work. All those impossible Saturday morning check mark workouts, fartlek starts, and side-by-side self-immolating training runs had put us in the position to claim our spot in the final.

The work invested — it could quite possibly save us from ourselves.

56

We sat on the bus listening to its hydraulics snort and wheeze, its undercarriage clank and squeak, as it took us around the course to the start. The Monday morning air smelled like summer the same way those last high school days smell before school's out, when you want to forget about all the exams you still need to write. If I'd allowed it, my mind would've drifted back to summer morning baseball games in Port Hope, family barbecues at the cottage, and playing in the yard for an hour after sunset.

Instead, I went to a different place in my mind. Rooted in my gut was the feeling of a storm always brewing, of disaster ahead. I hate optimism. Optimism equals stupidity. It is easier to go forward in time and live out the worst-case scenario. Then the present turns into a kind of gift, a second chance at an experience not yet lived. A chance to make it right the first time.

Doug signalled to the rest of us that it was time to drink our beet juice. Trent Stellingwerff, our team physiologist, had recommended we try it. Though inconclusive, some studies suggested that beet juice contained nitrogen oxide molecules able to counteract the lactate by-products in the bloodstream. I drank it while plugging my nose, thinking maybe I owed my mom a thank you for forcing me to eat the dark-purple root vegetable so often growing up.

When I stood up to get off the bus, I monitored my body: how did my weight feel in my quads? Effortless? Heavy? As we walked along the matted-down grass toward the pedestrian bridge, I took a few lunge steps, gauging the spring in my legs.

We moved along in one cluster of athletes from different countries and boat classes: Denmark, Romania, the Netherlands, Norway, Switzerland, Croatia, Spain, South Africa. A kaleidoscope of country colours shifted all around us. We reached the foot of the pedestrian bridge and passed through fans who gawked at us and cheered us on. Some part of me wanted to soak in the adulation before it all vanished.

The routine went smoothly enough: walk to tent, change, warm up on stationary bike. I tried to eat some more to make up for how quickly my bowels evacuated under the stress. On the way to the dining hall, I passed a few guys from the American eight. They'd won the other heat two days prior and now looked confident, returning my ferocious stare without a blink.

For nine guys who had spent so much time together, we were a sullen, quiet group under the white canopy of our team tent as we made final preparations. We drank our personalized sports drinks at precise intervals and warmed up together yet mentally apart from each other. Quiet. Focused. You'd never know how much of each other's lives we'd shared over the previous months. All the laughter, the pining after women, the jokes, the spats — all of the little things that had knitted us together day in and day out were buried away somewhere deep.

Malcolm made frequent eye contact with an expectant look on his face, ready to reassure any of us, though this offering was mostly a way to reassure himself. Will sat with music thumping in his ears, going to the place he needed to be for the race. The others, one at a time, disappeared and then returned after receiving their body activation from Murray. With each return, I felt a bit of relief from the regained contact with one eighth of the boat, one eighth of myself. There weren't enough chairs, so I sat on an orange Gatorade watercooler. Every once in a while the roar from the grandstands filled our tent and a nervous shiver went up the back of my spine. When Brian came in to give us the five-minute warning, I took a deep breath and looked up from the ground for the first time in several minutes.

Outside the tent, puffs of white clouds with grey underbellies dotted the blue sky. I looked up, stretching my fingertips toward them, feeling the muscles in my back and arms grow taught. Fingertips to toes, fingertips to sky. I liked to stretch this way often in the moments before a race. It helped to break up the nervous static electricity built up inside me.

We walked out to get our boat and hear a last word from Mike, the sun shining warmly on our necks. As we passed the metal gates that led out of the team tent area and turned left toward the docks, several fans walked by us on the opposite side of a tall fence, making their way around the back of the boathouse to take their seats in the south grandstands. Again, I was struck by a sense of otherness — that I more appropriately belonged in their ranks than amongst my teammates. I felt like an observer and participant at the same time.

Doug said something to do with logistics as we walked. I let it pass through my ears without registering, grateful that we had enough guys on our team paying attention to where we had to be and when that I could ignore him and simply follow the group.

We took our boat outside of the bays to weigh in, and then flipped it over so that Brian and the Empacher representatives could buff the hull, removing spiderwebs, fly poop, dirt, or any other contaminants that had accumulated overnight and might add frictional drag.

I had gone to the washroom three times already that day, but some of the beet juice and sports drink had collected in my bladder. I asked Brian if I had enough time, and he said two minutes. I made my way over to one of the two glass-enclosed spiral staircases on either side of the boathouse. They jutted out from the rest of the building like castle towers. The glass was aqua blue like the Olympic banners adorning the course. Inside, the blue-tinted light turned the red on my unisuit into magenta. I was careful to take one step at a time instead of the usual two or three in order to preserve my quads for the race. When I came back, the guys and the boat had vanished. A brief panic. I jogged back to the boathouse to find my teammates already at the back of the boat bay with Mike, the boat resting on boat slings in front of them. The daylight lit up their blank faces like a cluster of opossums whose nest had been discovered.

"It's on you guys now," Mike began, after I'd rejoined the group. "I can't do it for you. You need to go out there and bloody well focus." He was in the same fear-mongering state as the previous evening, and I tried to think beyond him as though trying to snap out of a bad dream. "You know my job is on the line. I *need* you guys," he said. He looked pale and glazed over with fear. I tried not to look at his face; fear is contagious. Was

I alone in my disbelief at what, to me, was Mike's abandonment? Perhaps Andrew and Brian and Malcolm were moved by Mike's personal plea from their years of training under him. Rob stood across from me with his strong arms folded across his chest, sticking out his chin and looking at Mike like a doctor trying to summarize in his head what was wrong with his patient. Then, despite my best efforts to ignore him, it got personal again. "Think about your son, Jerry. He doesn't want his dad to let him down, does he?" *This is who Mike really is,* I thought. *A deserter from the battlefield, a coward.*

Finally it was over and we were marching toward the water, the boat gunwales bobbing on our shoulders. The whole scene with Mike left me feeling like we'd already lost. As soon as we were out of earshot of the dock, Brian said that it was the worst speech he had ever heard, and to ignore it. "It's up to the nine guys in this boat right now," he said. "We're going to do it for each other — no one else."

We warmed up, and I felt like the entire world was watching with voyeuristic eyes, waiting for us to fail. This is the draw of the Olympic Games. Train wrecks and broken dreams are as captivating as the glory of victory. In less than an hour, we would find ourselves either having a spot in the final or packing our bags and wondering what could have been for the rest of our lives.

Our focus was good. Brian had stepped up in Mike's undoing and gave us all something to rally around. We allowed ourselves to enter into the rhythm smoothly. All senses attuned to the feeling of rolling up the slides together, slowing, dropping blades into the water, and driving legs, like Mike had coached — the coach momentarily dispatched, yet still with us in this way. I let my hands glide out in front of me to take each stroke, watching the small circle they made at the catch, thinking about Mike's favourite analogies: *Spin the wheel with your finger, a knife through warm butter, a bell tone at the catch.*

There was a slight delay getting onto the course, causing us to drift toward shore while we waited where the warm-up course joined the racecourse. The four of us on starboard had to push off the grassy hill with our oars when we were finally called. I wondered if I'd nicked my blade on a rock and how that might affect the hydrodynamics.

We were given lane one for the race, right beside the grassy bank. It would be hard to sense what was going on in lanes four, five, and six, but at least Malcolm, whose head was always on a swivel, would only have to look to starboard. I knew only we could stop ourselves from finishing in fourth place or higher to earn a spot in the final. The Ukraine crew, farthest from us in lane six, had not shown themselves to be at the calibre of the rest of the field in previous races. Australia, the Netherlands, and Great Britain all threatened our existence, and beside us in lane two, the Poles were the wild card. We were capable of beating them, but once in a while the Poles, with their shouts and slaps in the starting gates, put a heater together and surprised top crews.

Our boat holder lay on the starting gate dock, doing his best to not exist, lying still and looking down at the stern steadied in his hands. The water was perfect. Smooth oval ripples, enough to put some air under the boat. Six blue Olympic banner flags tugged against their tethers from a slight tailwind, the knock of the rings against the metal pole sounding like one-note chimes. These were my favourite conditions. A good omen.

A line of coaches straddling bicycles stood spread out on the bank nearest us, ready to start riding alongside us. I sat with my left arm extended straight, my body erect, breathing deep breaths and pushing them out with a tightening of my abdomen. Mike had once said exhaling was more important than inhaling, that you wanted to expel the carbon dioxide. Since hearing that, I'd developed the habit of forcing my breaths out with a whoosh like a train's air brakes releasing pressure.

"Focus on *our* race, boys," Brian said. Just then the British crew was introduced to the fans, and a roar of approval forced him to raise his voice. "We do this together."

The man in the starting tower began the eulogy: "Canada … Poland … Australia … Great Britain … Netherlands … Ukraine …"

"Attention."

The horn.

The electricity humming in my body finally found a current through my oar and into the water. The first strokes reminded me of the power available to me, something I always forgot in those paralyzing moments before the starting horn. By stroke thirteen, the moment we shifted gears from blast-off into a rhythmic forty-three strokes per minute, I was relieved to find I had also remembered how to row.

Our start was good. After 250 metres, we sat level in the field, except for the British, who had pushed boldly into the lead by a canvas. In my peripheral vision I made out the see-sawing bodies beside me. So packed with humanity, this event. Like an airport concourse or a busy shopping mall. Will's back strained toward me, released, strained toward me, released. I focused in on a particular constellation of freckles and moved with them until they became part of me. The pain started to creep through my body like a time-lapse of ivy spreading up the walls of a building. A mixture of anger and rage and despair. I felt trapped amongst these elite rowers. *Fuck them.* Enslaved to my own commitment for the sake of commitment, for the sake of something I couldn't even clearly define. Always the desire to escape, even with our Olympics on the line — a disgusting sentiment that spurned me deeper into a primitive rage until I was a hot bull snorting oxygen and chortling spit. *This is who I am.*

At 1,000 metres, the Brits had stretched out to a three-quarter-length lead on us. We now had a canvas on the Aussies and the Dutch. Slipping behind the rest of the field, Poland and Ukraine fought for their Olympic lives. Along shore, fans stood on smaller grandstands that led into the large grandstands near the finish. They were a stone's throw away, many waving tiny British flags, whistling and whooping. The sound was far away, beyond the churning water, the eight rolling seats, and the hum of blood pumping through my eardrums.

At 1,500 metres, a feeling of controlled death, as if I was happy in my suffocation knowing that I'd make it to the end, where my oxygen-starved body would restore itself with deep gulps of air. A comforting feeling. We were going as hard as we could, but this time we weren't going harder *than* we could — a subtle difference, a matter of focus, and with it the transformation of pain into something encouraging.

We were firmly in qualifying position behind the Brits down the final stretch, and with the Aussies pressuring us in third I knew we'd done enough to secure a berth in the final. The mostly British fans roared for their British men as the buoys turned from yellow to red, indicating the last 250 metres. The Dutch had, at some point, moved through the Aussies into third, but they sprinted too late to catch us. *Beep, beep, beep, beep.* Great Britain, Canada, the Netherlands, Australia. All four crews safely through to the A final. Poland and Ukraine finished fifth and sixth, respectively, and were eliminated from medal contention. They would race the B final for pride alone.

This time I didn't rock back and forth from the waist trying to escape my own skin. There was something left in me, in us: an extra gear that we hadn't needed to use. We'd nearly pulled even with the Brits when we crossed the finish line. I looked across the water, now grey from cloud cover. Mohamed Sbihi, their big five seat, keeled over his oar in pain. Greg Searle, in six, held himself up with both hands on the gunwales, waiting for his breath to return. They had used all their gears to beat us, and it showed. For once I understood why Mike was so adamant about hiding your pain after a race. Like a fighter seeing his opponent's knees wobble, I sensed weakness. All the emotion of the past two days balled up into one thought: *We're fucking coming for you.*

The hours before the race had felt like being on death row, with one last appeal before the electric chair. Immediately following, heart pounding along at 180 beats per minute, my inner fire ignited back into a hot, hungry furnace. Within an hour the endorphins would settle and my mindset would find its usual equilibrium, but for now I revelled in the manic rush of rage, violence, and conquest.

When we returned to the dock, Mike was there to greet us. Some colour had returned to his face. "Well done, guys. Well done," he said. I didn't acknowledge him.

An hour later, I stood under the shower head in our hotel bathroom, letting the warm water soak my head and bead off my nose and chin.

One more. Just one more.

57

In the evening after dinner, I decided I would go for a long walk and explore the surrounding suburbs. This would be my last. I couldn't risk worrying Andrew the following night, on the eve of the Olympic final. I exited the hotel under a deepening blue sky and walked until shops started to replace the rows of townhouses. When I came to the first major intersection, I turned right and began following a group of teenagers at a distance. On this night, they would help distract me from thinking about the Olympic final, my Armageddon.

How old were they? Sixteen or seventeen, maybe. I imagined being their age again, how preoccupied I'd been with girls, how I'd tag along with groups just like them in the hopes it might lead to some sexual encounter. All the testosterone at that age going toward local rivals — in sports, for girls, for notoriety at drunken house parties. They were years spent staking claims of tough brazenness. I was intellectually capable, yet drawn to the rawness of a street fight. I didn't fight often, but I pushed boundaries with brutish boys whose time in high school would be the peak of their social ascent; the kind of guys who eventually soften up when adult life dictates a need to get along with people in order to make a living. I never imagined the possibility of doing something on the world stage back then. Yet, there I was in Slough, an export of small-town Canada, with the same queasy gut feeling I'd had on bus rides to school all those years ago, knowing a fight was waiting for me at my destination.

The teens crossed a bridge and turned off the sidewalk onto a path lining a creek. I followed. The path was a skinny brown scar in the earth, winding its way around trees and dipping down to the water's edge at times. I slowed my pace and, as the excited chatter of the teens slowly disappeared, thought how improbable it was that I should find myself in this spot at this time. I skipped a few rocks across the creek and then stepped out onto a rock in the middle, careful to keep my Team Canada track pants and running shoes dry.

Now the worst-case scenario was that we might come last in the final, but at least we were in it. My expectations were back to where they had been going into the Olympics: we were the third-ranked crew with the potential to win. I tried to calculate our ranking based on the results so far. The Americans beat the Aussies in their heat, but how would they have stacked up to the field in the rep? Would they have beaten us? And the Brits — we'd nearly caught them at the end of the rep. I imagined Doug had it all worked out in his head. I could just ask him for the over/under.

When I returned to the hotel, it was a black silhouette against the dark blue of creeping night. I entered our hotel room and exchanged a look with Andrew: *We talked about this,* his face said. *You know I need my walks,* my face replied. Like an old married couple, no words needed to be exchanged.

At some point, one of the Beijing rowers had told me not to count on sleeping much the night before the final, but to make sure I slept well the nights before. I slipped into sleep that night knowing there was still one more day between us and the final. One more chance for my psyche to prepare itself.

58

The day before arrived. We did our one row for the day — a race simulation at three-quarter pressure and a low stroke rate — early in the morning, at 7:30 a.m. Exactly twenty-four hours later, we would do it again for the last time.

Life was a constant feeling of the wind taken out of your lungs, trips to the elevator with two or three teammates, silent elevator rides with only the Final Challenge raging through the quiet, ringing in my ears like a bad case of tinnitus. I had the urge to grab a handful of my teammates' muscles, like a farmer inspecting his animals, assuring myself of the quality of stock in our boat. I began anticipating the end, shook my head to free myself from the allure of post-Olympic freedom. I wanted a good ending, craved it with all my being. Time passed at the rate of one year per minute, and I passed the decades wanting one of those big, beautiful Olympic medals like a heroin addict wants the needle.

There is something mystical about the final approach. The Olympics had taken root in my brain, sucking up all my juices, owning me, pulling me toward it ever since the seed had been planted in 2008. But the closer I got, the more it began to push back and repel me. The Olympics, Mount Olympus, home of gods, of men and women who touch immortality, did not want to be conquered. It wanted to stay in the realm of aspiration, an ideal not meant to be achieved.

I was still the ten-year-old kid looking at my dad's copy of the *Toronto Star* and the profile on Derek Porter before the 1996 Games. Nineteen months is not enough time to acclimate to the possibility of becoming part of Olympic history, coached by the same man who had coached the guy from the newspaper to his gold medal in the men's eight in 1992.

Perhaps Mike was all too familiar with the force that pushes away many great athletes in the final moments that count for everything. Through all his crews' failures and victories, what could he do or say to get them to execute to their full potential? A question made anew with every new generation of athletes emerging under his tutelage.

This trip was not like other competitions, where we'd meander down hotel hallways and hang out with each other during downtime. I hadn't visited the rooms of any of my other teammates since arriving. Four hotel rooms, two to a room: Doug and Rob, Will and Gabe, Conlin and Malcolm, me and Andrew. Except for meals and the actual rowing, we stayed mostly isolated, as if in separate decompression chambers. Once in a while Brian, bored and lonely, would pop his diminutive figure into our door frame, offering some chit-chat to keep our minds from ruminating too much. When I did go to Malcolm and Conlin's room to double-check the meeting time that evening, it smelled like sweaty gym socks and musk, the human exhaust of two idling, revving, aerobic engines. Somewhere within a 20-kilometre radius, the Brits, Germans, Americans, Dutch, and Aussies were making final preparations. They would be well aware of Conlin and Malcolm's reputation as aerobic powerhouses. I tried to imagine their fear. It would help assuage my own if I could visualize the weight on their chests, too great, crushing them while my teammates and I endured.

Much of the day I spent with my elbow on a table, cradling my face in the soft tissue between my thumb and fingers, feeling my steady pulse, the warm breath from my nostrils blowing against the back of my hand. I was either on or off under this kind of pressure. Either give me the starting horn and let me unleash every atom in my body or leave me alone to recoil into myself as deep and far from the world as I could get. I would freeze the world if I could. Stop the hotel staff from moving. Stop the fifty-something tourists from chatting at the bar in the foyer. Waiting is a disease. I hate waiting.

At noon we finally had reason to break up some of those hours. We joined each other in the hotel banquet room for a buffet. The butterflies took away my appetite so that I ended up force-feeding myself mashed potatoes, mixed vegetables, and a few slices of ham. This was good: a grumbling stomach meant my nervous system would not fail me like it had before the heat.

I crunched down on a raw carrot. The sound echoed in my head. Doug sat next to me. He bit his lower lip and his eyes darted around the room, analyzing, calculating probabilities of various outcomes. Beside him Conlin worked through a heaping plate of food, and I felt his strength emanating across the white linen tablecloth. Heart of an innocent kid in the body of a beast. He was twenty-two years old. His best rowing was still ahead of him in quadrennials to come.

After lunch we returned to our decompression chambers to privately urge the afternoon onward. The hotel corridors had ceilings so low that Andrew nearly grazed the top of his head on the panels. We walked down the hall, and his head created a strobe effect as I followed — a flash memory of highway night drives with my family, the orange of street lights passing over my face in intervals. *Stay in the present*, I thought. Andrew laid down for his afternoon nap, set his alarm, and was out cold two minutes later. I lay on my bed with my eyes closed but still awake, looking at the insides of my eyelids lit up pink by the sun streaming through our window. Even if I couldn't fall asleep, I knew my body would still benefit from rest.

An eternity later, Andrew was up. An eternity after that, we finished dinner, a repeat of the scene at lunch. Time ticking by slowly. Pressure making me want to keep moving, like walking barefoot on scorching hot sand at the beach.

The day seemed to have dragged on forever, but now the sun set fast, as if lassoed and pulled downward by an invisible force. Darkness pushed out the remaining daylight until it glowed beyond the horizon like the fading tail lights of a passing car. We met in the boardroom for the last time. Mike was composed. Ever since pulling out of the death spiral after our performance in the rep, his tune had changed: still cautious, but no longer panicked.

Mike started the meeting with a smile as we sunk into black leather chairs. "Okay, let's talk through our approach tomorrow," he said, folding a piece of paper with his notes flat on the conference table. "You can count on the Germans setting the standard early and the British pushing them the whole way. We'll race our race like we did in the rep, but this time we'll pace off the Brits." Here Mike paused, letting us absorb the plan. "Brian, you'll tell the guys where they are and make sure you stay in contact with the Brits. We know they'll be gunning for the Germans, and we can't afford to be left behind. We'll use the Brits to keep contact," he said. "If you race to the best of your ability, you should be in a position to have a run at the Germans in the finishing sprint. You can't win it in the first five hundred metres, but you can lose it in the first twenty strokes. Hit it hard, but stay in control. The goal is to race your race for as long as possible. This will put you in a position to attack late in the race."

I liked what I heard. Tactics, not an appeal to our emotions. There was already enough emotion in that room to fill a lifetime.

"Brian, I'm giving you the discretion to decide when to start the sprint," Mike continued. "It's the Olympic final. Everyone will raise their game. In the last five hundred metres, it's over to you guys. How bad do you want it? How deep are you willing to dig?"

I imagined falling unconscious after my last stroke. The perfect race, as Mike had once said, would require a water rescue and eight stretchers. If we could override our unconscious reflexes, we would all choose to sacrifice ourselves, there was no question.

"How deep will you dig?" Mike repeated, the second time a statement more than a question.

It's the only important question in sport. This is what rowing is: finding out how much pain you can subject yourself to. Seeking it out.

The small room housed our collective wills as we mulled it over. *How deep*. I thought I could hear the light humming through the pot lights recessed in the crown moulding, but it was just the electricity in my own body. Will took a deep swig from his water bottle, the sucking sound of air being pulled back through the nozzle filled the small wood-panelled room. Everything that needed to be said had been said.

"Before you leave," Mike said, "I would like to share a poem I wrote for you, if that's okay with you guys."

We all nodded in agreement. Mike had written a poem for the 2008 men's eight crew before their final race, and now we were to receive ours. A rite of passage, an anointment by words. He spoke melodically, as if reading onstage, encapsulated in a cone of light from a single spotlight.

Our journey has been unforgiving,
Tomorrow you will face strong crews.
You have overcome all that has stood in your path,
You can hold your heads high, win or lose.

When others turn back, you stuck to your path,
Gritted your teeth and came back for more.
Through ice and snow on harsh winter days,
Braving winds and waters that were wild and rough,
You persevered with no complaints,
Just kept on going when the going was tough.

You are the fastest crew the world ever seen,
You have nothing to prove to me.
But now you have to prove to yourselves
That you can be as good as you can be.
To win would be a marvellous feat,
A show to the world for all to see.
One last request, never asked before,
Please win the race for me.

Please win the race for me. In the face of everything we'd been through, the request rang hollow. Clearly, Mike was under a huge amount of pressure being at his native country's Olympics. He was facing perhaps the defining moment of his coaching career, and with us he had an opportunity to cap his legacy in the sport. But it was my brothers in the boat who compelled me — not Mike's legacy. Above all else, a refusal to let each other down is what had gotten us this far, and it was what would get us across the finish line the next day.

59

I wake up yawning and stretching, muscles quivering, electric, alive. Windsor Castle is shrouded in mist, and the sky is grey. It feels like a good day for a funeral. I will skip the funeral and go to the Olympics. First thought conquered. A million more to go. Andrew is up after me: first to sleep, last to rise. When one of us is in the washroom, the other is preparing water bottles. Andrew's baritone voice is loud even though we murmur to each other. "Head down for breakfast in ten," he says, coming out of the bathroom.

At the breakfast table, I have no appetite. I wonder what kind of negotiation happens when the force-fed oatmeal, eggs, and hash browns arrive at my stomach. I expect my first bowel evacuation will come within minutes. The white linen tablecloth feels too smooth under my elbows; the smell of someone's coffee is strong. I have Spiderman senses. My teammates are silent, chewing, breathing, several let's-fucking-do-this glances are exchanged.

Back in the hotel room, I step into an old World Cup unisuit we've all agreed to wear during the morning pre-row — the two Team Canada Olympic unisuits are to be worn only in Olympic races. My feet are clammy and cold on the bathroom's tiled floor as I straighten my shoulder straps in the mirror, snapping them against my skin. I'm surprised by the anger written into the face looking back at me.

The course is quiet this morning. We row our race simulation, put our boat away, and return to our hotel. Eternity progresses to a later part of eternity — 12:00 p.m. Greenwich Mean Time for everyone else in London. I'm back in front of the mirror, this time adjusting the straps on my Olympic Team Canada unisuit. I'm not surprised to see my face is now even angrier.

Outside our hotel, our team manager and 1996 Olympian, Adam Parfitt, is waiting for us all to gather by the van. He's looking at his checklist and going over reminders as we arrive one by one. I feel the breeze against my skin, and my first thought is *Please, anything but a crosswind.* I want this final race to be about power and less about oarsmanship. I'm electric, touching my toes, stretching, moving to escape the swarm of thoughts that will plague me if I stay still. I make these movements smooth and strong so as not to unnerve my teammates, whose minds are also in orbit.

We shuffle into the van, and Andrew hits the gas. He drives us around a double-lane roundabout, and when he exits we're on the wrong side of the road. "Byrnes, you back in Canada? Wrong side, buddy," says Will. Andrew switches lanes, saying nothing. We say nothing. I'm rubbing my thumb along the inside of the plastic cup holder, feeling the plastic dimples, anticipating the wood grain of my oar handle; it will become an extension of me one more time. I hate myself for it, but I mourn for myself. Pain is coming. At intersections I look out the window and imagine the everyday worries of the people in their idling cars beside us. We are undercover commandos going to our mission, hidden among the working people of Slough.

The volunteers don't know us from any other spectators entering the parking lot. They over-direct us like greenhorn cops at an intersection. When one guy blows his whistle at us and steps in front to stop Andrew, I want to get out of the van and drive my fist into his chin, but I will save that violence for the race.

My body is highly tuned for what is coming in the next two hours. In just weeks from now, it will already get soft again, but right now it is an instrument of flesh, bone, muscle, and millions of pumping veins. "Gabe, our bodies are Ferraris," I'd said during the taper in Italy. "Jerry, you're thinking about Malcolm and Conlin. We're more like Dodge Neons," he'd responded, laughing.

We drive around the course, and I see the grey clouds reflected in the water, which flows toward us in tight ripples. It looks like a straight headwind, maybe a touch of cross. The wind will act like a cradling hand, offering some resistance to drive into. These conditions will reward power.

When we get off the bus, I see Florian Mennigen, seven seat from the German eight, getting off the shuttle bus ahead of us. I like Florian — we'd bonded in drunken German conversation after the 2011 World Championships — but I'm looking for weakness now. He looks meek, pale. They must win today, or their undefeated streak over the previous three and a half years will become meaningless. When our eyes meet, he gives me a knowing look. We're in this together. We are each other's obstacle to conquer.

The Germans are the worst kind of enemy. They are too gracious in victory, making it hard to hate them. I want us to spoil their streak and self-deprecate to them for a change. We'll tell them we can't believe our good fortune and expound on how capable a crew they are. Just like Florian, Richard, Kristof, and Max have done to me in the beer tent each time they've beat us.

The eight-language-speaking UN delegate is making announcements as we pass over the pedestrian bridge and walk alongside the boat storage area. My head is swollen with pressure, and my heart and gut have conjoined somewhere in the middle of me. I immediately make a trip to the washroom — the third one today — knowing I'll be back to empty my bladder one more time before shove-off.

Brian has us take our Empacher out of the boat bay and onto stretchers to be polished and buffed one last time. We mill around as the Empacher rep uses an electric polisher to bring the yellow hull to a shine so perfect I worry about our subsequent fingerprints causing drag. These moments of lull lend themselves to fatiguing tornadoes of thinking. I avoid the tornado by cycling through a checklist: *check shoes in boat, check rigger hardware, check oarlock, beet juice, bike, hydrate, Murray activation, hydrate, stretch, breathe, breathe, breathe.*

We return the boat to the racks in the boat bay and make our way to our team tent. The cheers of the crowd are closer than before. I manage my energy now, using anger to fend off the tingling nerves that will cause sheepishness if I let them. My brows pull inward so that a roll of skin pops out in the middle of my forehead. This facial expression is second nature to me. I was an angry kid. Rob does it even better. He is on the bike now, with a demonic look on his face, music pumping through earbuds, already coated in a film of sweat. Malcolm is nodding almost imperceptibly as if acknowledging a conversation partner who is not there. Doug is putting three-quarter pressure — more like seven-eighths pressure — on one of our two ergs, the whir of the flywheel filling our tent.

When it's my turn to receive my body activation from Murray, I feel time is running out. I'm like a baby bird being nudged out of the nest, forced to fly or slam into the ground. I'm so nervous, my genitals have shrivelled up and hardened into nubs that push against my spandex. This makes me self-conscious as I lay flat on my back on Murray's massage table and he begins chopping my quads with lightning-fast combinations, like Bruce Lee. I'm relieved when he tells me to turn onto my stomach. He continues by slapping my hamstrings, shaking the collection of muscles in my back, digging an elbow into me at times, beating me with fists. I am an old rug being cleaned.

When I stand up again, my body is nearly as red as the Team Canada fabric of my unisuit. I am ready for the fight of my life.

Mike and Brian have spent this time in the boat bay going over the boat several more times to make sure all the riggers, backstays, oarlocks, and foot stretchers are secure. It is time for us to join them. We walk past the other white canvas team tents with our chests puffed out, staring straight ahead. When we arrive, Brian is running a finger wrapped in cloth along the insides of our slides from underneath the boat. Mike is doing the same. It's the first time I've seen Mike actively work on the boat this close to a race.

They stop what they're doing, and we gather in a semicircle around Mike.

"Okay, let's get ready to go," Mike says.

This is it. One final word from Mike Spracklen, our leader.

"You may be nervous … you may be nervous.… Remind yourself to be calm, to be in control. Think it's good to be nervous. You've got to turn those nerves into adrenaline, then power. No one has more power than you guys. No one deserves it more than you guys. You take off, stay with the leaders, stay in control, change into pace. That's the key: change into pace, hold the pace. You hold it, hold it, hold it. Power, power, power," he says, slapping the back of one hand into the palm of the other three times for emphasis.

"Then it's a fight. Those guys out there are going to fight their necks off. Those people will give their lives to get on that podium. You fight with them, you go with them, or you take in their wake. There's no reason why you can't stay alongside them. And it's inch by inch by inch, fighting, fighting, fighting. And when they take a bit, you fight harder, and when they take a bit more, you fight fucking harder!"

A pause. All eyes are fixed on Mike.

"Don't want people crying in the stands. That's not why they're here," Mike says. He looks at us, burning in this last statement with an icy gaze, like a victim of physical abuse, afraid the next blow might kill him.

I sense fear all around me, but it floats on top of an unbreakable resolution. Some of the fear is my own, some is my teammates'; a steady stream of it comes from the other boat bay, where the Dutch are circled around their coach receiving final instructions.

"No one is more powerful than you guys," Mike says again.

I can't feel my body. I want to press my legs against foot stretchers and pull on an oar to remind me of my strength. *Get me in the boat. Let's fucking go.*

"Put yourself in the race, and have confidence in that power."

"It's time, Mike," says Brian.

Mike smiles and acknowledges Brian with a glance. He looks at us like a sergeant inspecting his line of troops. He pauses at Conlin. Looking up, he says to Conlin, to all of us, "It's your time."

We give our lanyards to Mike and shake his hand, one by one. He starts opposite Rob to his right and makes his way around to me. I'm the last to exchange a lanyard for a handshake. Mike drapes it around his neck. Our blank faces, like nine mug shots, hang from him.

"One last thing," Mike says quietly. "Please win this one for me."

We leave Mike in the back of the boat bay and march the boat to the dock. A forced smile appears on his face, but it's wilting away with every step we take. We walk, and I feel like I'm three feet outside my body looking back at myself. The nerves spread across me like an unending orgasm, wave after wave. I worry my nervous system will be flooded and put into shock before we reach the dock. The Olympic final is next.

"Ready, up," Brian orders. We're on the dock now, the water sloshing under our weight. We lift the boat high over our heads towards the cloudy sky, roll it down to our hips, and place it into the water so carefully you can barely hear the splat. I bump into Rob while reaching for my oar and it feels like getting trap-blocked by an offensive lineman. I take comfort in this. We take our places and strap into our shoes.

"Hands on. Ready, shove," says Brian.

We push off together with a powerful thrust. A million volts of electric nerves release through this first physical act. Ports place their blade edges against the dock and push us out the rest of the way. We're free — free from the other rowers scattered about the pavilion, free from the hurried steps of coaches, free from waiting and thinking. The water is grey like the sky, and it's an odd sensation to feel like we've crossed a barrier. No one can interfere now. No spectator can run onto the track in rowing. The water is our domain.

Brian is all business as he talks us through the warm-up. We've heard it all before, and his tone of voice tells us this is no different than any other race; we will prepare like we always do.

A shadow swallows me from behind, and then the walls of the pedestrian bridge are on either side of us. Our strokes echo loudly against the concrete.

My nerves have settled a little now that we've taken some strokes. I can feel my body again. The easy strain against the oar, legs first, then body opening and arms pulling through to a satisfying finish. Every stroke I take will be the best stroke I've ever rowed. We pass under the shadow of the grandstands, and even now I try to improve, try to find perfection.

I can tell by how the pull on my shoulders feels at the catch that we are rowing together as one. Brian coos over the PA system *Yeah, boys*, and *That's it, boys*, and *Nice, boys*, and *Keep giving me that smooth rhythm, boys.*

The Germans row past us and into view as we approach the bottom of the warm-up course. Their oars are perfect to my eye, in and out together as if all oars are attached by string to the same finger of a giant puppeteer hiding in the grey clouds above. There is something unforgiving about the bands of black and red and orange making up the German flag painted on their blades, flashing at us with each catch like the frill of a provoked lizard. Although our rowing is not as crisp, I believe we can match them if we have our best race.

The warm-up course is getting busy now, and Brian is jostling for position, being aggressive. I would like nothing more than to smash into the other crews at ramming speed, board their vessels, and attack them with my fists. I need to muster all the anger left in my furnace. I don't dare stop stoking that part of me. It is the angry asshole in me who will help us win a medal, not the friendly Jeremiah known to friends and family.

The Aussies come in and out of view as we blast through our final hard twenty. They have faux-hawks and tattoos on bulging muscles, but they're a little too impressed with themselves. At least, that's what I tell myself. The Dutch pass by next, and they always look a bit frightened to me. Maybe that's why they wait until the last possible moment to sprint to try to catch the leaders; they're afraid of the pain, want to delay it as long as possible. *Yes, they're scared,* I tell myself. Even Roel Braas in their five seat, the physical specimen who I'm convinced was designed in a petri dish by Dutch scientists, looks unnerved.

We're into race pace pieces now. Brian's been talking to us in a calm, soothing voice. He's like a horse whisperer. I'm nervous as ever about the over-rate piece. What if I lose the handle and get ejected from the boat? I don't have a choice. "This is our chance to open things up. Let's get it up around fifty-five. Over-rate. Here we go."

Brian reminds us to keep some length on the slides, and it goes fine. We do a five- and ten-stroke start. Both are smooth, powerful, fluid.

"Okay, long start, twenty-five strokes," says Brian. This is the last piece before the race. Just before we take off, the Americans charge past us in the middle of a hard twenty. By the time Brian says go, the Americans' wake reaches us and threatens to disrupt the set of our boat. No problem. Portside blades eat it up as we power through. Doug, Conlin, Andrew, and Will have always had the better blade work compared to us on starboard.

It's time. All the work has been done: the warm-up, the drama of the heat and repechage, the hundreds of hours slaving away on Elk Lake, the personal sacrifices, the mind games with Mike, the single-mindedness of the last three and a half years. All for this moment. Our moment.

Special relativity is in full force. A spectator in the stands is experiencing time as they always do, ticking along steadily. For us, time is elastic and warping. Right now I feel like time is sliding downhill, accelerating, taking us with it. I'm helpless to stop it.

We're sitting in a cluster of warships, arranged in order by lane number, waiting for the voice of God from the starting tower to call us onto the course. The sky is grey; the water is grey; the flat, grassy bank is scorched to the colour of straw. Thoughts of my family in the stands start to rise and are instantly suppressed. I dip my hands in the water instinctively and wet my oar handle. It needs to be moistened often, as the cool breeze dries it out.

This is not the Olympics, this is just a race. I can't imagine racing at the Olympics. It's something you dream of as a kid, not something you actually do. I wish I could stick a key through my skull and turn off parts of my brain. I can't begin to imagine the computational analysis going through Doug's head.

"Sitting up," Brian says. "Ready ... row."

The rowing is the only thing familiar about this situation. When I squeeze my legs down and pull on my oar, I can stop thinking. It's the torturous waiting that undoes me.

We pass under the little bridge into the lanes, slicing through red lane markers into lane five. Great Britain is already midway through their simulated racing start. It's just us and Brian now. His familiar voice is our lifeline.

"Ports, hold; starboards, tap it around. Back it down together now," he says.

We straighten in our lane and then push forward on our oars to move the twenty metres back into the starting gate. Rowing forward is like writing with your weak hand. We start moving so fast I worry my oar will snap out of my hands — I've never lost hold of my oar in competition, yet the fear persists.

"Easy, let it run," Brian says, as we coast into parallel with Germany on our port and Australia on our starboard. "Let's tee it up here, boys. Twenty-five-stroke racing start. Focus now." His voice drops to nearly a whisper. "First two are long and strong. Sit straight and drive legs from three to five. Strokes six to ten, start bringing in the body and lengthening. On my call, we drive into rhythm on thirteen." We've heard it a million times before, but the pressure does something to my memory and I'm grateful for the reminder.

As Brian brings us to attention, I know the Germans and Aussies are pretending to ignore us when really they are staring at us through their peripheral vision. Everyone's psychology is vulnerable. We blast out of the gates, and by the fifth stroke it feels like we're flying. The switch into rhythm is clockwork. We get the race into our bodies from strokes thirteen to twenty-five. We learn how today will feel with the wind, the bit of chop shivering across the water, the boat's response to our exertion.

Doug takes his third pee of the warm-up, pointing his member over the side of the boat and dribbling on himself as the stream loses pressure. We back the boat down again. This time we have farther to go; we've chewed up nearly 200 metres in just twenty-five strokes. We get closer and closer, moving toward the biggest fight of our lives. Our bodies have been opened, and the blood is pumping like a geyser now. I remember a quote from Jake Wetzel, six seat in the 2008 Canadian men's eight, saying this moment is like being stuffed into a cannon, the fuse lit, waiting for it to explode. He's right, there's no escape.

My heart is in my throat. I swallow it down, but it keeps rising back up. We're in the gates now. Every breath is an effort. I might not breathe at all if I don't purposefully expand my chest and pull oxygen deep into my lungs. My body is preparing for a ninety-second fight to the death. I need to override the adrenaline, to channel it for a longer fight that might last nearly six minutes with the headwind.

"Let's fucking do this, boys," says Malcolm. Andrew slaps me on the shoulder for encouragement. It jars me out of my own head. Rob and Conlin are back there, I know, like wildebeests, their muscles twitching. Gabe is looking over his shoulder from bow seat, touching us up with small jabs at the water, keeping us straight in the lane. I envy this responsibility that occupies his attention. I don't look left or right, but if I did, I would see Richard Schmidt in the German five seat rocking back and forth on his slides, taking deep breaths. To our port, I'd see the Australian seven seat, Sam Loch, nodding to himself and slapping his bulging chest and shoulder muscles.

"Ladies and gentlemen, the Olympic final of the men's eight," a British voice says to the crowd, who cheer in response. My brain is in overdrive: *Fend off the shock, snuff out bad thoughts, stay loose, feel the strength of my teammates.*

"In lane one, the Netherlands, stroked by Mitchel Steenman, coxed by Peter Wiersum," the announcer's voice echoes over a PA system spread out down the course so that everyone can hear.

"In lane two, Great Britain —" Immediately a roar of approval from the home crowd swallows up the rest of the announcement introducing their stroke, Constantine Louloudis, who, at twenty years old, is rumoured to be some kind of rowing prodigy. Their coxswain is Phelan Hill. The side of his face is familiar to me by now. He's got an overbite that protrudes, lips that curl outward, and a sneering tone of voice that reminds me of the cronies who provoked fights in high school but never got into one themselves.

"In lane three, the United States of America, stroked by Jake Cornelius and coxed by Zach Vlahos." The Americans have had an easier path here, and I hope their heads are filled with false confidence so that fear and panic will consume them when they find themselves unable to move away from this stacked field of contenders.

"In lane four, Germany, stroked by Kristof Wilke and coxed by Martin Sauer." The Deutschland-Achter are one win away from sealing their place in history as one of the most dominant men's eight crews ever. As close as they are, I know they've never felt as far away as now. *Come on, Deutsche brüder, make one mistake. That's all we need.*

"In lane five, Canada, stroked by Will Crothers and coxed by Brian Price." A small cheer from our Canadian fans follows. Someone in another boat lets out a loud cry, like a tennis player hitting a late-match winner. Other rowers let out angry, primitive shouts and growls. The sound of hands slapping thighs is becoming more frequent as time ticks along, insensitive to our growing panic. I don't need to slap my thighs; I can see my quad muscles quivering with electricity. They are alive and ready.

"In lane six, Australia, stroked by Nicholas Purnell and coxed by Tobias Lister." The Aussies' tanned brown shoulders and strong arms push out against their golden yellow unisuits. I remember my arrogance crossing over into rowing as a football player, thinking my upper body mass would help me overpower the competition. I wonder if — I hope — the Aussies have made a similar miscalculation.

"Netherlands."

A new voice, familiar. It is the voice that controls my intestines and churns them at will. *Okay, you bastard. Here we go.*

"Great Britain."

I have been holding on to my rigger in front of my shins, steadying myself. I let go and put both hands on my oar, sliding forward into position.

"United States."

I take one last glance back at my blade in the water, ensuring it sits plumb.

"Germany."

I feel as if our boat is rushing towards the edge of a giant waterfall. I'm afraid, but determined. Courage is not the absence of fear. Courage is pushing through the fear.

"Ca-na-da."

He's slowing down. Why is he slowing down? Shut the fuck up. Focus, focus, focus.

"Australia."

There is no more thinking. I am only an animal now, with one purpose: self-sacrifice.

"Get ready to squeeze," says Brian, calm and quiet.

"Attention."

The horn blares, as when an assembly line starts up in a factory, the light in front of us switches from red to green, and forty-eight men stomp on their footboards with enough wattage to power a small town for a day.

The first stroke is long and strong. We get on the second stroke fast. All around us it sounds like a levee has broken with the roar of water erupting behind blades. We build rate and power while sitting up with strong backs. I breathe. I stay loose in my upper body as I slam my legs down again and again. Tension is not fast; our power is smooth and athletic. My oar handle grips well from the sanding I gave it an hour ago. My inside hand flicks the oar from feather to square with ease. We've overcome inertia now. We're flying across the water.

"In two," shouts Brian. In a blink, we're driving into rhythm. All around us the frantic pitch of coxswains shouting through PA speakers rides on top of our thunderous strokes. Brian's voice rises above them all, and I swear to God I will never be more obedient to anyone in my whole life as I will be to Brian for the next five and a half minutes.

"Yep, forty-four right there. That's the one, boys. Send six in two, one, *now*!" says Brian. "Brits are pushing, Brits are already pushing. Keep sending the six."

I search the tone of his voice for clues. *Is he worried? Does he smell blood?* He is excellent — maybe the best coxswain in the world — at managing our perception.

"Legs dominate. Yep, and again. Yep, and again. Seat and a half on the Aussies, and moving, and moving. Keep dominating that one cut." Brian talks to us at the pace of an auctioneer. We focus on each race call together, pushing the last six inches of the finish, then one powerful cut through the water together. Eight minds and bodies coming together to row as one. Brian gives us one order after another, renewing our focus every few seconds by rallying us around one element of the stroke at a time.

"Brits are doing exactly what we expected and pushing very early," Brian cautions. "Put those hard hats on, boys, we're going to fucking work here. One cut, legs here, and again. Yeah, boys."

We're approaching 500 metres, and I feel my body's aerobic engine switch into full gear, taking over from the expended anaerobic rocket fuel that got me this far, like a space shuttle shedding its booster rockets.

"Here we go, boys. One hundred through the middle, sawing that wood. In two …"

We cross 500 metres in third place, only a couple tenths of a second up on the Dutch. Germany and the Brits are charging out in front, but the whole field is staying close. No one dares fall behind this early. We think about nothing except the best hundred strokes we can muster — make it finite, trick our brains into forgetting about the torture waiting in the final 500 metres, where we will begin anew and search our souls for something more. This Final Challenge has given me more adrenaline than ever before and I must be aware of the pain it is masking as we charge toward the 750-metre mark. I know the mask will fall away, somewhere between 1,000 and 1,500 metres, leaving me drowning in lactic acid, begging for escape.

"Remember, guys, this is where Mike said we make the British fucking pay. They haven't got much more than a quarter length here, boys. We close the fucking gap with long legs. Set in two, one, two — let's fucking move. *Yeah, boys!*" Brian's voice is desperate and hungry, every *Yeah, boys,* groaning out of him as if he's lifting us on his shoulders. Our position is precarious. It's a game of chicken. Even the Dutch aren't saving anything. We have a quarter-length overlap on the German leaders, yet we're only one and a half seats up on the last place Americans, and even less on the Aussies and Dutch.

"Inside leg, outside arm whip. Right here. Make the British pay. Making 'em pay here, boys. Keepin' it lively." Brian comes at us in torrents now, and I pray to God he won't run out of things to say. I need to hold on to his voice as we enter the void of the third 500.

"Four seats on the Aussies, four on the U.S., one on the Dutch. Keep cycling the hands. Let's go, boys!" I am embracing the pain. I will not let my teammates down. We'll march into the fire together, until our competitors melt from the heat and disintegrate. Brian calls Conlin by name, and the next five strokes feel like a ninth rower has been added to the boat. We feed off the energy and force our oars through the grey, choppy water. The lactate is spreading its tentacles everywhere now, sneaking up my spine and causing my head to buck backwards at the finish. The final sprint is still too far away to mentally anchor to it. This is no man's land, where body and mind burn mercilessly.

"Two minutes to go here, boys!" Brian shouts. I'm lost without him. *Keep talking to me, Brian.* We're up two seats on the Dutch, then three seats. We're one-quarter length back from the Brits and Germans, who are trading bows for first place. I'm trapped in my own body now. My heart doesn't beat so much as hum. The lactic acid has become a million spiders crawling all around under my scalp, looking for an opening to get in and put an end to me.

"Quarter length to both boats. Pushing on the Germans. Guys, they've got nothing fucking left. Their six man's got nothing left. This is our call. This is our day! Bows and down. *Now!*"

We die and come back to life over and over. Every stroke now. There are 300 metres left, and Brian's voice stays elevated. The noise from the crowd is thundering down on us now, rolling over our backs and vibrating our rib cages. I'm too tired to breathe. The final sprint will come at the cost of complete asphyxiation. Will's see-sawing back morphs into a blurry outline. Brian yells to be heard over the frenzy of thousands screaming, and water churning, and our own anger and hope and despair and pain coagulating into something more than I can bear.

Final 300 metres of the men's eight Olympic final at Eton Dorney. The Canadians are the fifth crew from the grandstands.

"Four on the Dutch. Bronze medal here. Gold is right there!" Brian yells.

The grandstands appear on either side of us, and the crowd is screaming down on us. Somewhere our families are roaring *GO CANADA!*

"Here we go, boys. Time to go after it. Will is going to flip the switch. One more. Seven *now*!"

The buoys turn red. Two hundred and fifty metres to go. Thirty strokes for the rest of our lives. Will charges us into our first seven-stroke lift. It's everything I can do to stay with him. It's finite now. A hand reaches down into me and pulls me up for one last fight. We feed off each other. Everything will be left on this course, on this day. This moment is every last thirty strokes of every god-damned-to-fucking-hell workout we've ever done together.

"Closing on the Brits. Seven now, finishes and through. Send power! Three seats! Three seats to silver!"

There's nothing more I can do. *Fucking Christ, come on!* It's the work now. Have we done enough? I'm nothing more than muscle memory. I'm rowing ugly, bucking strokes, throwing my back into the bow, pressing my feet, pulling my arms.

"One seat to silver! Push on 'er, boys!"

I am breaking down, fighting, fighting, desperate.

"Even for silver! Ten *now*. All power!" Brian screams.

The British have nothing left. I have Brian, Will, Andrew, Malcolm, Conlin, Rob, Doug, and Gabe. I wouldn't trade them for anyone else in the world.

Last ten strokes. Where are the Germans?

"You got a seat. We're in silver, boys. Power to the finish. Yes, boys. Power it. Fucking right. Power it. Another one!" Brian is jubilant, yelling down the final strokes when he knows we've done enough to secure second place.

The Germans win it. We take the silver, and the British hold on to bronze as the rest of the field finish within a second of each other: U.S.A. fourth, Australia fifth, and Netherlands sixth. The finish horn sounds off like a flurry of firecrackers, beeping six times in rapid succession.

The silver may as well be platinum, for the euphoria that erupts inside me. Humans aren't built for this combination of anguish and joy and relief all at the same time. *I am an Olympic medallist! We are Olympic silver medallists!* I flop backward into Andrew's lap, waiting for the pain to subside. It feels like it will be permanent this time. The crowd thunders on in appreciation of the closest Olympic final in the history of the event. I pull myself up and lift my arm in triumph. It is heavy, like my blood has been transformed into mercury and my bones into lead.

Rob, resurrected from the blackout of the final strokes, finally yells out in celebration. Malcolm won't stop telling us how proud he is, what this race means to him. I tell Brian, in babbling saviour-worship, I'm coming to his house every Sunday night for dinner for the rest of my life to relive this moment. Now Andrew has got hold of my shoulders; he's shaking me. Will reaches behind and clasps my hand. I grab on, my face etched with pain. We did it; we did it.

"We're out of the Bronze Age, fellas," Gabe quips. "Silver sounds pretty good to me."

I look back at my teammates as waves of euphoria wash over my body. Doug pokes his head around Rob's shoulders with a shit-eating grin, foam

Pain mixing with joy as Will and I celebrate moments after crossing the finish line of the Olympic final.

at the edges of his mouth. Conlin is wide-eyed, mouth agape. He looks like he's ready to race back to the start line. He probably could.

"Great fucking race, Germany," says Will to Kristof and his German teammates. They are worthy champions, celebrating their victory. But they're more relieved than anything. For them, this race was about not losing, not screwing up their incredible string of victories in the final hour. For us, it was about rising out of the bowels of defeat and achieving our best result on the most important day. *Carpe diem*. We pump our fists in the air and shout and soak in the moment. If you saw only the celebrations, you'd think we'd won the race. This is the beauty of sport: you can lose and still feel like a champion.

"Be proud of that, boys. Be fucking proud of that," says Brian.

An official steers his launch alongside us and barks at Brian to keep moving toward the podium dock. Brian lights into him, then takes his time commandeering us the 50 metres to the south grandstands.

I climb onto the dock, knees first. We're on the podium now — giddy, grinning, still in disbelief.

We look for our families in the sea of red shirts in the stands. I see my little sister, Julia, first. She's waving, with a huge smile on her face, jumping up and down. I'm looking for Ethan, but my little boy is hidden behind the shoulders of standing, screaming Canadians. My sister grabs him by the armpits and lifts him up high. I see him and yell his name and blow him kisses. He is shell-shocked by it all, smiling self-consciously, waving both hands at me. He will remember this moment forever.

Finally, I see my sister Jenny, my mom and dad, and Amy. I want to climb my way up to them and hug them all at once.

We stand side by side facing the crowd, freely taking it all in, structure and routine gone now. The medal ceremony begins. The Brits receive their bronze medals first. They rowed a brave race and led the Germans at times, but now, crestfallen, they accept their medals with the body language of missed opportunity. They show grace to their fans, who roar in approval.

When it's our turn, Gabe is first to bow his head and receive his medal. He shakes hands with the Olympic official, holds up the chunky medal, and kisses it. His two brothers are screaming louder than anyone in Great Britain,

2012 Canadian men's eight celebrate their silver medal on the podium in London.

probably the world. They are shirtless, with CAN-ADA painted on their chests in red. We'd all heard Gabe recount stories of the Bergen brothers like folklore — the way they had beat on each other growing up, the intensely competitive family, including a father who had rowed for Canada at the 1976 Montreal Olympics. No one is prouder right now than the Bergen clan.

The official continues down the line, and each of us is introduced over the PA system and cheered by the crowd. When it's my turn, I bow low and the official loops the medal over my head. The medal pulls the purple lanyard tight against the back of my neck, and I can't believe how heavy it is. It must weigh ten pounds. I take it in my hands and run my fingers over the raised surface in awe. It reads: XXX Olympiad London 2012. In the foreground, Nike, the goddess of sport, rises partially bare-chested out of the ancient Greek Parthenon. Touching her little silver breast is the most action I've gotten in months.

Finally, the Germans are announced as Olympic champions. They receive their medals, and their national anthem plays to close out the ceremony. I see my German-born mom in the stands. She gets to hear her

Throwing Malcolm into the water from the podium dock.

national anthem and see her son win an Olympic medal for Canada — the best of both worlds.

It's rowing custom for only the winner to throw their coxswain into the water, but we're so excited we all grab hold of Malcolm, swing him by his arms and feet three times, and launch him into the water. Gabe jumps in after him, then, like dominos, the rest of my teammates jump in. I'm staying on the dock. Four years after falling out of my single every few strokes, a part of me is still grateful we didn't capsize today.

EPILOGUE

What we call the beginning is often the end, and to make an end is to make a beginning.

— T.S. Eliot (from "Little Gidding")

After the medal ceremony, we took to the boat for the last time as a crew. We all switched our usual seating order, with Brian rowing horribly in five seat and me coxing horribly from Brian's tiny seat in the front of the boat, my big haunches forcing me to sit atop the gunwales. We went across the course to salute the Canadian fans in the north grandstands. Gabe and Malcolm shouted instructions at Brian to get his oar in sync, and Will coached me on the correct calls to avoid running aground. Then we docked for the last time together at the same place where we'd shoved off to take hold of our fate only an hour before. Mike and Peter Cookson stood smiling under the bright grey

Assuming coxswain duties for our celebratory final row before putting our boat away for good.

sky. "Well done, guys," Mike said as we hugged him one by one. No seething undertones, no urgent insistence — just the voice of a satisfied coach.

We hurried from the dock to the media tent for a press conference, where the British media scrutinized the British eight and Malcolm gave Mike credit for our silver medal performance. I want to write that all my ill will toward Mike evaporated as my teammates and I hugged him after the race. Truthfully, with my brain still scrambled from the lactic acid I felt inclined to attack Mike, the way a survivor might attack someone who'd run out on their family during a crisis. When I tried to say as much en route to the Canadian Press headquarters later that day, Conlin and I nearly came to blows as he defended Mike with all the indignation of a loyal husky defending its master. Now, several years later, I hold no grudges against Mike. It's because of him that this story even exists to be written down. Let me be clear about it: thank you, Mike.

After the last interviews — where we were impossibly tasked with summing up our experience in five sentences or less — we greeted our families

First hug from Ethan after the Olympic final.

and friends. Ethan ran to me, and I picked him up and squeezed him so hard his head nearly popped off. When I let him down, he was still clutching me, not wanting to let go. Julia and my mom were in tears of sympathetic relief and wonderment. Amy and my older sister, Jenny, couldn't get the smiles off their faces. My dad's voice was painfully hoarse after screaming "Go Canada!" at the top of his lungs during the final 300 metres. He was still whooping, laughing, coughing, and losing his voice mid-sentence. My best friend, Chris Donegan, and his dad, Tom, had come over to London to watch the race after visiting family in Ireland. They stood with Guinness beers in hand, glassy-eyed from the alcohol as much as the emotion. Tom said something incoherent, and Chris and I laughed.

On the second day after the race, after we'd fulfilled our media obligations, we paired off in groups to pursue various attractions: the athlete-exclusive Oakley House, to check out the build-your-own custom sunglasses bar; Canada House at Trafalgar Square, to meet friends and family and cheer on our Canadian teammates in other events; and German

Canadian family, friends, and fans celebrating after our silver medal performance at the London 2012 Olympics.

Celebrating with my family at Canadian Olympic House. *Left to right*: my mom, Bettina; Jenny; me; Julia; Ethan; my dad, Jonathan; Amy.

Haus, to drink with our German competitors as friends in the charitable atmosphere of post-competition relief (and where, later, copious drinking had me speaking the best German of my life).

On day three, Conlin and I decided to take the tube downtown to Trafalgar Square to begin our celebrating (our earlier spat over Mike had fizzled out as quickly as it had started). Our event had ended on day five of the Olympic program, so we were among the very first medallists set loose upon London. The medals were heavy and chunky in our pockets. We kept them in satin sunglass bags to protect against nicks. "Let's bust them out," said Conlin, slipping the medal around his neck. I followed his lead, and within seconds a sea of bodies surrounded us. Outstretched arms groped at our medals, cameras snapped away incessantly, people wedged their bodies in sideways to get to us, and kids squeezed their heads between legs to catch a glimpse. Insane! For the moment, we were major celebrities — a most peculiar, surreal experience.

EPILOGUE

London breathed energy and excitement. At night, we bypassed lines at every club as if we'd been given a key to the city. We exchanged selfies and autographs for rounds of free-flowing beer. At one point, Conlin shot me a look from across the bar. Five grasping hands pulled his Olympic medal tight around his neck. He mouthed the words *What is going on*?

When the bars closed, we went to the casinos. My body was remarkably efficient at transferring the alcohol into my bloodstream and up to my brain, which led to poor decisions such as trying to bet my silver medal on red at a roulette table, swimming in the Serpentine triathlon course in Hyde Park mere hours before daybreak on the morning of the triathlon race, and having a tendency to swing my silver medal over my head like a lasso (only to find out one morning that I'd torn through half the purple lanyard and nearly sent the medal flying into the night).

We partied hard for eleven straight days until the closing ceremonies. The strangest event was a private party thrown exclusively for Olympians at a London club. Many of the medallists were in celebrity shock, trying to fathom who they were now, not realizing the long journey that lay ahead to reclaim an identity based on one's day-to-day self and not on an Olympic medal or Olympian status. Among these athletes were incoherent and ballooning egos whose listening skills were temporarily shut down. The opposite extreme was the many more Olympians who had fallen short of their dreams, who felt they'd squandered their once-in-a-lifetime opportunity. An Australian rower I spoke with struggled to make sense of things: "Yeah, we had so much potential, but we couldn't pull it together when it counted." His tone sounded blasé, but beneath these simple words he was clearly struggling to make sense of a gargantuan effort that had led only to disappointment. Was it worth the sacrifices? Could he have prepared better, or differently? Questions that will haunt an athlete all their lives. The dejected, too, would be tasked with reconciling their identity, their future peace, with something other than Olympic failure. I wouldn't understand how similar both journeys are until years later.

After the Games ended, I joined my family for a vacation in Portugal. There, the Olympics quickly became wrapped up in history. I walked the sunny, cobbled streets of Lisbon, trying to process my new status as an Olympic medallist. At the end of a harbour pavilion stood a busker painted head to toe in shiny silver — a living statue act. Tourists flocked to him for pictures in exchange for a couple of euros. My silver medal was like his silver skin: it was painted on me now, a thin layer of silver covering all other aspects of my identity.

I drove through the interior mountains of Portugal with my parents on the last leg of our trip. We stayed in hostels, and I spent one night wrapped around a toilet bowl under buzzing florescent lights. It was my worst bout of diarrhea in years. One week earlier I had been in peak physical condition, and then there I was, incapacitated by my bowels and muttering to my mother for assistance. Some people mistake an athlete's mentality for that of a soldier — the notion that we athletes will persevere through any conditions. This is true only in a narrow sense. Athletes do everything in their power to optimize their environment for peak performance within set parameters, but soldiers are trained to respond to the best of their abilities in *any* circumstance. It's why my initial response to illness was *I need an IV, electrolytes, salted crackers, and an air-conditioned room to rest in*, instead of *I need to swallow these pills my mom gave me, wait until sunrise, and then drag myself into the back of our rented Fiat so I don't steal a day from my parents' vacation.*

In truth, I was as much in awe of the Olympic cape around my neck as anyone, both during my five minutes of fame and in the months following. I experienced a new phenomenon: remembering that I was an Olympic medallist randomly throughout the day. *Wow. Me? Incredible.* I couldn't get used to it.

When I got back to Canada, the euphoria spiked again as my friends and family greeted me in contagious excitement. Amazement and curiosity supplanted familiarity: who was this guy they'd known so well, who had disappeared for a few years and then resurfaced with an Olympic medal?

In the months following, I received the odd phone call from old friends, some whom I hadn't spoken to in years, congratulating me and telling me how proud they'd felt after the race. Without fail, I recognized a common desire in them to understand how I'd pursued such a daunting goal. How does one begin? I heard reflection in their voices, consideration of their own paths in life and whether they'd given themselves a fair shot at their dreams.

An Olympic celebration gala, meeting the prime minister, a parade in Toronto, and school and hospital visits left me and my fellow Olympians dazzled. I nearly cried several times per day — a mix of post-Olympic relief and gratitude. I felt like I had survived the greatest test of my life. Yet how could I feel this way when, while visiting a hospital cancer ward, a young hairless boy who was undergoing chemotherapy held my medal and smiled up at me serenely? Surely the relativity of human experience is the biggest gag of all, that I would feel like a survivor when I shook this sweet boy's weak, pale hand — this boy who was fighting to live.

Amy, Ethan, and I stayed in Victoria for two years after the Olympics. I decided to use some of the tuition credits Sport Canada grants its athletes to take courses in jazz drumming at the Victoria Conservatory of Music. During one challenging lesson, I shocked my teacher when I hit the snare drum as hard as I could in frustration. I expected to achieve a level of mastery within a time frame that was unrealistic. Rowing was a unique opportunity to exploit the athleticism I'd built up through other sports all my life. I couldn't expect to become one of the world's best drummers in less than four years.

As the months passed, my teammates made their decisions to continue or retire. Andrew retired from rowing to pursue an engineering career, get married, and start a family. Malcolm did the same, although he went to medical school to become a doctor. Gabe finished the undergrad degree he'd been chipping away at during his rowing career and finally got married to Lindsay Jennerich. He was on track to become a teacher, but I bet he'll start his own woodshop. Doug Csima resumed his career as director of care at a retirement facility, got married, and has since had two sons. Brian Price finally moved on from his long coxswain career to become a bank branch manager in Orangeville, Ontario, where he lives with his wife and two daughters. Will Crothers, Rob Gibson, and Conlin McCabe all eventually returned to full-time training and went on to compete in the Rio Olympics. It's hard to fathom the amount of sustained effort these athletes and friends of mine are capable of. Truly incredible. And while Rio did not result in medals for Canada's men's rowing crews, the Canadian women's lightweight pair of Lindsay Jennerich and Patricia Obee — our training partners leading up to the London Olympics — earned a hard-fought-for silver medal of their own.

Aside from my own reservations about continuing with the sport, it was now my turn to be flexible in planning our future with Amy and Ethan in mind. Amy had made my journey possible. Despite a long and gut-wrenching uncoupling, she'd supported me in the pursuit of my dream, and I couldn't have done it without her. At one point in 2011, I'd said, "If you stick by me these next two years and let me have my shot at this, you can decide where we live afterwards." In the summer of 2014, the time had come to keep my promise. Amy's small camping and RV resort she had renamed West Pines now required her full attention. And she was getting married, moving on fully into the next phase of her life. We agreed to move to nearby Peterborough — roughly equidistant between Toronto, our families in Cobourg, and Amy's business up north.

The move back to Ontario meant officially starting a new chapter in my life. My carding cheques had ended, and I supported myself through paid speaking engagements while I worked on this book. The speaking engagements were great at first, but over time I couldn't manufacture enthusiasm for telling my story again and again. I began to feel fake — an empty shell of my past. Anxiety crept into my life in a way it never had before, as if I was only now processing the mental toll the Olympics had taken on me. I tried to sweep it aside as a phase that I would get through and did my best to get on with things.

Thoughts turned to finding a job, any job really, to shore up my dwindling savings. Old colleagues from the bank vouched for me and helped me land a contract analyst position in Hamilton, Ontario. I spent a day pulling out boxes filled with binders of old training materials and trying to reactivate a part of my brain that had lain dormant for four years. When I arrived in Hamilton to work on a new loan for a local manufacturer, it turned out there had been a miscommunication between HR and the district vice-president, and they weren't expecting me. "No worries," said the DVP. "We'll set you up in an office this week and have you work on some annual reviews."

When I got to my temporary office, it was bare except for one printed-out poster taped to a bulletin board. It pictured a men's eight crew rowing into morning fog, with the caption "Get to Work: You Aren't Being Paid to Believe in the Power of your Dreams." This was no practical joke, I later confirmed.

It was a coincidental and timely reminder that what had started as a dream quickly transformed into several years of extreme output.

A goal achieved is never how you dreamt it to be; the thing you had worked so hard to achieve now simply drags behind you, insisting, against your nature, that you embody it for the rest of your life. I panicked, thinking I had only delayed real life and now, with less money and an intensity not fit for white-collar environments, I had nowhere to go. Where to begin?

Word travelled fast through the office that an Olympian had come to work on a temporary assignment. While my new co-workers asked me the usual questions — *What was the pressure like? How did you feel when you won the medal? Who won gold?* — I was anxious to get back to reviewing my training materials. I felt incompetent, and the Olympic halo over my head had become a distraction. Behind my smiling acknowledgements, I was caving and falling into depression.

They had scheduled me to work for two weeks in Hamilton, but I lasted only two days. Not only were my analytical skills rusty, but the bank had completely overhauled its software systems and I required new training to get up to speed. We agreed the set-up wouldn't work as planned, and I returned to Peterborough.

It was December 2014. The Olympics were two and half years behind me. Trapped in my own head with no Spracklen dictating my days and no teammates to vent with every day in the locker room, I started to free fall into an abysmal cocktail of my worst qualities. I set unrealistic goals for this book, for my speaking career, for my aspirations as a musician, and I became brutal on myself, stopping all progress. The inner critic previously silenced by massive physical output now ran me into the ground as I sat alone in an empty house in a new town with no clear direction. When Ethan came home from school, I lectured him on resilience, goal setting, and discipline — mostly to remind *myself* of what it would take to get through this unanticipated transitional phase.

After the Games, my body blew one gasket after another — three herniated discs, to be exact. Between my bad back and torn finger tendons, I'd attempted rowing only twice since the Olympics, each time lasting less than 2 kilometres. Mentally, what should have been easy thirty-minute workouts at the YMCA three days per week now required as much willpower as the second Saturday row at the end of a week of full-time training. The body may lie, but the mind-body connection is real, and my mind told my body it was okay to finally let go in the year after the Games.

My ego, somehow, ballooned and cratered at the same time. I was useless and incompetent, yet too good for most jobs. Burning through the last of my savings, I applied to a Canada Post part-time letter carrier position and landed an interview. I hoped it would buy me time to get my shit together. A week later, a burly postal worker greeted me at the Canada Post sorting facility in Peterborough and guided me to a room filled with ten other eager candidates. We were given a five-minute time limit to answer two-digit multiplication and division questions. My anxiety walled off my logic and reasoning faculties. I stumbled through. Next, we were given a table of addresses to memorize in thirty seconds and rewrite in their proper place from a scrambled list. My mind went blank, and my ears rang. I knew these tests were coming, but I hadn't prepared. Had I become a mule, capable of working only if flogged by someone else? A blast of icy February wind hit me as I exited the facility, a new low point reached.

Then, finally, a glimmer of hope. When I'd first moved back to Ontario, I had gone to visit the Canadian Olympic Committee offices in Toronto. I had met a few of the directors and done my best to learn about their roles. During one meet-and-greet, the CEO, Chris Overholt, had entered the room wearing a crisp white dress shirt and peppered me with questions. We hit it off. Over the months, I periodically checked in with Chris in the hopes that an opportunity with the COC might emerge. Finally, six months later, it did. The COC had decided to invest in the development of an athlete transition program called Game Plan, a joint initiative between the Canadian Olympic and Paralympic committees and the federal government, and they needed a manager to work on the program. When I saw the job posting, I got busy. I studied the structure of the Canadian sport system and all its players (a highly fragmented landscape), and spent a day refining my cover letter and resume. Finally, I stood up on the linoleum floor of the rented house I could no longer afford, straightened my arm, and clicked the send button with a dramatic, downward-pointed finger.

When I got the email saying I had been selected for an interview, a light flickered inside me, but only dimly. I knew many capable Olympians would be applying for the role. Wincing as I paid for a new bespoke suit, I began acting the part of a confident young man who was entertaining multiple prestigious career paths.

I travelled to Montreal by train for the interviews, practising a smooth, assured smile the whole way, softening my piercing stare in the reflection of the window as the trees and farmers' fields rushed by.

I needed to hide what was going on inside me. The symptoms I'd experienced before a major international rowing race found their way into every event in my life now: heart pounding out a pulse that I swore others could see and hear, shallow breaths that made it hard to speak, racing thoughts, coursing adrenaline. But I was an Olympian. I would overpower these symptoms.

I walked through the glass doors of the Canadian Olympic Committee office determined to succeed. Just as Mike used to say our bodies lied when pushed to extremes, I took the ill-informed approach that mental weakness was a lie I could overcome with sheer willpower.

At first, it worked. I landed an offer after a lengthy process that felt more like a political appointment than a job application process. *Relief*, like I'd entered the boathouse out of the winter cold, like another major rowing race had just ended and my breath was returning. But the people who experience the most relief are never relieved for long. Mine would be short-lived.

My first day on the job involved attending a meeting with two people from the COC management team and several management consultants at their downtown Toronto office. The sun shimmered off the towering skyscrapers as I walked among white-collared creatures again, decked out in the same grey clothes and shiny dress shoes, herded together yet isolated from each other.

I was introduced as the Olympic medallist with a business background, someone who could lend a valuable perspective to the project. Within minutes of hearing the project plan, however, and then continually over the next days, weeks, and months, I realized there was no substance behind the plan — only beautiful PowerPoint slides, buzzwords galore (*holistic approach*, *module development*, *segmentation matrix*, *stakeholder buy-in*), and skillful deflection of any direct line of questioning. As is endemic of the Olympic movement, soaring promises had been made, well-wishers without a real plan had weighed in, unrealistic goals were set with no resources allocated to achieve them, and I began to realize that I, in my weakened state, had not parachuted into a steady job. I had just found my next fight.

The money replenishing my bank account, steadily, every two weeks, stymied my financial woes. But as I prepared to entrench myself against the posturing and petty politics riddling my new environment, one source of stress was traded for another. This wasn't just a job; this was personal. Feelings of dishonour crept in: Was I betraying my fellow athletes by allowing myself to be bought, like so many others in the Olympic movement? Would I make the many small reconciliations people make over time to justify their privileged station in life, convincing themselves they deserve what they don't?

Three months into the job, I prepared to be fired as I wrote up a scathing criticism of several elements of the Game Plan program. Chris didn't fire me. Instead, he gave me the reins: you're the leader of the program, he said, with the caveat that sometimes you have to fit round pegs into square holes. So, I spent the next year trying to hammer round pegs into square holes. Instead of being an athlete-centred program, we used our limited resources to help slow-responding corporate partners find ways to tell "genuine" marketing stories. And underneath the posturing, there remained the difficult issue of how to improve athlete transitions and well-being — what could we actually do to help? I wanted to succeed so badly that my anxiety and depression deepened when things didn't go well. Depression for me shows up as anger (surprised?). As an athlete, I could count on releasing all that anger temporarily with a physical effort strong enough to force away coherent thought. I couldn't count on that anymore. Days now ended with my brain cooked and no physical outlet, as my butt went from car seat to train seat to office seat.

I battled a steady rotation of consultants who tried to work me instead of work *with* me. They created a distortion field that paralyzed the leaders tasked with making the decisions necessary to move us forward. The situation drove me into rage most days. I squelched the rage, packed it away deep in my belly, where it consumed me from the inside out. In my mind, the program was paralyzed and I would be fired any day. Anxiety and depression eventually crippled me to the point where I sat, overwhelmed and useless, staring at my computer monitor with a deep sense of foreboding. Whole days of productivity evaporated, with nothing but the sound of the ventilation system humming away above my head. My heart raced as people walked by my cubicle, for fear they would see through my mask and realize I was a fake.

My problem is I don't reach out until I'm in a crisis. I told myself I didn't deserve to feel the way I did: racing thoughts, wild emotional swings, brutal self-talk, perpetual fight mode. Who was I to feel this way when others had real problems? Those with terminal cancer, soldiers with PTSD, members of my own family who were battling more severe mental illness — a long list of those who actually deserved concern. I was an Olympic medallist. If anyone should suck it up (*pussy*), it was me. But mental illness does not discriminate, it is not a weakness of character, and like any wound, it can get worse if left untreated — a message that needs to reach more athletes.

In the summer of 2015, I called the athlete helpline we had put in place for active and recently retired athletes who needed confidential counselling support. My own recorded message greeted me: "Hi, welcome to the athletes' and coaches' helpline. I'm Jeremiah Brown, 2012 Olympian and Game Plan national manager." The voice was assured and authoritative — well-disguised. I dialed through the options, almost hung up impatiently, and then finally connected with a counsellor. I was expecting a patronizing, soft-spoken therapist spouting fluffy hoo-ha, but instead the guy was practical and action-oriented like me. We talked options. He helped me reframe things from all-or-nothing tunnel vision to being able to see different paths forward again. It was good.

Five years after our final Olympic race, and two and a half years into my work with the Canadian Olympic Committee, I still find myself slipping into the same self-destructive patterns, but less frequently. I've developed better self-awareness and learned to manage my environment to avoid descending toward crisis mode. I don't notice the sound of the ventilation system humming overhead anymore. Mostly, I feel competent and engaged, and I see the way forward. Game Plan has made a real difference in many athletes' lives already, thanks in most part to the people on my team who work with athletes every day across Canada. It's not quite the endorphin kick of a hard workout, but I get a little shot of adrenaline every time we get positive feedback from an athlete we've connected with one of our athlete counselors, an employer, a scholarship opportunity, or mental health services.

I don't think sport made me who I am; I think sport suited who I already was — that same kid who would blow up if his sisters beat him at a game of Snakes and Ladders. I believe many athletes achieve the highest levels in their sport precisely because of genetic predispositions that put them at greater risk of developing mental illness. If I'm honest with myself, I've always oscillated between the lowest of lows and highest of highs with not much time spent in the middle. Intense exercise is an antidepressant, and for many athletes it can mask an underlying vulnerability for years. It's easy to become addicted to the high that follows an intense workout, yet we find it hard to think of exercise as a form of addiction. For people like us, it's always going to be a question of how to channel the energy and the wild swings between the poles.

My Olympic silver medal now sits in its black case resembling a giant engagement ring box in the cupboard above my microwave. It's something that makes my family and friends proud and wows many who hold it. "It's so heavy," they say. It's true, it makes my neck sore after a while, pulling me down into the past as it does, a reminder of those four years between 2009 and 2012 and what is possible when you go all in.

A year after the Olympics, when Ethan was eight years old, he brought home three dog-eared, stapled pages from school. On the front, the title: *A Book All About the Best Dad in the World.* On the second page, Ethan's description of me: *My dad's name is Jeremiah. He has creamy black hair. For work, he rows. I think he's funny when he is happy and in a good mood.*

Sounds like a worthwhile next goal to me.

ACKNOWLEDGEMENTS

Thank you (in boating order) to Brian Price, Will Crothers, Andrew Byrnes, Malcolm Howard, Conlin McCabe, Rob Gibson, Doug Csima, and Gabe Bergen for being tough bastards and great teammates, and for accepting me into your world (eventually).

Thanks, Mike Spracklen, for doing what you do. The body lies, and I've not trusted it since. You revealed a path, and the path was brutal at times, but it's sure made for lots of introspection in the years following. A firm handshake to you.

Doug White, with whom the journey began in earnest, thank you for teaching me how to row and believing in me from that first meeting at the HoJo. I'll never forget it.

Thanks, Amy, for taking the high ground, for being a wonderful mother and the best parenting partner, and for the great relationship we've arrived at. Couldn't have done it without you.

Julia, we seem to be each other's keel when pushed over by life's winds. Thanks for moving across the country to help me out. And Jenny, your spirit, warmth, and kindness were felt from Ontario all along. Thanks for the phone calls and for your steadfast belief in me over the years. I love you both very much.

Dad, you always do the right thing and you go about it quietly. Thanks for getting me out of jail, for the loans (we're squared up, right?), for the counselling, and for not putting me in a foster home during those teenage years. You're a great partner in life. And Mom, thanks for giving me the straight goods when I need it, always in a caring way. Though it was not very helpful that time you told me about your nightmare of me drowning the night before another stormy row on Shawnigan Lake.

Ethan, thanks for the laughs, for the love, and for putting up with me more than anyone else must. It ain't always easy. Love you, my boy!

Tom McCarthy and Kate Fillion, thanks for believing in my writing ability when I wasn't sure what I had on my hands.

Thanks, Margaret Bryant, Dominic Farrell, and the entire Dundurn team for your professionalism and belief in this book.

To the many other teammates, coaches, friends, family, and colleagues who've supported me along the way, some mentioned in this book, some not, thank you.

PHOTO CREDITS

Alistair Boubly: 35
Bettina Brown: 184, 266
Jennifer Brown: 18
Jonathan Brown: 305
Canadian Press: 296, 297
Bert Cocu: 294, 298
Kevin Light: 134, 142, 160, 193, 196, 225
Mike Murray: 170
Unattributed: 306
Amy West: 303, 304